The Four

Peter J.
Leithart

THE
FOUR

a survey of
the Gospels

canonpress
Moscow, Idaho

Also by Peter J. Leithart

Against Christianity

Ascent to Love
A Guide to Dante's Divine Comedy

The Baptized Body

Blessed Are the Hungry
Meditations on the Lord's Supper

Brightest Heaven of Invention
A Christian Guide to Six Shakespeare Plays

Deep Comedy
Trinity, Tragedy, and Hope in Western Culture

From Silence to Song
The Davidic Liturgical Revolution

A Great Mystery
Fourteen Wedding Sermons

Heroes of the City of Man
A Christian Guide to Select Ancient Literature

A House for My Name
A Survey of the Old Testament

Miniatures & Morals
The Christian Novels of Jane Austen

The Promise of His Appearing
An Exposition of Second Peter

A Son to Me
An Exposition of 1 & 2 Samuel

Wise Words
Family Stories that Bring the Proverbs to Life

To Darcy

"Christ behind me, Christ before me,
Christ beneath me, Christ above me"

Published by Canon Press
P.O. Box 8729, Moscow, ID 83843
800-488-2034 | www.canonpress.com

Peter J. Leithart, *The Four: A Survey of the Gospels*
Copyright © 2010 by Peter Leithart

Cover and interior design by Laura Storm.
Cover illustrations: *Lion,* Peter Paul Rubens (1577–1640); *Muzzle of an ox as seen from the front* (c. 1501–1505), Albrecht Durer; *Figure Study of Christ,* Peter Paul Rubens (1577–1640); *Eagle* from *Taccuino di disegni,* Giovannino de' Grassi (d. 1398).

Library of Congress Cataloging-in-Publication Data

Leithart, Peter J.
  The Four : a survey of the Gospels / Peter J. Leithart.
     p. cm.
  Includes bibliographical references (p.   ) and index.
  ISBN-13: 978-1-59128-080-4 (pbk.)
  ISBN-10: 1-59128-080-X (pbk.)
  1. Bible. N.T. Gospels--Textbooks. I. Title.
  BS2556.L45 2010
  226.007--dc22

                                             2010033841

11 12 13 14 15 16 17 18 19 20   9 8 7 6 5 4 3 2

CONTENTS

INTRODUCTION

Christology appears to be one of the most complicated, technical, jargon-ridden areas of Christian theology. Beginning with the church fathers, theologians developed a sophisticated conceptual apparatus and vocabulary for dealing with Christological issues. To get it right, we need to distinguish between person and nature, know the difference between substance and subsistence, know that there can be union without mixture and distinction without separation, and believe that the Word is en-hypostatically related to an anhypostatic human nature.

Even those who agree with the orthodox formulas of Nicea and Chalcedon do not always function within the same Christological framework. J. N. D. Kelly long ago distinguished the mainly Alexandrian Word-flesh Christologies from the mainly Antiochene Word-man Christologies. The former tend to maximize the confession that the Word of God was the subject of the story of Jesus and to minimize the full humanity of Jesus, and at the heretical margins turned into Apollinarianism (which denies that Jesus has a human soul). Since the Eternal Son acts in Jesus for our salvation, Word-flesh Christologies are soteriologically monergistic, but since they tend to minimize the historical Jesus they lean toward docetism, characterizing salvation as escape from the material world. Word-man Christologies insist on the full humanity of Jesus, but tend to divide the human nature from the divine nature, and at the margins turned into Nestorianism. Soteriologically, Word-man Christologies lean toward synergism, since salvation is the product of the cooperative work of the divine Word and the human nature. Neither the Word-man nor the Word-flesh is heretical or orthodox in itself, but both have tendencies toward one or another heresy.

Chalcedon's formulation of the relation of the two natures in the one person has been particularly difficult to manage, no doubt because the council was an effort, not always or altogether coherent, to combine different strains of patristic Christology. Among the many disputed questions is, Does the Word constitute a single Person by uniting divine nature and human nature, or does the one Person of the Word precede the incarnation and remain the same Person in the incarnation? Is the incarnation about two natures coming together to *form* a single Person, or is it about a single Person taking on a second nature? Is the formula, Divine Nature + Human Nature = the one Person of the God-Man? Or is it, Person of Word + Human Nature = the one Person of the God-Man?

Chalcedon's creed appears to answer the question straightforwardly:

> [O]ne and the same Son, our Lord Jesus Christ, at once complete in Godhead and complete in manhood, truly God and truly man, consisting also of a reasonable soul and body; of one substance with the Father as regards his Godhead, and at the same time of one substance with us as regards his manhood; like us in all respects, apart from sin; as regards his Godhead, begotten of the Father before the ages, but yet as regards his manhood begotten, for us men and for our salvation, of Mary the Virgin, the God-bearer; one and the same Christ, Son, Lord, Only-begotten, recognized in two natures, without confusion,

without change, without division, without separation; the distinction of natures being in no way annulled by the union, but *rather the characteristics of each nature being preserved and coming together to form one person and subsistence,* not as parted or separated into two persons, but one and the same Son and Only-begotten God the Word, Lord Jesus Christ; even as the prophets from earliest times spoke of him, and our Lord Jesus Christ himself taught us, and the creed of the Fathers has handed down to us (emphasis added).

The fathers at Chalcedon say that the one person is *formed* by the addition of a human nature to the divine nature of the son: "coming together to form one person and subsistence." That's been the opinion of many orthodox Christians since the fifth century, but it was definitely *not* the opinion of Cyril of Alexandria, the great opponent of Nestorius. For Cyril, nearly everything hinged on the continuity of the Person of the Word from the pre- to the post-incarnate state; it all depends on the fact that the God-man is not some "new" Person, but the very Son of God in the flesh.

The sixteenth century contributed to Christological conflict as well. Reformation debates between Calvinists and Lutherans added new intensity to traditional questions about the *communicatio idiomatum,* the communication of attributes from one nature to the other. Do the attributes of one nature become the attributes of the other nature? Does the human nature of Jesus become omnipresent and omnipotent? Conversely, does the nature of God the Son take on human attributes of limitation, finitude, weakness? Or, as Calvinists argued, do we *attribute* the characteristics of each nature to the single *Person* of the God-man, without any *actual* "transfer" of attributes across the boundary of the natures? If we say, "The Son of God was finite," are we simply saying, "The human nature is finite, but since that human nature belonged to the Son of God, we can *say* that the Son of God experienced human limitations. Even though he didn't. Not really"? Or do we really mean, "The Son of God went through the human experience of limitation"?

If the complications of orthodox Christology are bewildering, the array of heretical options is more so. Barth deftly classifies Christological heresies as either "Ebionite" or "Docetic"—the former treating Jesus as the "apotheosis of man" and the latter treating Jesus as the embodiment or personification of some Idea, so that the specific actions and character of Jesus of Nazareth are an arbitrary husk that we discard to get to the nut. The Ebionite uses Christology as a springboard for a thoroughgoing humanism; for the Docetist, the Savior could just as easily have been Jason of Athens as Jesus of Nazareth. The intriguing thing about this classification is that both of these theories were originally theories about *Jesus,* not about the Eternal Son as such, yet Barth uses them to discuss dogmatic errors regarding the Eternal Son. For Barth, of course, there could be no knowledge of the "Eternal Son as such," since He reveals Himself only as Jesus.

By focusing on two "fundamental" Christological errors, Barth makes it look easy. But these two errors elaborate themselves in dozens of different specific directions. Among the "Docetic" heretics are "Monophysites" (also known as "Eutychians," after a monk named Eutyches), who believe that after the incarnation there was only one nature (*physis*) in Jesus; but there are also Apollinarians, who believe that the Word occupies the space of the human soul in Jesus. Perhaps Barth would place Nestorians among the Ebionites, since they treat the human nature almost as a second person. But where do we place the Adoptionists and Monarchians and Sabellians and Patripassians and Psilanthropists and all the rest?

And what's the point? Whatever happened to the Gospels in all this? Haven't we left the living, risen Jesus buried in a cave of jargon and metaphysics?

Classical Christology has its distortions. It has pitched its tent almost exclusively at the margins of the gospel story. The few narratives of Jesus' birth, along with John's great prologue, have been central to discussions of the nature of the Incarnation; the stories of the crucifixion have played a central role in the development of atonement theologies, though not nearly so great a role as Paul's discussions of the death of Jesus. The period between birth and death, the life and ministry and miracles of Jesus, have played very little role in the development of Christology. For some Protestants, the avoidance of the gospels partly results from embarrassment about Jesus' appalling lack of attention to justification by faith alone and His puzzling, and no doubt ironic, insistence on obedience. But the minimal use of the gospel stories in Christological discussion started long before the Reformation. For all the intense attention, debate, and exegesis, and for all the technical terminology and distinctions, Christology remains, two millennia into church history, in its infancy.

On the other hand (and there is always another hand): The Christological technicalities of the early Church, the Reformation, and the modern age are not intended to move Christians away from the gospels but to provide coordinates for reading the gospels. Christological controversies are about hermeneutics as much as anything else. They raise and answer the question, Whom are we reading about when we read the gospels? Who is the hero of the story? Answering "Jesus" is correct, but insufficient. Is the Jesus we read about in the gospels a God or a man? Or is He God now and then and man at other times—God when He's doing God-things like miracles but man when He is weak, God when

He's full but man when He's empty? Most importantly, who is that on the cross? Does Jesus suffer on the cross as a shell of a man abandoned by His better, divine half, or is God dying? And, if the latter, whatever could that mean?

And classical Christology provides the *right* coordinates. Orthodox Christology insists that the hero of the gospel story is the Son of God who has assumed human flesh. Everything Jesus does and says and suffers is what the Son of God does and says and suffers. Jesus is never a human shell, emptied of divine presence. He is, from the moment when the Spirit overshadowed Mary to knit Him in His mother's womb, to the last cry of dereliction, the Son of God.

This, especially the cross, was always the stumbling block of heretics. How can the exalted, pure Creator have such intimate contact with the grossness of human flesh? How can *God* enter a womb and be born? On the face of it, isn't that just *absurd?* How can God sweat blood and die in anguish? Arians said, God can't; so Jesus must be a secondary, not-quite-god. God can't do those things, so He sends an exalted creature to do His dirty work. Nestorians also said, God can't; so some happenings in the life of Jesus—birth and death especially—are happenings to the human, not the divine, nature, while other happenings happen to the divine nature. Docetists said, God can't; so it's all appearance; the Son has no real human flesh. These denials are only common sense, common Greek sense especially.

The Church, against all sense and through protracted struggle, consistently rejected those hedges and safe havens. Orthodoxy has always been a risk-taking enterprise, but it is nowhere so adventurous as in Christology. Bowing to Scripture, the Church said: *God the Son,* wholly eternally equal to the Father, took on flesh, *God* was born, *God* suffered human hunger and thirst, *God* took the lash and the spitting on His own flesh, and *God* died in that flesh on the cross.

Orthodoxy said that God experienced a human birth, lived a human life from the inside, finally died the death of man in order to destroy the power of death, and rose to become the first of the new human race.

The Church has insisted that none of this compromised the utter and complete Lordship of God in the least. On the contrary, Jesus' life as the incarnate Son *reveals* the Lordship of God. It is one of Barth's most invigorating contributions to theology to insist that, far from being a compromise of God's sovereignty, the incarnation is *proof* of God's sovereignty. God the Son is so utterly and completely Lord that He can enter a womb and be born as man, hunger and suffer weakness, die on a cross, and yet all the while remain wholly Himself, the living Creator of heaven and earth who needs nothing of what He has made. To heretics who can't bring themselves to believe that God can so thoroughly identify Himself with His world and to the timid orthodox who want to maintain a buffer (however thin) between God and His creation, the orthodox answer is, Our God is great enough even for this; He is great enough even to become weak, poor, empty, man. To those outside the church, who scoff at our crucified God, we can boast: "Our God can die. Can yours?" Thus, and only thus, do we make our boast in the Lord, our Lord Jesus.

Orthodox Christology has also insisted on the Lordship of God the Son by identifying the incarnate God with the God of Israel. If this book has a single guiding insight, it is N. T. Wright's astonishing summary of Jesus as the incarnation of Yahweh:

> Let us suppose that *this* God were to become human. What would such a God look like? This is the really scary thing that many never come to grips with; not that Jesus might be identified with a remote, lofty, imaginary being (any fool could see the flaw in that idea), but that God, the real

God, the one true God, might actually be like Jesus. And
not a droopy, pre-Raphaelite Jesus, either, but a shrewd
Palestinian Jewish villager, who drank wine with his
friends, agonized over the plight of his people, taught in
strange stories and pungent aphorisms, and was executed
by the occupying forces.[1]

As Wright says, "To say that Jesus is God is of course to
make a startling statement about Jesus. It is also to make a
stupendous claim about God." That is the stupendous claim
that orthodoxy has always made about Jesus. That is the
wild gospel that the entire, apparently staid, apparatus of
classical Christology is designed to protect.

* * * * *

As much as possible, I tried to write this book, as I wrote
my Old Testament introduction, *A House for My Name*,
from the "inside." Rather than hovering over the text and
picking it apart, I attempted to interpret the Old Testament
by telling the story of the Old Testament. That has proven
harder, finally impossible, with this book. Chapters 1–2 are
written in this vein, as I tell the story of "intertestamental"
Israel using the coordinates provided by Daniel's prophecies
and follow with a "harmonized" story of Jesus. Chapter
3 is terribly technical, and even when I get to the specific
gospels, I am forced to step outside the text and go "meta."
The alternative would be to follow the model of the gospels
themselves and simply tell the story of Jesus four different
ways. That would be a challenging and useful task, but I lack
the imagination to accomplish it.

This book is the product of over a decade of teaching
the Gospels to my students at New St. Andrews College.

1. N. T. Wright, *Who Was Jesus?* (Grand Rapids: Eerdmans, 1992),
52.

Through their papers, questions, and observations, my own understanding of the gospels has deepened, and I am grateful for their contributions. During the spring of 2009, I led a graduate seminar on the gospel of Mark, and that was stimulating and helpful not only for my writing of the chapter on Mark but for my work on the gospels as a whole. Kurt Queller of the University of Idaho generously shared his insights into Mark and the other gospels, and I am grateful to him for his insights. Jeff Meyers has lectured several times at Biblical Horizons conferences, and I have always benefited from his teaching. Of course, James Jordan, as always, is behind this work. And, finally, I thank my former student, Brad Littlejohn, who helped this project along by turning lecture notes into coherent prose.

This book is dedicated to my granddaughter, Darcy Bella Jane Tollefson, who has the distinction of being the Leithart grandchild who broke the gender barrier. As *The Four* goes to press, Darcy spends her days perfecting her sitting-up technique, learning to rock on hands and knees while avoiding a face-plant, teething on anything that comes within mouth-shot, charming everyone with blue eyes that are always wide with wonder. She cannot yet say the name of Jesus, or count to four, but she belongs to Him and He to her, and as she grows I trust that she will come to know that the breadth and length and height and depth of the Christ of the fourfold gospel, her Life, the One in whom she lives and moves: "Christ behind me, Christ before me, Christ beneath me, Christ above me."

CHAPTER I

THE NEW
COVENANT

One night in the second year of his reign, King Nebuchadnezzar of Babylon has a puzzling dream that leaves him sleep-
less the rest of the night. In the morning, he calls together
his wise men and magicians and demands that they recount
the dream to him and interpret it. They stall, and the king
eventually gets so enraged that he orders the commander of
his bodyguard, Arioch, to execute all the wise men.

Earlier, Nebuchadnezzar invaded Palestine and brought
back some Jews to train for service in his kingdom. Daniel is
one of the young men from Jerusalem studying at the Babylonian court. He is one of Nebuchadnezzar's wise men. When
Arioch comes to execute Daniel, Daniel turns to Yahweh
for help. Daniel has his own vision in the night (Dan. 2:19)
in which Yahweh reveals the mystery of Nebuchadnezzar's
dream. Daniel saves the day by telling Nebuchadnezzar that
in the dream God shows Nebuchadnezzar what He is going
to do in the "end of days," the "latter days" (Dan. 2:28).

Yahweh also reveals to other prophets what He plans to
do in the "latter days." According to Isaiah, during the latter
days the mountain of Jerusalem will become the "chief of
the mountains" and the destination for Gentile worshipers
(Is. 2:1–4; cf. Mic. 4:1–5). Under Yahweh's orders, Hosea
lives out the story of Israel, loving an adulteress as Yahweh
has loved adulterous Israel. In this way, Hosea prophesies

that Israel "will come trembling to Yahweh and to His goodness in the last days" (3:5). Jeremiah rejects false prophecies of peace and warns that Yahweh's anger would continue until "He has performed and carried out the purposes of His heart." But he promises that in the "latter days" Israel will come to understand the purpose of her exile (Jer. 23:20). Ezekiel prophesies that Gog will assault Israel in the "latter days" (38:16), but He assures Israel that Yahweh will blaze up to judge him with pestilence and blood (vv. 17–23).

Jeremiah 31 describes this period as a "new covenant":

"Behold, days are coming," declares Yahweh, "when I will sow the house of Israel and the house of Judah with the seed of man and with the seed of beast. As I have watched over them to pluck up, to break down, to overthrow, to destroy and to bring disaster, so I will watch over them to build and to plant," declares Yahweh. "In those days they will not say again, the fathers have eaten sour grapes, and the children's teeth are set on edge. But everyone will die for his own iniquity; each man who eats the sour grapes, his teeth will be set on edge. Behold, days are coming," declares Yahweh, "when I will make a new covenant with the house of Israel and with the house of Judah, not like the covenant which I made with their fathers in the day I took them by the hand to bring them out of the land of Egypt, My covenant which they broke, although I was a husband to them," declares Yahweh. "But this is the covenant which I will make with the house of Israel after those days," declares Yahweh, "I will put My law within them and on their heart I will write it; and I will be their God, and they shall be My people. They will not teach again, each man his neighbor and each man his brother, saying, 'Know Yahweh,' for they will all know Me, from the least of them to the greatest of them," declares Yahweh, "for I will forgive their iniquity, and their sin I will remember no more." (vv. 27–34)

Hebrews 8 makes it clear that Jeremiah is ultimately referring to the covenant established in the death and resurrection
of Jesus. But Jeremiah's original prophecy is about Israel's
return from Babylon (vv. 6, 8, 10, 12, 17, 21, 23). Yahweh
promises to "sow" the land with people and animals (v. 27).
He has been destroying Israel but promises to build her again,
and especially to rebuild the temple and city of Jerusalem
(v. 28; cf. vv. 38–40). Centuries before Jesus comes, Israel is
already living in Jeremiah's "new covenant."

Years after Nebuchadnezzar's disturbing dream, after
the Persians conquer Babylon, Daniel is reading Jeremiah's
prophecy and he is reminded that the Babylonian exile was
to last "seventy years" (9:1–2; Jer. 25:11–12; 29:10). Seventy years has gone by, so Daniel asks Yahweh to keep His
promise and liberate Israel from exile (Dan. 9:3–19). Gabriel
appears to tell Daniel that the seventy years of exile will end.
But Gabriel also says that there will be a continuing exile,
another "seventy" period, a period of "seventy weeks":

> Seventy weeks have been decreed for your people and your
> holy city, to finish the transgression, to make an end of
> sin, to make atonement for iniquity, to bring in everlast-
> ing righteousness, to seal up vision and prophecy and to
> anoint the most holy place. So you are to know and discern
> that from the issuing of a decree to restore and rebuild Je-
> rusalem until Messiah the Prince there will be seven weeks
> and sixty-two weeks; it will be built again, with plaza and
> moat, even in times of distress. Then after the sixty-two
> weeks the Messiah will be cut off and have nothing, and
> the people of the prince who is to come will destroy the
> city and the sanctuary and its end will come with a flood;
> even to the end there will be war; desolations are deter-
> mined. And he will make a firm covenant with the many
> for one week, but in the middle of the week he will put a
> stop to sacrifice and grain offering; and on the wing of
> abominations will come one who makes desolate, even

until a complete destruction, one that is decreed, is poured
out on the one who makes desolate. (Dan. 9:24–27)

Each day of the seventy weeks represents a year, so that the
whole period is 70 x 7 or 490 years. The seventy-week period begins with the "decree to restore and rebuild Jerusalem"
(v. 25). Daniel is prophesying in the first year of "Darius," a
throne name for Cyrus (9:1).[1] The "decree" is the decree of
Cyrus, which permits Israel to return to the land to rebuild
the temple (2 Chr. 36:22–23; Ezra 1:1–4). The end-point of
the period is the coming of "Messiah the Prince" (Dan. 9:25).
The period from the exodus to the temple is 480 years (1 Kgs.
6:1), and the period from the "new exodus" from Babylon
until the coming of the Messiah will be 490 years. Messiah
is going to be a new Solomon in the latter days, building a
new, more glorious temple after the new exodus.

Today, Christians usually refer to the period between Israel's return from exile and the beginning of Jesus' ministry as
an "intertestamental" period. Like the phrase "Middle Ages,"
it is a misleading term. The phrase "Middle Ages" was in-
vented by writers of the Renaissance who believed that the
world was in darkness between the end of Rome and the beginning of the Renaissance. They disliked the Christian civilization that developed between 500 and 1400, and spoke of
it either as a "dark age" or as an unimportant "middle age."
When we call the period between Malachi and Matthew an
"intertestamental" period, we are saying that the period between Malachi and Matthew is not very important.

"Intertestamental" is misleading for another reason. The
word "intertestamental" means, literally, "between the testaments." We call this period by this name because it is the
period of time between the writings of the Old Testament

---

1. James B. Jordan, *The Handwriting on the Wall: A Commentary on
the Book of Daniel* (Powder Springs: American Vision, 2007), ch. 12.

and the books that make up New Testament. When we use the word "intertestamental," we are assuming that the word "testament" refers to a collection of writings. But the Bible never uses the word "testament" to refer to writings. In Scripture, "testament" is another word for "covenant." Yahweh's covenant is the marriage relationship that He enters with human beings, especially with Israel, which includes His commitment to bless His people and the demands He places on them. "Testament" or "covenant" refers to the whole collection of rites, signs, rules, orders, and offices that make up the life of God's people.

When we understand "testament" in the biblical sense, "intertestamental" is clearly a misleading label. It implies that there is a period between about 500 B.C. and 4 B.C. where the covenant between Yahweh and Israel lapses. If this period is "inter-testamental," then the history of God's dealings with the world that starts with Adam suddenly ends with Malachi. The phrase implies that Yahweh is in a covenant with Israel from the time of Abraham to the time of Nehemiah, but then after Nehemiah there are 500 years of blank pages in the story.

That is not what happened. On the contrary, a prophecy late in Daniel shows that the history of this period repeats the history of Israel from the time of the patriarchs to the period of David.

A. A mighty king, Daniel 11:1–4
   B. Egyptian captivity, Daniel 11:5–10
      C. Apostasy and desolation, Daniel 11:21–35 (as in the time of the Judges and 1 Samuel 1–4)
   B'. New Saul, Daniel 11:36–45
A'. New David, Daniel 12:1–3[2]

2. This reproduces a section of an outline in Jordan, *Handwriting*, 498.

From another angle, the period that Daniel calls the "latter days" repeats the history of Israel's monarchy: A united kingdom (Dan. 11:1–3) is divided (11:4), and wars between "Northern" and "Southern" kings follow (11:5–10). After a desolation that results in judgment on the temple (11:31), faithful Jews suffer tribulation (11:33), though they will receive help to endure (11:34). Finally, Michael, another Cyrus, will come to deliver the people from their new exile (12:1–3).[3]

Though often ignored in studies of both the Old and New Testaments, the period between the return from exile and the coming of Jesus is a unique period of redemptive history. It has its own unique features as much as the Mosaic or Davidic periods do. This period begins with a new exodus, the restoration from Babylon. It continues with the re-building of the temple, which repeats both the conquest of the land under Joshua and the building of the temple under Solomon. It involves a new relationship between Israel and the Gentile nations. When she comes from Egypt, Israel is formed as a priestly nation. Yahweh exalts David's house and makes Israel a monarchy, a nation of kings. With the restoration from Babylon, Israel enters a third phase of history. Nestled among the nations, Israel becomes a prophetic people, called to witness to the world.

Times of the Gentiles[4]

How is Israel's life different during the "latter days"? One of the main differences is political. Israel is no longer an independent kingdom, as she is from the time of Saul to the time of Jehoiachin. Instead, Israel is subject to Gentile powers.

3. Jordan, *Handwriting*, 501.
4. I am dependent throughout this section on various writings of James Jordan, who speaks of this period as "the first phase of the New Covenant."

This is the point of Nebuchadnezzar's dream. In the night, he sees a statue with a head of gold, breast and arms of silver, belly and thighs of bronze, legs of iron with feet of a mixture of iron and clay. These materials represent a series of empires that will rule during the period between Daniel and the coming of the kingdom of God. Nebuchadnezzar, King of Babylon, is the head of gold, and the other materials represent the Persian, Greek, and Roman (including Roman-Herodian) powers.[5] This is the political order that Yahweh is instituting for this period of Israel's history. Eventually, a stone cut without hands, representing the kingdom of God, will strike the feet of the statue and grow into a mountain that fills the whole earth (2:34–35, 44–45). Daniel later sees a vision of four beasts coming from the sea, and these beasts represent the same four Gentile powers that will eventually give up their dominion to "one like the Son of Man" and his saints (Dan. 7). Daniel's vision of the "seventy weeks" makes a similar point. Seventy is the number of the Gentile nations (Gen. 10), so a seventy-week period is a time of Gentile domination.

Yahweh reveals to Daniel the broad sweep of the history of the "latter days," but he also gives a detailed vision of Israel's history (Dan. 10–11). He quickly tells the story of Alexander's conquest of Persia (11:1–3) and then of the division of Alexander's kingdom (11:4), before focusing on the contest between the kings of the North and South—the Syrian Seleucids and the Egyptian Ptolemies (11:5–45), who fight over control of Israel, the "beautiful land."[6]

During the "times of the Gentiles" (Lk. 21:24), Yahweh organizes the Gentiles in a way He never did before. Under the Mosaic and Davidic covenants, the Gentile areas are simply outlying areas. Prophets occasionally speak to

5. Jordan, *Handwriting*, ch. 7.
6. Jordan, *Handwriting*, chs. 19–23.

Gentile rulers, but the Lord never before mapped out the Gentiles and placed Israel in their midst. Beginning with the exile and restoration, the Lord organizes the Gentiles into the "*oikoumene*."[7] It's important to see that this *oikoumene* is part of God's plan. Gentile empires form an international "temple," housing Israel in its midst. The materials that make up the statue that Nebuchadnezzar sees are the materials of the temple, and the beasts of Daniel 7 are cherubim-like beasts who protect Israel. During the latter days, Israel is going to have a temple, but as importantly, Israel is going to be housed in the temple of the Gentile empires.

God originally organizes the earth into three zones: the garden, the land of Eden, and the outlying world. In the wilderness, the Mosaic system is also divided into three zones. At the center of the world is the tabernacle, Yahweh's tent; it is surrounded by the holy camp of Israel; and outside the camp is the wilderness of the world. Once Israel enters the land and Yahweh gives them peace from their enemies, He puts together something more complex. At the center of the world is Solomon's temple on Mount Moriah; surrounding the temple is the chosen city of Jerusalem, the city of David. Jerusalem is within a land of promise, a land flowing with milk and honey, which expands beyond the boundaries of the original inherited land; and outside the land of promise are the Gentiles.

When Israel comes out of exile, they do not return to the same land. At least, the land is not in the same condition as before. Instead, they enter a new land, which has been upgraded from a "land of promise" to a "holy land." In English, the phrase "holy land" is a common term for Palestine, but it occurs only twice in the Old Testament. Psalm 78:54 tells us that Yahweh brought Israel to His "holy land," and Zechariah tells us that when Israel is gathered to

7. The term is from Jordan.

Yahweh, He will "possess Judah as His portion in the holy land" (2:12). After the exile, holiness is no longer locked up in the temple. It spreads to the whole city of Jerusalem and to the whole land.

Because Israel has more contact than ever with the Gentiles, the prophets promise that during the latter days there will be a great expansion of Gentile mission. Isaiah begins his prophecy with the promise that the nations will stream to the mountain of Zion (2:1–4) and ends with a vision of nations offering to Yahweh in His house:

> "[T]he time is coming to gather all nations and tongues. And they shall come and see My glory. I will set a sign among them and will send survivors from them to the nations: Tarshish, Put, Lud, Meshech, Tubal and Javan, to the distant coastlands that have neither heard My fame nor seen My glory. And they will declare My glory among the nations. Then they shall bring all your brethren from all the nations as a grain offering to Yahweh, on horses, in chariots, in litters, on mules and on camels, to My holy mountain Jerusalem," says Yahweh, "just as the sons of Israel bring their grain offering in a clean vessel to the house of Yahweh. I will also take some of them for priests and for Levites," says Yahweh. "For just as the new heavens and the new earth which I make will endure before Me," declares Yahweh, "So your offspring and your name will endure. And it shall be from new moon to new moon and from Sabbath to Sabbath, all mankind will come to bow down before Me," says Yahweh. (Is. 66:18–23)

Yahweh's Servant will become a light to the nations, so that salvation will reach to the ends of the earth (Is. 49:6). When she is restored from exile, Jerusalem will also become a light, so the nations will "come to your light, and kings to the brightness of your rising" (Is. 60:3), bringing their wealth with them (v. 5). Yahweh will make good on His declaration:

"My house shall be called a house of prayer for *all nations*" (Is. 56:7).

Jeremiah had the same hope. Gentiles will recognize that their idols are nothing, and they will come to Yahweh from the ends of the earth (Jer. 16:19–21). Yahweh will prove Himself the true God by restoring Israel from captivity. When the nations see Jerusalem rebuilt and cleansed, "they shall fear and tremble because of all the good and all the peace that I make for it" (Jer. 33:1–9). Yahweh saves Israel for His own name's sake, to defend Himself among the nations after Israel has profaned His name (Ezek. 36:23). When Yahweh gathers His people in, He will give "renown and praise among all the peoples of the earth" because He restores Israel's fortunes (Zeph. 3:20). After He turns Israel's fasting to feasting, then

> It will yet be that peoples will come, even the inhabitants of many cities. The inhabitants of one will go to another saying, "Let us go at once to entreat the favor of Yahweh, and to seek Yahweh of hosts.". . . So many peoples and mighty nations will come to seek Yahweh of hosts in Jerusalem and to entreat the favor of Yahweh. . . . "In those days ten men from all the nations will grasp the garment of a Jew saying, 'Let us go with you, for we have heard that God is with you.'" (Zech. 8:20–23)

Zechariah ends his prophecy with a vision of a future feast of booths, when the remnant of "all the nations" will worship before Israel's God (Zech. 14:16–21).

This is not entirely new, and it is what Yahweh aims at from the beginning. He promises Abraham that He will make him a great nation and bring blessing to the Gentiles through his seed. Solomon has such a great reputation for wisdom that wise men come from all over the ancient world to Jerusalem. Throughout the Old Testament, the Lord draws Gentiles to salvation. But Gentiles are brought into contact with Israel and Israel's God on an unprecedented scale during and after the exile. Joseph anticipates this by his elevation to the right hand of Pharaoh, but between Joseph and the exile, no Jew has the same high position in a Gentile empire. Daniel does, and so do Nehemiah and Mordecai. By the time Paul is traveling throughout Asia Minor, he finds synagogues everywhere he goes, which include not only Jews but Gentile God-fearers as well. The Abrahamic promise is already being fulfilled before Jesus arrives on the scene. God scatters Israel from the land because of her sins. But He turns that judgment to a blessing by using the dispersed Jews to make Him known to Gentiles.

A Priest on the Throne

Israel is in a new political situation after the exile. After Nebuchadnezzar took the last Davidic king in slavery to Babylon, the Davidic kingdom is not restored. She lives under the authority of Gentile empires, and in certain respects these Gentile rulers take the place of the Davidic kings who ruled Israel in earlier times. Saul and then David are Yahweh's "anointed," and Israel is to submit to them as Yahweh's own representative. At the exile, Jeremiah tells Israel to submit instead to Nebuchadnezzar, and Isaiah looks ahead to see Cyrus as the new "anointed" (Is. 45:1).

Through much of this period, Israel herself is ruled by high priests rather than by kings. This is not accidental, but part of Yahweh's new covenant with Israel. According to Zechariah 6, the crown was given to the high priest, who held it until God kept His promise to bring a new David:

> Take silver and gold, make an ornate crown and set it on the head of Joshua the son of Jehozadak, the high priest. Then say to him, "Thus says Yahweh of hosts, 'Behold, a man whose name is Branch, for He will branch out from

where He is; and He will build the temple of Yahweh. Yes,
it is He who will build the temple of Yahweh, and He
who will bear the honor and sit and rule on His throne.
Thus, He will be a priest on His throne, and the counsel
of peace will be between the two offices.'" Now the crown
will become a reminder in the temple of Yahweh to Helem,
Tobijah, Jedaiah and Hen the son of Zephaniah. Those
who are far off will come and build the temple of Yahweh.
Then you will know that Yahweh of hosts has sent me to
you and it will take place if you completely obey Yahweh
your God. (vv. 11–15)

The branch is a frequent image of the restored Davidic monarchy, and in the Bible the temple-builder is always a king,
not a priest. No priest sits on a throne elsewhere in the Old
Testament. Zechariah prophesies that royal privilege will be
given to priests. Yahweh gives royal privileges to the priests
until the time of the Messiah's coming. At that point, the
priests are supposed to give the crown over to the Branch.
During the period between, though, the priests will exercise
royal as well as priestly duties. As we see below, this is precisely what happens after the Maccabean Revolt.

At the same time, Yahweh institutes some changes in
the rules for the temple and priesthood. Ezekiel envisions a
spectacular new temple-city at the end of his prophecy, and
Zechariah also sees visions of a new temple. From the time
of the exile, though, the priesthood was confined to the sons
of Zadok, a sub-class within the clan of Aaron, which was
itself a clan of the tribe of Levi (Ezek. 43:19; 44:15; 48:11).
Ezekiel announces that in the new temple only the sons of
Zadok will draw near to priest to Yahweh.

After the exile, Israel no longer worships idols. She has for
a long time. Throughout the period of Judges, she turns to
the gods of the nations, and Ahab and Jezebel are the most
aggressive idolaters among the kings of Israel and Judah.
Once she returns to the land, Israel is no longer tempted by

Baals and Ashteroth. There are no idolatrous shrines dotting the landscape. Zechariah, Haggai, and Malachi, prophets of the post-exilic period, do not preach against Baal. Nehemiah does not have to break down pagan idols in the temple, and neither does Jesus. What Ezekiel promises Israel after the exile actually occurs: "I will take you from the nations, gather you from all the lands, and bring you into your own land. Then I will sprinkle clean water on you, and you will be clean; I will cleanse you from all your filthiness and from all your idols" (Ezek. 36:24–25).

Idolatry is still a problem, but it is a new form of idolatry. Instead of worshiping the gods of the Gentiles, Israel turns the privileges she has from Yahweh into idols. Already Jeremiah tells the people of Jerusalem and Judah not to trust in the temple (Jer. 7:1–11), but they do not learn. When Jesus comes, He still has to warn them that the temple could not protect them from God's wrath (Mt. 21:12–13). Yahweh marks Abram and his descendants with circumcision, but the Jews are not supposed to trust in their circumcision. By removing flesh, circumcision symbolizes the fact that Israel has no hope in herself. But the Jews turn circumcision into an occasion for boasting. Circumcision becomes an idol. Yahweh expresses His will to Israel through the law, but the law itself instructs Israel to love the Lord above all (Deut. 6:4–6). Pharisees and scribes idolize the law itself instead of worshiping the author of the law.

Throughout the Old Testament, when Yahweh sets up a new covenant arrangement, His people rapidly sin and spoil the good things He has given them. The same is true during this period of the new covenant. Yahweh restores Israel to her land, gives her the name "Judahites" or "Jews," and promises to be the protecting Yahweh of Hosts. He gives them influence among Gentiles and sets up a Gentile imperial system that will protect Israel during this period. Instead of witnessing to Gentiles, the Jews intermarry with them, both literally (Ezra; Nehemiah) and spiritually (by compromising with Greek ways of life). Instead of gratefully submitting to Nebuchadnezzar and his imperial heirs, the Jews resist the Gentiles, often violently. Instead of accepting the Zadokite priests, the Jews after the Maccabean revolt never restore the Zadokite priesthood that was ended earlier.

By the first century, Jews are divided between compromised Hellenists (Sadducees) and nationalists like the Pharisees. Jews either resist Gentile Romans or virtually worship Caesar. They make converts, but they teach them evil ways of living (Mt. 23:15). They are not happy with the temple of the restoration because it lacks architectural splendor, and many are awed by the temple of the Idumean Herod. Gentiles, even Gentile converts, are often despised. In the temple, the Jews set up a "court of the Gentiles," which has no precedent in the Old Testament sanctuaries.

When Israel fell from the covenant during the Old Testament, Yahweh sent invading armies to oppress them. In the latter days, this happens again. But the oppressors are worse than ever. Instead of Gentiles, Yahweh sends hoards of demons. By the time Jesus comes on the scene, the new covenant has been spoiled beyond recognition.

Review Questions

1. What does Nebuchadnezzar see in his dream in Daniel 2?

2. What does the phrase "latter days" refer to?

3. What is wrong with using the phrase "intertestamental period" to describe the time between Malachi and Matthew?

4. What is the "seventy weeks" prophecy about (Dan. 9)? Why does the Lord use the number seventy?

5. What is the "*oikoumene*"?

6. How are the Jews supposed to relate to the Gentile powers that rule during this period?

7. How do the Jews fall from this new covenant?

Thought Questions

1. What do you think the New Testament writers are talking about when they use the phrase "last days"? See Acts 2:17, 2 Timothy 3:1, Hebrews 1:2, and 2 Peter 3:3.

2. Nehemiah spends a lot of time repairing the walls of Jerusalem. Why? How does that fit with what we have learned about the "last days"?

3. What is Jeremiah's point about the ark in Jeremiah 3:16? How does that fit with what we have learned about the "last days"?

Alexander and After

Daniel provides a number of overviews of the "latter days" or the "new covenant." The *oikoumene* is a statue made of different materials, which will be struck by the kingdom of God (Dan. 2). It is a series of beasts—a lion, a bear, a winged leopard with four heads, and "a fourth beast, dreadful and terrifying and extremely strong" with iron teeth to devour all the other kingdoms (Dan. 7:1–8).

Daniel also gives a detailed prophecy about the events in Israel during the same period. Twice he describes Alexander's conquest. During Belshazzar's reign, he sees a vision of Alexander's conquest of Persia:

> Then I lifted my eyes and looked, and behold, a ram which had two horns was standing in front of the canal. Now the two horns were long, but one was longer than the other, with the longer one coming up last. I saw the ram butting westward, northward, and southward, and no other beasts could stand before him nor was there anyone to rescue

from his power, but he did as he pleased and magnified himself. While I was observing, behold, a male goat was coming from the west over the surface of the whole earth without touching the ground; and the goat had a conspicuous horn between his eyes. He came up to the ram that had the two horns, which I had seen standing in front of the canal, and rushed at him in his mighty wrath. I saw him come beside the ram, and he was enraged at him; and he struck the ram and shattered his two horns, and the ram had no strength to withstand him. So he hurled him to the ground and trampled on him, and there was none to rescue the ram from his power. Then the male goat magnified himself exceedingly. But as soon as he was mighty, the large horn was broken; and in its place there came up four conspicuous horns toward the four winds of heaven. (Dan. 8:3–8)

The ram with the two horns is the Medo-Persian empire, and the goat that defeats him is Alexander. Later, in a vision during the first year of Darius the Mede, Daniel tells the same story more clearly:

[T]hree more kings are going to arise in Persia. Then a fourth will gain far more riches than all of them; as soon as he becomes strong through his riches, he will arouse the whole empire against the realm of Greece. And a mighty king will arise, and he will rule with great authority and do as he pleases. But as soon as he has arisen, his kingdom will be broken up and parceled out toward the four points of the compass, though not to his own descendants, nor according to his authority which he wielded, for his sovereignty will be uprooted and given to others besides them. (Dan. 11:2–4)

Two centuries before it happens, Daniel sees that Greece will become the next dominant power in the Mediterranean world. It happens in the fourth century before Christ. After Alexander conquers the Persians at the battle of Issus in 333

B.C., he marches south and takes the off-shore fortress of Tyre. During the siege, he sends a message to Jerusalem asking for provisions and help. The high priest, however, has promised to support Darius III of Persia, and refuses to help Alexander. Enraged, Alexander vows that once he finishes with Tyre, he will punish the Jewish high priest. Finally he conquers Tyre, and as he marches toward Jerusalem, Jaddus, the high priest, becomes frightened. He dresses in his "garments of glory and beauty" and leads a procession of priests and citizens out of the city to meet Alexander. When Alexander sees the priests "clothed with fine linen, and the high priest in purple and scarlet clothing, with his mitre on his head, having the golden plate whereon the name of God was engraved," the conqueror comes and pays his respects to Jaddus and the God of Israel.[8]

Whether this happened or not, it is true that Alexander never conquers Jerusalem. But if Alexander himself has little effect on Jerusalem or Jews, the culture he brings with him has a huge impact. From Macedonia, through Palestine, to Egypt and beyond, Alexander spreads Greek culture wherever he goes. Nearly every Jew becomes Hellenized to some degree by the time of Jesus. Some aspects of Greek culture pose no threat to Jewish religion. Jews in Palestine, and of course Jews in Asia Minor, Greece and Macedonia, and the Italian peninsula, speak Greek. Jesus Himself probably knows enough Greek to deal with the merchants, Roman officials, and other Gentiles occupying the land. Paul, a Pharisee of the Pharisees, writes in Greek. Jews adopt Greek customs as well. Jesus and His disciples recline during meals, a custom that Greeks introduce to Palestine. There was a theater in Caesarea, so close that Jesus and His disciples can

---

8. The story appears in Flavius Josephus, *Antiquities of the Jews,* 11.317–345. It may be apocryphal.

watch a play by Euripides if they want to.[9] What is called "Hellenization" (Hellas is another name for Greece) is not a one-way process. Jews are influenced by Greeks, but Greeks also admire and sometimes adopt the habits and ideas of the Eastern Mediterranean. According to 1 Maccabees a Spartan king, Areus, writes to the high priest Onias claiming kinship with the Jews, and claiming that the Spartans too were descended from Abraham.

Learning how to be faithful in response to Hellenism is one of the huge challenges for Jews living in the latter days, dwelling in the *oikoumene*. Jews have a hard time agreeing about how to meet that challenge. Jews fight with Jews about how far they can adopt Hellenistic customs.[10] It is one thing to speak Greek, or recline at the table. For some Jews, watching a Greek play at the theater is more of a problem. Many Jews go much further. Though they do not worship Greek gods, they begin to practice Greek customs that many other Jews find abominable. Some, like Philo of Alexandria, Egypt, interpret the Bible in the light of Greek philosophy. Both in Jerusalem and throughout the Mediterranean, Jews adopt Greek names, customs, habits, and enthusiasms.

Fights about Hellenization are closely related to fights about the law. When some Jews see Hellenistic customs seeping into Jewish life, they want to stop it. They find all the places in the Torah that require them to be separate from the rest of the world. They emphasize the need for Jews to avoid Gentiles and Gentile ways of life. Other Jews notice how often the Bible talks about the Jews' ministry

9. N. T. Wright, *New Testament and the People of God* (Minneapolis: Fortress, 1992), 157.

10. My summary of intra-Jewish conflicts below is dependent on E. P. Sanders, *Judaism: Practice and Belief, 63 BCE–66 CE* (Harrisburg: Trinity Press International, 1992).

to the Gentiles, and they emphasize that the Jews should be on good terms with their Gentile neighbors. The first group represents the "Pharisaical" wing of Judaism, and is tempted toward hatred of non-Jews. The second group represents the Hellenized "Sadducean" wing of Judaism, and is tempted toward compromise with the Gentiles.[11] The first group is tempted to rebel against the Gentile rulers that Yahweh has set over Israel; the second group is tempted to join the Gentile rulers in fighting against other Jews. These conflicts and tensions between Jews are simmering within Judaism for many years before they become open battles.

Kings of North and South

When Alexander dies, his empire is divided among several generals. As Daniel says, "his kingdom will be broken up and parceled out toward the four wings of heaven" (11:4). In Egypt, Alexander left behind the Ptolemaic dynasty, which lasted until Cleopatra. The Ptolemies, whom Daniel identifies as the "king of the south," dominate Israel during the 200s B.C. In 198 B.C., however, another of the dynasties that follow Alexander defeats the Ptolemies. These are the Seleucids, and they are based in Syria. Antiochus IV "Epiphanes" takes over in 175 B.C., and during his reign the simmering conflicts among Jews explode.

Daniel tells the background of these events in detail.[12] Initially, the "king of the South," Ptolemy I, will be strong (11:5). Seleucus is originally given power over Babylon, but

11. The formation of Pharisaical and Sadducean "parties" or "denominations" in Judaism comes later than this period, and other factors shape their responses to the issues facing Judaism. But the divergent tendencies are already evident at the beginning of the period of "Hellenization."

12. Throughout the remainder of this chapter, my interpretation of Daniel 11 is primarily a summary of Jordan, *Handwriting,* 546–614.

has to flee to the safety of Egypt, where he becomes a commander in the army of Ptolemy. Equipped by Ptolemy, Seleucus recovers the territory of Syria and becomes the founder of the Seleucid dynasty. About fifty years later, in 250 B.C., the Ptolemies and Seleucids attempt to forge an alliance by marriage, when the "daughter of the king of the South," the Ptolemaic princess Berenice, is sent to the "king of the North to carry out a peaceful arrangement" (Dan. 11:6). The marriage ends in divorce and murder, and the Seleucids and Ptolemies go to war. For much of the second century B.C., Palestine is under the Ptolemies. As Daniel sees it, the Ptolemies bring "desirable vessels of silver and gold" into "captivity into Egypt" (Dan. 11:8). In Daniel, "vessels" are people (cf. Dan. 1, 5), the precious treasure of Yahweh. Daniel prophesies another Egyptian oppression of Israel.

Under this Egyptian domination, the worst persecution of Jews occurs in the time of Ptolemy IV (222–204 B.C.). After fighting the Seleucids in the North, he stops in Jerusalem on his way home to Egypt. When he tries to enter the temple, the high priest, Simon II, the Just, bows and prays for mercy, and the Lord responds by shaking Ptolemy "as a reed is shaken in the wind." He falls helpless to the ground. When he returns to Egypt, he recovers and takes vengeance on Jews in Alexandria by crowding them into the hippodrome and then releasing drugged elephants to trample them to death.[13]

Out of this warfare comes the Seleucid ruler Antiochus III, called "the Great." He is the "triumphant king" whose career is summarized in Daniel 11:10–20. His large armies flow over his enemies like a "flood" (11:10), and he overcomes the arms of the South (11:15). None stand before his face, and he has all of the "beautiful land" in his "hand"

---

13. 3 Maccabees. This is a much-doubted text, but there is likely a germ of truth behind its fanciful stories: The Egyptians did persecute Jews, and the Seleucids were therefore greeted as liberators.

(11:16). Because the Ptolemies were attacking Jews, the Jews are happy with Antiochus. They support him in his fights with Egypt, and in return Antiochus grants the Jews favor. He adopts a policy of toleration, lets the Jews govern themselves and retain their worship, and even provides funds to restore the temple, animals for sacrifice, and wheat and oil for the temple service.[14]

When Antiochus "turns his face to the sea lands" (Dan. 11:18), conquering Macedon, Thrace, and Greece, things do not go so well. He intends to ally with Hannibal, the great general of Carthage, against Rome. But the Roman general Lucius Scipio defeats him at Thermopylae and Magnesia. Antiochus becomes a Roman vassal, and sends his son, the future Antiochus IV, to Rome as a hostage. Antiochus III is himself assassinated when he tries to pillage a temple of his own god to pay tribute to the Romans. As Daniel says, "he will stumble and fall and be found no more" (11:19). Following Antiochus comes Seleucus IV (187–175 B.C.), who has to send out a "tax collector" through the "Jewel of his kingdom" to raise funds for the Roman tribute (11:20).

Through the reign of Antiochus III, the Jews remain on good terms with the Seleucid rulers, and that initially continues in the reign of Antiochus IV, who is the "angry king" of Daniel 11:21–35. Daniel calls him a "despicable person" who does not have the "honor of kingship" (11:21). Antiochus is a usurper who steals the kingdom from his nephew Demetrius, but he is a despicable person in the eyes of God because he eventually defies God's commandments.

Much of what he does, however, is inspired by Jews. He gets in the middle of a battle between Hellenized Jews and faithful Jews who keep to the covenant of God. Under Antiochus, a "group of renegade Jews" arises who encourage the rest of the Jews to make alliances with the Seleucids. "We

---

14. Josephus, *Antiquities,* 12.3.3–4.

should go and make an agreement with the Gentiles round about; nothing but disaster has been our lot since we cut ourselves off from them," they say, and many Jews agree. As a result, some Jews "went to the king and received authority to introduce pagan laws and customs. They built a gymnasium in the gentile style at Jerusalem; they removed the marks of circumcision and repudiated the holy covenant; they intermarried with Gentiles and sold themselves to evil."[15]

Antiochus is closer to these "renegade Jews" than to others, and he gives these Jews what they want. At the time of Antiochus' enthronement, the high priest is Onias, a faithful and devout Zadokite. Simon the Benjamite slanders Onias to Antiochus, reminding Antiochus that Onias has resisted paying tribute to Seleucus IV. Onias's brother Joshua offers the Syrians money, promising to pay tribute regularly, if Antiochus makes him High Priest. Antiochus agrees, removes Onias from his position, and makes Joshua High Priest. Joshua Hellenizes his name to Jason and makes "his fellow-Jews conform to the Greek way of life." He establishes "a gymnasium at the foot of the citadel itself" and makes "the most outstanding of the young men adopt the hat worn by Greek athletes." Because of Jason, "the priests no longer showed any enthusiasm for their duties at the altar; they treated the temple with disdain, they neglected the sacrifices, and whenever the opening gong called them they hurried to join the sports at the wrestling school in defiance of the law. They placed no value on the dignities prized by their forefathers, but cared above everything for Hellenistic honours."[16] Jason holds the high priesthood for only three years before Menelaus pays the Seleucids even more money, and gets to be high priest. Menelaus is not even a priest, but a Benjamite.[17] This shows the "despicable person" at work. Antiochus'

15. 1 Maccabees 1:11–15.
16. 2 Maccabees 4:7–17.
17. Jordan, *Handwriting*, 576–577.

father required the Jews to perform temple worship as the law requires. Antiochus IV is not interested in the law. He ends the Zadokite priesthood without a second thought.

Antiochus also offends Jews by violating the temple. In 169 B.C., he is involved in wars with both Egypt and Rome. To replenish his treasury, he plunders the temple. Like many of the kings of Judah before him, he "entered the temple and carried off the gold altar, the lampstand with all its fittings, the table of the Bread of the Presence, the libation cups and bowls, the gold censers, the curtain, and the garlands. He stripped the gold plating from the front of the temple, seized the silver and gold, the precious vessels, and whatever secret treasures he found, and carried them all away when he left for his own country."[18] Again, the blame falls as much on the apostate Jews as on Antiochus. Menelaus already plundered the temple and sent treasure to Antiochus, and when he goes to help himself to the temple treasures, Menelaus is there to escort him in.[19]

On another occasion, Antiochus enters the temple and sets up a pagan altar and offers sacrifices to Zeus.[20] In 1 Maccabees this is called the "abomination of desolation," and 2 Maccabees adds, "King Antiochus sent an elderly Athenian to compel the Jews to give up their ancestral customs and to cease regulating their lives by the laws of God. He was commissioned also to pollute the temple at Jerusalem and dedicate it to Olympian Zeus; the sanctuary on Mount Gerazim he was to dedicate to Zeus God of Hospitality, as requested by the local inhabitants."[21] While this incident offends many Jews and provokes a reaction, it is not the incident that Daniel describes as the "abomination of desolation."

---

18. 1 Maccabees 1:20–24.
19. 2 Maccabees 5:15–20; cf. Jordan, *Handwriting,* 578.
20. 1 Maccabees 1:4.
21. 2 Maccabees 6:1–2.

According to Daniel, the abomination that brings desolation is not something done by Antiochus himself. It is done by Jews who forsake the covenant:

> [H]e will come back and show regard for those who forsake the holy covenant. Forces (arms) from him will arise, desecrate the sanctuary fortress, and do away with the regular sacrifice and they will set up the abomination of desolation. By smooth words he will turn to godlessness those who act wickedly toward the covenant, but the people who know their God will display strength and take action. (Dan. 11:30–32)

Not Antiochus himself, but "arms from him" desecrate the sanctuary. These arms, in Daniel, are the Jews "who act wickedly toward the covenant." The specific incident is probably the murder of Onias III, the deposed High Priest, who rebukes Menelaus for taking gold from the temple treasury. The blood of the faithful priest is the detestable act that brings desolation to the temple.[22]

Eventually, Antiochus tries to force the Jews to adopt Hellenistic customs. He makes everyone in his kingdom "become one people and abandon their own customs." Many Jews obey the decree. They "willingly adopted the foreign cult, sacrificing the idols and profaning the Sabbath." Because of his decree, "whole-offerings, sacrifices, and drink-offerings" are forbidden, Sabbaths and festivals are profaned, and the temple and priests are defiled. "Pagan altars, idols, and sacred precincts were to be established, swine and other unclean beasts to be offered in sacrifice. The Jews were to leave their sons uncircumcised; they had to make themselves in every way abominable, unclean, and profane, and so forget the law and change all their statutes." Antiochus backs up his decree with threats: "The penalty for disobeying the

---

22. Jordan, *Handwriting,* 578.

royal command was death."[23] Syrian officers "put to death women who had had their children circumcised; their babies, their families, and those who had performed the circumcisions were hanged by the neck. Yet many in Israel found strength to resist, taking a determined stand against the eating of any unclean food. They welcomed death and died rather than defile themselves and profane the holy covenant. Israel lay under a reign of terror."[24]

The motives of Antiochus are somewhat hard to figure out. He has no hostility to Jews as such. For Antiochus, the motive is political. Rome controls Egypt, and Antiochus needs to make sure that there are no Roman allies within his territory.[25] As Daniel sees things, his attacks on the Jews and the temple are the result of the detestable acts of apostate Jews. It is the desolation that always follows abominations.

Resistance

While Jews are being slaughtered, the Lord provides "a little help" (Dan. 11:34). That comes from the Maccabees. Resistance to Antiochus and to the apostate Jews allied with him comes mainly from outside the nobility and large Hellenized towns. It comes from the countryside. A priest named Mattathias lives with five sons in the village of Modin. One of Antiochus's officials comes there and tries to force them to sacrifice. Mattathias refuses, and kills a Jew who begins to sacrifice and also the official who is enforcing the royal decree.[26] This becomes a sensational event, and Mattathias and his sons have to flee to the mountains. Mattathias dies

23. 1 Maccabees 1:41ff.
24. 1 Maccabees 1:60–64.
25. Jordan, *Handwriting*, 579.
26. 1 Maccabees 2:23–25.

soon after, and is succeeded by his son Judas, who takes the nickname Maccabeus (which means "hammer-like").

Judas is a military commander of the first order, a perfect commander for the kind of guerilla war that the Maccabees are forced to fight. While Antiochus is fighting against Persia, for example, he leaves Palestine under control of Lysias, who raises an army under the command of Gorgias: five thousand infantry and one thousand cavalry. Gorgias camps at Emmaus to prepare to attack the Maccabeans near Jerusalem, while Judas camps at Mizpeh. Gorgias decides to search out the rebels. When Judas hears that the Syrians have divided their forces, he leaves Mizpeh to a position just south of Emmaus. At dawn, he attacks the Syrian camp and defeats the smaller force based there. Instead of pursuing the defeated armies, Judas recalls his men to Emmaus to await Gorgias. Meanwhile, Gorgias goes to Mizpeh during a night march and finds the Jewish camp abandoned. When he returns to Emmaus, he discovers his own camp in flames and retreats to the coast. Gorgias never actually fights Judas during this sequence of events. Judas makes him look foolish.

Judas defeats Lysias again at the battle of Beth-zur, and in the aftermath of this battle, Judas and his men march to Jerusalem and take the temple mount. On December 25, 164 they consecrate the altar in Jerusalem and began the sacrifices—his is the origin of the feast of Hanukkah. It is a restoration of pure worship. "He [Judas] selected priests without blemish and faithful to the law, and they purified the temple, removing to an unclean place the stones which defiled it. They discussed what to do about the desecrated altar of whole-offerings, and rightly decided to demolish it, for fear it might become a lasting reproach to them because it had been defiled by the Gentiles." To begin their worship, "they took unhewn stones, as the law directs, and built a new altar on the model of the previous one. They also repaired the temple and restored its interior, and they consecrated the temple courts. New sacred vessels were made; the lampstand, the altar of incense, and the table were brought into the temple. They burnt incense on the altar, and they lit the lamps on the lampstand to shine within the temple. When they had set the Bread of the Presence on the table and spread out the curtains, their work was completed." On that day, "sacrifice was offered as laid down by the law, on the newly constructed altar of whole offerings. On the anniversary of the day of its desecration by the Gentiles, on that very day it was dedicated with hymns of thanksgiving, to the music of harps and lutes and cymbals."[27] It is the beginning of the Jewish feast of "Dedication" or "Hanukah."

Judas also takes the opportunity to fight against a number of Israel's traditional enemies and to expand into traditional Israelite territories, such as Edom and Gilead. Despite his many successes, Jerusalem is still divided: Hellenizers hold the citadel (the Acra) and the rebels hold Zion. The story becomes more complicated at this point, because another Seleucid, Demetrius, arrives on the scene in 162, to fight Antiochus V, the son of Antiochus IV, who has taken over the kingdom. The Jewish rebels make the best of it by allying with one faction of Syrians against the other. They also seek help from the Romans, which raises the stakes considerably for the Syrians. It is only under Simon, a brother of Judas, that the Acra is taken in 141.

Judas's successors hold onto the territory he had won, and they are able to secure a testy peace with the Syrians. However, one problem remains: the High priesthood remains to be filled. The Maccabees have removed the apostate priest Menelaus, but they gave it to Alcimus, whom 1 Maccabees calls "Alcimus the apostate" (7:9). Alcimus has slaughtered

27. 1 Maccabees.

a delegation of Hasidim who were seeking reconciliation between the priesthood and the rebels. Judas challenges the High Priest but is killed in battle before being able to do anything about it; his brother Jonathan succeeds him, and he finally convinces the Syrians to allow him to hold the office of High Priest in 153. That marks the end of the Zadokite priesthood. The Maccabeans are descendants of Aaron, and therefore priests. But Ezekiel says that after the exile only the descendants of Zadok can be priests. The Maccabeans' revolt never restored a suitable high priest. From that time, the High Priest took over as both religious and military leader of Israel. Some Jews conclude that the high priests after Jonathan are illegitimate, and therefore that the whole temple worship is illegitimate. A group known as the Essenes believes that Judaism is so corrupt that they cannot remain part of it, and they migrate to the desert and establish a community near the Dead Sea.

The Maccabean revolt is "help," but only a "little help." It is not the final restoration that Daniel is looking for.

Review Questions

1. According to legend, why didn't Alexander the Great conquer Jerusalem?

2. What is "Hellenization"?

3. How do different groups of Jews react to Hellenization? How does this affect the way they interpret the Torah?

4. What dynasty rules after Alexander in Egypt? In Syria?

5. Who is Jason? What did he do?

6. Who is Antiochus Epiphanes? What did he do?

7. How did the Maccabean revolt begin?

8. In what ways was the Maccabean revolt successful?

9. What did the Maccabeans do with regard to the priesthood?

Thought Questions

1. Examine 1 Samuel 1–4. How is this like an "abomination of desolation"?

2. Who was Zadok? Use a Bible concordance to find out.

3. How *should* the Jews have responded to "Hellenization"?

Hasmoneans, 143–63 B.C.

Judas's brother Jonathan continues to expand the territories controlled by the Maccabeans. He in turn is succeeded by the third brother, Simon, who in 143 is able to expel the Syrian garrison from Jerusalem. Jerusalem becomes a free, and Jewish, city. For a number of decades, Israel is an independent state ruled by the High Priest. The High Priest becomes hereditary, passed down from the Maccabean brothers to their descendants. This begins the "Hasmonean" dynasty, named for an ancestor of the Maccabees.

Simon's reign is the high point of the Hasmonean dynasty, seen by Jews as a restoration of the glory of Solomon. It is a time when "the people farmed the land in peace" and the land "produced its crops and the trees in the plains their fruit." The land is at peace so old men can sit "in the streets, talking together of their blessings" and young men dress "in splendid military style." Towns have "food in plenty" and Simon gives them "weapons for defense, so that his renown spread to the ends of the earth. Peace was restored to the land, and throughout Israel there was great rejoicing. Everyone sat under his own vine and fig tree, and there was none to cause alarm. Those were days when no enemy was seen in the land and every hostile king was crushed. Simon gave his protection to the poor among the people; he fulfilled the demands of the law, and rid the country of renegades and evil men. He enhanced the splendor of the temple and furnished it with a wealth of sacred vessels."[28]

Simon's successors are not as well-liked or successful. Aristobulus is the first to assume the title "king." He is followed by Alexander Jannaeus, who expands the kingdom to nearly the size it had been during Solomon's reign. But Alexander is a horrifically violent man. During a festival, he stands at the altar ready to sacrifice when some of the Jews began to throw citrons at him. They insult him, claiming that his ancestors were slaves. Alexander sends in troops and kills six thousand Jews. After that, he puts up a wall of wood around the altar and temple to prevent the mobs from attacking him again.[29]

Many of the Jews organize themselves against Alexander. Alexander beats them in a number of battles, and eventually many of them retreat to the fortress in the city of Bethome. Alexander sets siege to the city, and after taking it brings the captives to Jerusalem. There, as he is "feasting with his concubines, in the sight of all the city, he ordered about eight hundred of them to be crucified; and while they were living, he ordered the throats of their children and wives to be cut before their eyes. This was done by way of revenge for the injuries they had done him." It is the first time that a Jewish ruler has used crucifixion. This was the source for his nickname, "Thracian," given because the Jews regarded the people of Thrace as "barbarous and cruel folk."[30] The great dream of Judas and Simon had come to this: The dynasty that started with resistance to tyranny ends up producing tyrants.

The Hasmonean dynasty finally comes to an end in the mid-60s B.C. with a civil war between Hyrcanus II and Aristobulus II. The former is chosen by his mother, Salome

28. 1 Maccabees 14:8–15.
29. Josephus, *Antiquities,* 13.13.6.
30. Josephus, *Antiquities,* 13.14.2.

Alexandra, to succeed her, but the people support Aristobulus. Antipater, the father of Herod the Great, gets involved
after Aristobulus defeats Hyrcanus. While Antipater and
his allies besiege Jerusalem, the Roman general Pompey
moves into Palestine from Syria and waits to see what will
happen. Aristobulus becomes impatient, and he begins organizing military resistance to the Romans. His suspicions
aroused, Pompey besieges Jerusalem and takes it after three
months, and he caps off his conquest of the city by entering
the temple and the most holy place. He puts Hyrcanus II in
the office of High Priest and divides the district into several
areas. The cities in the coastal region become independent;
the Decapolis (ten cities in trans-Jordan) is combined into
a free league; Samaria becomes an independent region; and
the High Priest is left with control only of Jerusalem, Judea,
part of Galilee, and Perea. That area itself is divided into
five districts in 57 B.C.

Herod and Rome

Pompey's arrangements may have worked, but Aristobulus
continues to make trouble, and Pompey's own civil war with
Caesar distracts him. God is arranging history to bring a
third ruler onto the stage. After the triumphant king (Antiochus III) and the angry king (Antiochus IV), God brings
the "ungodly king" (Dan. 11:36–45). This king corresponds
to the boastful little horn that Daniel sees arising after the
clash of the ram and the goat (Dan. 8:9). Antiochus Epiphanes foreshadows the little horn, but he is not the little horn,
or the ungodly king. That title belongs to Herod the Great.

Daniel sees Herod as the "climax of the history of Adam,"[31]
the man who strives to be God:

---

31. Jordan, *Handwriting,* 597.

> Then the king will do as he pleases, and he will exalt and
> magnify himself above every god and will speak mon-
> strous things against the God of gods; and he will prosper
> until the indignation is finished, for that which is decreed
> will be done. He will show no regard for the gods of his
> fathers or for the desire of women, nor will he show regard
> for any other god; for he will magnify himself above them
> all. (11:36–37)

Herod rises to power on the coattails of his father, Antipater. In the latter days of the Hasmonean dynasty, Antipater is able to work his way into a strong position. At his
death, he divides his area among his sons. Herod receives
Galilee and his brother Phasael becomes the power in Judea.
Because of an attack from Parthia in the east, Herod's brother
and Hyrcanus, still high priest, are eliminated around 40
B.C. Herod sees an opportunity to gain sole power. He rushes
to Rome, gains the support of Octavius, and returns with
the title, "King of the Jews." Several years later, he captures
Jerusalem (37 B.C.), marries Mariamne from the Hasmonean
dynasty, and begins his extensive building projects, including a rebuilding of the temple, which he begins in 19 B.C.

Herod is a skillful and unscrupulous politician. When
Caesar is assassinated by Brutus and Cassius, Herod comes
into the favor of Antony, who rules along with Octavius. Despite the favor of Antony, the first years of Herod's kingdom
are troubled by Cleopatra, who is eager to bring Palestine
back under Ptolemaic rule. When Octavius defeats Antony
at Actium in 31 B.C., Herod quickly changes sides and gains
the support of Octavius. Octavius confirms Herod's position
as king and solidifies his rule. Herod not only furthers Octavius Augustus's interests in Palestine, but also helps with
building projects in the Eastern Mediterranean, all to pro-
mote Augustan policies and prestige.

Herod is never popular with Jews. He wipes out the Has-moneans, and though he gets circumcised[32] and makes a show of being Jewish, he is an Edomite, a descendant of Esau. Rebuilding the temple does not make him legitimate in the eyes of hardcore Jews. Perhaps that is because he puts a Roman eagle above the gate.[33] Herod's family life is anything but peaceful. He has two sons by Mariamne, Alexander and Aristobulus. They are brought up in Rome, and are acceptable to Jews because of their Hasmonean background, but their other brothers become envious. Both are executed in 7 B.C. Another of Herod's sons, Antipater, is executed three years later, again on suspicion of plotting against Herod, only a few days before Herod's death. Herod eventually executed Mariamne as well. His slaughter of the infants at Bethlehem is characteristic of his violent, paranoid style of rule.

After his death, Herod divides his kingdom among three sons: Judea and Samaria to Archelaus, Galilee to Antipas, and northeastern territories to Philip. Several of these Herods appear in the New Testament. Archelaus, who is mentioned in Matthew 2:22, rules Judea from 4 B.C. to 6 A.D., but his rule is so repressive that it becomes intolerable to the Jews. Augustus's allies in Judea warn that if Archelaus is not re-moved there will be a full-scale revolt. So Augustus makes Judea a Roman province administered by prefects appointed by the emperor. As a result, when Jesus is tried, a Roman governor, Pilate, presides at the court. Galilee stays under Herodian rule longer. In Galilee, Herod Antipas is the one who kills John the Baptist (Mt. 14:1–12) and later tries Jesus (Lk. 23:8–12). In his efforts to gain power, he tries to be-friend Caligula, but it backfires. He asks for the title of king,

---

32. Herod insisted, for example, that Syllaeus, an Arab suitor to his sister Salome, be circumcised (Josephus, *Antiquities*, 16.225).

33. Jordan, *Handwriting*, 608.

but instead is exiled to Gaul. In 38 A.D. Agrippa, grandson of Herod the Great, becomes king and rules the same territory as his grandfather: Judea, Samaria, and Idumea. This is the Herod who executes James, puts Peter in prison, and is killed after being acclaimed as a god (cf. Acts 12). Another Herod Agrippa appears in Acts 25.

By the time of Jesus' birth, Israel's history has come full circle. Herod the Great is a new Saul. That is tragic for Israel. But it also gives them hope: If Saul is on the throne, can a new David be far behind?

Review Questions

1. What is the Hasmonean dynasty?
2. Describe Simon's rule.
3. What kind of ruler was Alexander Jannaeus?
4. How did the Romans get involved in Judea?
5. Describe Herod the Great's rise to power.
6. What kind of ruler was Herod the Great?

Thought Questions

1. Whom does Jesus call a "fox" in Luke 13:32? Which Herod is Jesus talking about? Why does He call him a fox?

2. What happens to Herod and Pilate at the time of Jesus' trial? See Luke 23:12.

3. Look at John 19:15. Keeping in mind the history reviewed in the chapter above, explain the irony of that verse.

4. In a concordance, look up some of the passages in Acts that refer to Roman officials. How does Luke portray the Romans? Are they good or evil?

CHAPTER 2

THE STORY OF
JESUS[1]

"Seek the peace of the city where I have sent you into exile," Jeremiah says to the people of Judah as they are carried to Babylon by Nebuchadnezzar. Some of the Jews, like Daniel and his friends, Ezra, Nehemiah, Esther, and Mordecai, follow Jeremiah's instructions. Many Jews do not. By the early first century A.D., the tensions between Jews and Romans are very high.

During the decade between A.D. 26 and 36, when Pilate serves as the Roman procurator in Jerusalem, Pharisees clash with Romans on a regular basis.[2]

- Pilate moves the Roman army from Caesarea to Jerusalem for the winter, and brings along images of Caesar. He knows it will upset the Jews, so he moves them into the city at night. When Jews learn about it, they plead with Pilate to remove the images, but he refuses and threatens to kill them all. The Jews "threw themselves

1. My understanding of the gospels and life of Jesus has been so thoroughly shaped by the work of N. T. Wright, especially *Jesus and the Victory of God* (Minneapolis: Fortress, 1997), that I could footnote virtually every sentence of this chapter with a citation from that book. That would be tedious; so here I acknowledge that this chapter would have been very different, and probably could not be written at all, without Wright.

2. I have drawn this list of incidents from Wright, *People of God*, 174.

upon the ground, and laid their necks bare, and said they would take their death very willingly, rather than the wisdom of their laws should be transgressed."[3] Pilate is so impressed that he tells his troops to move the standards back to Caesarea.

- To raise money to pipe water into Jerusalem, Pilate takes money from the temple. Tens of thousands of Jews mob together and call for Pilate to return the money to the temple, and some of the Jews insult the Roman governor. When the Jews refuse to leave at Pilate's request, Pilate sends in the troops and massacres them.[4]

- Pilate massacres Galileans in the temple, so that the blood of sacrifices mingles with the blood of the animals (Lk. 13:1).

- Pilate places Roman shields in his palace at Jerusalem, and Jews become annoyed.

- In Samaria, a prophet calls all the people to gather to Mount Gerazim. Many Jews come with weapons, and Pilate stops them with a "great band of horsemen and foot-men." He kills some, others get away, and he captures many. Later, he slaughters all the prisoners.[5]

Rebels rise up in Galilee and Judea on a regular basis. These are often called "robbers" in our Bible translations, but that gives the wrong impression. They are not simply robbers stealing money. They are revolutionaries trying to make life very difficult for the Roman government, so that the Romans will leave the holy land. They are Robin Hoods or Jesse Jameses, folk heroes to many Jews. They are like

3. Josephus, *Antiquities,* 18.3.1.
4. Josephus, *Antiquities,* 18.3.2.
5. Josephus, *Antiquities,* 18.4.1.

the Iraqis and Afghans who set car bombs outside American military bases trying to get the Americans to run home. In the cities, there are *sicarii,* "dagger-men" known for their clever assassinations. They sneak up behind their target in a crowd, kill him, drop the knife, and immediately join in the loud laments over the dead body. No one knows who has done the deed.

There is a storm on the horizon, and almost all the Jews are expecting something to happen, something very big. They know that the Lord promised to destroy all Israel's enemies, to make Israel the "chief of the mountains" (Is. 2:1–4), and to raise up a new David to make war and then sit on the throne (Is. 9:7; Jer. 23:5; 33:15; Ezek. 34:23). Daniel even gives them a calendar (Dan. 9:24–27). He says that the Messiah will come to finish everything up within seventy weeks, four hundred and ninety years. That time has past, but the Jews are sure that the Lord has not forgotten His promise. He is going to come to help Israel as He did when she was in Egypt, when she was oppressed by Philistines, when Assyria threatened Jerusalem in the days of Hezekiah. Israel's best days are still ahead of her. This hope is what made the Jews of the first century do what they do.

Not all the Jews are hoping for something new to happen. Sadducees aren't. Most of the priests are Sadducees, and they have many privileges and much wealth. As long as the Romans protect the temple, and protect the Sadducees' privileges, they are content to have Romans in their land. They seem to be following Jeremiah's instructions, but they are not really. They have compromised and are not very faithful to the covenant with Israel anymore. The Sadducees think everything is just fine the way it is, and they hope it will last forever.

The Pharisees are people of hope. The Pharisees are strict about keeping the law, and strict about avoiding compromise with the Romans and other unbelievers. To that extent, they follow Jeremiah's instructions. But they also believe that the Romans are unclean and pollute the holy land. They want the Romans to go, and they are more than willing to use whatever means they can find to get rid of the Romans. Some are even willing to take up weapons and start a war. They resist the Romans, but the way they resist shows that they are more Roman than they think. Romans think the world is ruled by the sword, and many Pharisees agree. They forget that it is not by power nor by might but by the Spirit. Pharisees have compromised as much as the Sadducees have.

At the same time, the Pharisees do not think the Romans are the main problem. They believe the problem is that Jews are unfaithful. The Romans have power because Yahweh is punishing the Jews for their unfaithfulness. The Pharisees believe that the way to save Israel is to make sure that Israel is very, very pure. They want every Jew to follow the same strict holiness code that the priests followed. Once Israel is very, very clean, then the Messiah will come to deliver the faithful Jews from the Romans, destroy the unfaithful Jews and Romans, and raise up the true, faithful Israel as the greatest nation on the planet.

Even the Essenes are people of hope. They move out of the land of Israel sometime after the Maccabees replace the Zadokite priests. They don't believe that priests are legitimate, and so they refuse to participate in the temple worship. But they do not leave the land to live near the Dead Sea because they have given up hope. They leave the land because they are sure that the land is corrupted by the Romans, the temple corrupted by false sacrifices, and the priests polluted. But they do not expect to stay in the wilderness forever. Someday, they believe, Yahweh will come to destroy all the false Jews, scatter the Romans, and lead the true Israel—the Essenes, of course—into the land, just as He led Israel into the land under Joshua. The Essenes do not go to the wilderness because they like the wilderness. They go because they believe that is where the true Israel gathers, before they begin a conquest.

The ingredients are all there for a great explosion. The Romans mainly want to keep the peace and use the resources of the Middle East, but they are often brutal. Even though they give the Jews a great deal of freedom, they think the Jews are strange and do not understand them. They cannot understand, for instance, why the Jews get so upset about images and pictures, which are the main part of every Roman temple. So the Romans blunder on, sometime slaughtering Jews, sometimes ignoring them. Meanwhile many Jews hate the Romans for being in their land, and they believe God is on their side and will come to help them throw off the Roman yoke.

Judea and Galilee are powder-kegs whose fuses are burning short. They are ready to blow. In the first century, Palestine is nearly as volatile as that area of the world is today. It does not take a prophet to realize that the Romans and the Jews are headed for a catastrophe. But a prophet comes. In fact, two prophets.

Prepare Ye the Way

When Herod the Great rules in Judea, the angel Gabriel who appeared to Daniel appears again, this time to a priest named Zecharias while he is offering incense in the temple. He has good news for Zecharias and his wife Elizabeth. Though the two are very old and served the Lord faithfully, they had no children. Now, the angel says, in their old age, the Lord is going to give them their life-long wish. They are going to have a son. But Gabriel's announcement is bigger. He is the angel who delivered visions to Daniel; now, he is coming to tell Zecharias that the Lord is ready to fulfill those visions. Zecharias' son is not just any son. He will be a great prophet, filled with the power of Elijah. Elijah lived in the time of the tyrant Ahab, and John will live in the time of the tyrant Herod. He will do Elijah's work, turning the people back to God. He will prepare a people so that when the Lord comes, He will find a people prepared for His coming (Lk. 1:8–17).

John's ministry is a preparation for the ministry of Jesus. Jesus is the coming King, the new David. John is not the new David, but merely a servant of the king. When an ancient king goes to visit a distant district of his kingdom, he sends one of his servants ahead to get things ready. The servant makes sure that the city is clean, the people ready to receive the king. That is John's ministry. He prepares the way for the Lord. He is like a new Samuel preparing for a new David.

John's ministry takes place in the wilderness, where the Essenes are. He is in the wilderness for the same reason. They went to the wilderness because they are preparing for a new conquest, and so is John. He starts baptizing in the wilderness because he is getting the people ready for a new Joshua to come and lead them in conquest.

John's message is a message of judgment. Wrath is coming, he says, and if Israel is going to escape or survive that wrath, then they needed to repent of their sins and turn to the Lord with their whole heart. Keeping the purity laws of the Pharisees is not repentance enough. They need to repent even of the sins of the Pharisees. Otherwise, they will be destroyed in a clash with Rome. "The axe is already laid at the root of the tree," John says (Lk. 3:9). He is alluding to a prophecy of Isaiah which described Assyria as the Lord's axe against the northern kingdom of Israel (Is. 10:15). Rome is the new axe in the hand of the Lord, and He is getting ready to swing. The judgment that John talked about is the threat of the Romans finally destroying the rebellious Jews. John is gathering people together who will be saved from that judgment, who will pass through the fire of the Roman war against Judea and be preserved as the "remnant," the burned but lively seed of the new Israel.

Multitudes come to John asking for baptism. They want to be part of this new Israel. They want to be among the people ready to welcome the King who will fulfill all their hopes. When Jesus arrives, He finds a people prepared for Him, a people prepared by John.

A Virgin Shall Conceive

In the small town of Bethlehem in Judea, the same angel who has appeared to Zecharias in the temple appears to the young virgin Mary. If the angel gives a surprising announcement to the old priest and his wife, he comes with a mind-blowing announcement to Mary. Zecharias and Elizabeth are too old to hope for children, but they know that the Lord has opened the womb of Sarai and Hannah (Gen. 18:1–15; 21:1–7; 1 Sam. 1). Mary, though, is not yet married, and she is a virgin. There is no possibility for her to have a child. Whenever God gives a miracle child to an old couple, it is a sign that He is beginning something new. An old couple having their first child means a new life. But a virgin who conceives must mark the beginning of a new creation.

The angel not only gives Mary the news that she will conceive and have a child, but tells her that the child will be born when the Spirit overshadows Mary (Lk. 1:35). Just as the Spirit overshadows the water at the beginning of the world, and forms the first creation, so the Spirit is going to overshadow Mary to form a new creation in her womb. Hers will be the womb of a new world. No wonder Mary sang about the overthrow of the world's wicked rulers and the exaltation of the righteous people of God (Lk. 1:46–55).

When Mary becomes pregnant, her fiancée, Joseph, wonders what has happened. He knows that Mary is a faithful Israelite girl, but he thinks she must have fallen into temptation and conceived a child. He is ready to put her away quietly to protect her from scandal when an angel appears to him, as an angel has appeared to Mary. The angel assures Joseph that he has nothing to worry about, since the child Mary is carrying is conceived by the Spirit. The angel tells Joseph that Mary's conception fulfilled a prophecy of Isaiah (Mt. 1:23; Is. 7:14). In Isaiah, the sign of the virgin conceiving is a sign that Judah is going to be delivered from her enemies. The child that Mary conceives is the one who will fulfill all of Israel's hopes.

When he is still a young child, magi from Persia come to Jerusalem. They have seen a sign in the sky that tells the birth of a great king, and they come to Jerusalem looking for that king. Herod the Great consults the priests, who tell him that the prophet Micah has foretold that the birth of the Messiah is to happen in Bethlehem. So Herod sends the magi to that town looking for Jesus. The Lord sends an angel to warn Joseph of the danger from Herod, and Joseph takes his young family and flees to Egypt. When Herod dies, Joseph moves the family back to the land, but goes to Nazareth, in the Northern region of Galilee, rather than settling in the district of Herod's son in Judea. Even while he is still an infant, Jesus is already creating turmoil, shaking the thrones of kings, striking fear into the king of the Jews.

Jesus' life between his birth and his baptism is almost a complete blank. We see him next when He is twelve years old, traveling to Jerusalem with his mother and father for Passover (Lk. 2:41–52). It is an important episode. Mary and Joseph have taken Jesus to the temple once before, so that Mary can perform the rites of purification that the law required (Lev. 12). But when he goes to Jerusalem at twelve, he is aware of what is happening. He is twelve, his age matching the number of tribes in the nation of Israel. He goes to Jerusalem at the time of a feast, just as He returns to Jerusalem many years later at the same feast of Passover. When he visits Jerusalem at twelve, he stays in the temple, discussing the law with the scribes and priests, who are astonished at his teaching. Later, he will return to Jerusalem, stand in the same temple, and teach the people. Later, the Jewish leaders will again be astonished at his knowledge of the law, but their astonishment will give way to fear and hatred, as Jesus' words and his actions expose their own wickedness.

When Jesus goes to the temple at the age of twelve, his parents lose track of him. They start back home, thinking that Jesus is among the traveling pilgrims, but then they discover he is missing. They finally return to Jerusalem and find Jesus in the temple. This takes three days, and the three days when Jesus is missing foreshadow the three days he will be "missing" in the tomb. His entire visit to Jerusalem at twelve foreshadows his later arrival in Jerusalem, his teaching in the temple, his arrest and trial, his crucifixion, and his reappearance from the grave three days later.

Review Questions

1. What are Jeremiah's instructions to the Jews in exile?

2. What do the Pharisees want to happen? How do they think it will happen? What are they doing to *make* it happen?

3. What do the Sadducees hope will happen?

4. Who are the Essenes? Where are they? Why? What do they expect to happen?

5. What does Gabriel say John is going to do?

6. Why is it important that Jesus was conceived by Mary the virgin?

Thought Questions

1. When did Herod the Great die? Compare to Matthew 2. What conclusions can you draw about the year Jesus was born?

2. Suppose the magi were reading the Old Testament. How would they know that a star signified the birth of a king? Use a concordance to answer the question.

3. Given what you learned above about the Pharisees, why does Jesus spend so much time with them?

4. Can you think of Christians today who are like the Pharisees? The Sadducees? The Essenes?

Anointed by the Spirit

John's ministry as a prophet prepares the way for Jesus. His work also foreshadows the work of Jesus. John is filled with the power and spirit of Elijah, and he is preparing the way for a prophet like Elisha. John is like Elijah in many ways. Like Elijah he directly confronts a wicked king, for Herod is like Ahab in many ways. Not only is he a wicked king, but he is fascinated and frightened by John as Ahab is with Elijah. Herod is also married to a bloodthirsty queen, as Ahab is, a queen who is ready eventually to offer up John's head as the dessert course at Herod's birthday party.

Elijah and Elisha's ministries differed in some ways, and so do John's and Jesus'. Just as Elijah does, John is preparing a people who remain faithful in the midst of the decline of Israel, through the judgment. Then, like Elijah, he hands over the leadership of that people to another, to Jesus. Jesus will do all that John does, but do it more fully, with a "double portion" of the Spirit of John. Like John, Jesus is a prophet confronting the wicked powers that rule Judea, but Jesus goes after the "power behind the power." The most important difference between the ministry of Elijah and that of Elisha is that Elijah is a lone prophet and Elisha formed

a community of disciples. That does not exactly fit John
and Jesus, because we know that John has his own disciples.
But the disciples of John are not nearly as prominent in the
gospel story as the disciples of Jesus. In Elisha's ministry,
the sons of the prophets formed the core of a faithful Israel within Israel, a renewal movement within the northern
kingdom of Israel. Jesus' disciples play the same role. He
chooses twelve because that is the number of the tribes of
Israel. Jesus wants the twelve to become the "patriarchs" of
a new Israel.[6]

John knows that he is only a servant preparing the way for
the coming of the king, the royal prophet. When Jesus shows
up and asks to be baptized, John thinks it is inappropriate.
Jesus is the greater, and the greater should baptize the lesser.
Jesus insists that it is necessary if he is going to fulfill all righteousness, and John agrees and baptizes him. While Jesus is
being baptized, the heavens split open and the Father speaks,
commending His beloved Son, Jesus. Meanwhile, the Spirit
descends like a dove on Jesus, and remains on Him. This is
the beginning of Jesus' ministry. The Spirit that comes on
Him prepares Him to preach, to heal, to bring judgment and
righteousness (Is. 61:1). The Spirit that clothes Him is the
Spirit that clothed Gideon, Samson, and Saul to fight battles.
The Spirit is the storm cloud that catches Jesus up and makes
Him like a tornado or hurricane storming through Galilee
and Judea.[7] By the Spirit, Jesus is anointed to be the king, a
new David. By the Spirit, He becomes like another Elisha,
inheriting a double portion of the Spirit of His predecessor.
By the Spirit, He is equipped to confront the wicked in Israel
and to deliver His people from their oppressors.

---

6. For more, see my *1 & 2 Kings* (Grand Rapids: Brazos, 2006).

7. Thanks to my co-pastor, Toby Sumpter, for the vivid image of the
Spirit as storm.

The Spirit of Yahweh becomes Jesus' constant companion, guide, and power. Wherever Jesus goes, He goes in the power of the Spirit, a storm blowing through Israel. The first thing the Spirit does is drive Him into the wilderness, where He fasts for forty days and where the devil tempted Him. We know of only three of the temptations—to make stones into bread, to throw Himself from the temple, to bow down and worship Satan. Jesus resists every one of the temptations, and eventually the devil leaves Jesus. The devil is not done with Jesus. Throughout the rest of His work, the devil tempts and tests Jesus through the temptations and tests that the Jewish leaders pose to Him. Eventually the devil returns in force to inspire Judas to betray Jesus and to tempt Jesus to abandon his mission.

Like John, Jesus generates opposition and hatred. John's death is an important turning point in Jesus' ministry. It is a sign that Herod is ready to purge the movement that John has started, and the excitement about Jesus' appearance is already beginning to cause problems. When Herod beheads John, Jesus knows that it is too early for him to confront the Jewish leaders directly. As he often does during his ministry, He withdraws and begins a ministry in Galilee (Mt. 4:12–13).

Just as importantly, John's death foretells where Jesus' ministry is going. Like John, He too will be put to death as an enemy to kings and emperors, a threat to good order.

A Light Dawns

Jesus' ministry in Galilee fulfills a specific prophecy of Isaiah (Mt. 4:15–16), but more generally Jesus' ministry fulfills all of the promises and hopes of Israel. He is the greater David who has come to conquer Israel's enemies and rule in justice. He is the greater prophet like Elisha and like Moses, who moves about the land helping and healing. He is the greater priest who teaches the law. Though he fulfills all of Israel's hopes, not everyone in Israel recognizes that He is doing that. Some, especially the leaders, conclude that Jesus is a dangerous threat to the future of Israel. Jesus' ministry fulfills the hopes of Israel, but it does so in surprising ways.

There are two main reasons for that. One reason is that Jesus is attacking the true enemy of Israel instead of the enemy that many of the Jews recognize.[8] Many of the Jews think that the greatest problem for Israel is the Roman occupation. If they can get rid of the Romans, everything will go well. Jesus knows that the Romans are not the real problem. In the wilderness, He confronts the real threat to Israel, the devil. Throughout His ministry, Jesus is at war with the devil and the demons who serve him. Casting out demons is one of Jesus' most common miracles. He comes to deliver Israel, but to deliver Israel from the real oppressor. He comes to free Israel from the slavery that started in the garden of Eden, not primarily the one that started with Pompey.

Because of this, Jesus does not show the same hostility to the Romans and their agents that many of the Jews do. He does not consider Gentiles unclean, and does not keep His distance from the Jews who serve the Romans. He heals a centurion's servant and commends the faith of the centurion: "I have not found such great faith, no, not in Israel" (Mt. 8:10). To some Jews, this is a deep insult, a sign that Jesus' priorities and ideas are far out of line with tradition. Jews think that everyone must take sides, and they believe Jesus is on the Roman side. Plus, He spends far too much of His time with tax gatherers. He welcomes one into the company of His disciples, eats with them, and treats them

---

8. This is one of the main themes of N. T. Wright's *New Testament and the People of God* and *Jesus and the Victory of God*.

with compassion. Tax gatherers are Jews who serve the empire. Other Jews not only hate them because they serve the Romans, who are invaders, but because they are unclean. Because they have regular contact with Gentiles, tax collectors are polluted, and anyone who eats with them becomes polluted too. Jesus is crossing a line he shouldn't cross when he eats with publicans.

The second reason why Jesus' work is surprising follows from this. Some Jews think that their problem is "out there." Israel does not have problems of its own. Jesus focuses attention instead on Israel's own sins and problems. He focuses on Israel's disobedience. He knows that if Israel continues in the direction they are going, provoking the Romans, assassinating Gentiles, planning a war with Rome, then the Romans are going to destroy the temple and the city of Jerusalem. Many Jews think that they have to oppose the Romans, with violence, to be faithful to the covenant. Jesus says the opposite: Opposing the Romans with the sword is unfaithful to the covenant. Jesus calls the Jews back to the original demand of Jeremiah: "Seek the peace of the city where I send you into exile."

Israel has been unfaithful to the covenant in many other ways as well, and Jesus' ministry is all about exposing that unfaithfulness, teaching the Jews an alternative pathway for the future, and calling for and provoking the Jews to repentance. One of the great sins of the Jews is to misuse and abuse the law. The Pharisees and scribes distort the law in many different ways. At bottom, many of the Jewish leaders abuse the law because they rely more on traditions of interpretation than on the law itself. If the tradition of the elders requires them to wash their hands before meals, they demand that everyone wash hands before meals. And they are puzzled and offended when Jesus' disciples do not wash their hands. Meanwhile, they ignore what the law actually says about all sorts of things—about honor to parents, about love for their neighbors, about doing justice for the poor and vulnerable.

Sometimes, they use the law to divide Israel into the clean and unclean, the true Jews and the outcasts. The Pharisees apply purity regulations in a way that keeps many Jews in a state of impurity. Pharisees do not just keep their distance from Gentiles, or from Jews who have too much contact with Gentiles. They keep their distance from other Jews who do not keep the law in the same way they do, Jews that the Pharisees identify as "sinners."[9] The law is supposed to lead Jews to love their neighbors; the Pharisees use the law to justify avoiding their neighbors.

The Pharisees and scribes also misuse the law by finding tiny loopholes that allow them to do what they want. They know the law demands that they keep vows, but they distinguish between different sorts of vows so that some vows are more binding than others (Mt. 23:16–22). They also spend all their time and energy making sure they keep the smallest details of the law. They pay a tenth of even the tiniest seeds to the temple, but they ignore the law's demands for mercy, truth, and justice (Mt. 23:23–24). Their reason for tithing is to avoid consuming food that belongs to God. They make sure they give God His portion before they take their portion, so that they do not commit sacrilege by eating God's food. That is a good thing to do. Jesus says that they should pay close attention to the details of the law. But Jesus also says that they lose track of the more important teachings of the law. They are so afraid of eating an unclean gnat that they do not even notice they are swallowing down a

9. On the controversial point of how to define "sinner," I am following the lead of E. P. Sanders.

camel—which is equally unclean and much bigger—whole (Mt. 23:24). The Pharisees' abuse of the law is comical.

As a result these abuses, the Jewish leaders, especially the scribes and Pharisees, turn the law into its opposite. The law is intended to bring life and to enable Israel to flourish under God's blessing. Torah gives wisdom and is full of nourishing and delicious fruit. The Pharisees cut a few branches from the tree of life and use them as clubs to beat other Jews to a pulp.

Jesus never opposes the law or teaches his disciples to ignore the law. The opposite is true. Jesus teaches the people the right way to keep the law. He calls Israel to keep the law because keeping the law will enable Israel to flourish in the land, even with the Romans surrounding them. Jesus attacks the Pharisees and scribes as "hypocrites" who miss the real purpose of the law, and He teaches that the law is intended for life and health instead of for death.

Sabbath and Table

Jesus' teaching on the Sabbath illustrates the point. Many readers of the gospels think Jesus is opposed to the Sabbath. At least, Jesus makes exceptions to the Sabbath rules. If this is true, it means that Jesus agrees with the Pharisees that Sabbath-keeping means refraining from picking grain in the fields and from helping people and animals. But when things are really extreme—when someone is starving or a person is about to die—you can make an exception.

That is not what Jesus says about the Sabbath. He does not think the Pharisees are mostly right about the Sabbath. They miss the basic point of the Sabbath. Jesus does not think that healing someone on the Sabbath is an "exception" to the Sabbath rules. He thinks the opposite: Sabbath-keeping means doing good, healing, relieving distress. The Sabbath laws themselves require Israelites to *give* rest to their sons, servants, and even animals on the Sabbath. That's what Jesus does on the Sabbath: He *gives* rest by raising people from their sick beds, by cleansing lepers, by healing withered arms. When Jesus tells the Pharisees that they can get an ox out of a ditch on the Sabbath, He is not making an exception. Getting stuck in a ditch is not restful for an ox, any more than it is for you. Pulling him out of the ditch is a way of keeping the Sabbath, because it gives relief to an animal. Jesus does not attack Jewish Sabbath-keeping because He thinks Sabbath-keeping is wrong. He attacks Jewish Sabbath-keeping because they are not really keeping the Sabbath.

The Sabbath issue highlights another important part of Jesus' ministry. Jesus spends a lot of His time in Galilee teaching and preaching. But He also *does* things. He gets into trouble with the Jews because of what He says, but He gets into as much or more trouble because of what He does. He does not just talk about what to do on the Sabbath. He *does* things on the Sabbath that the Jews don't think should be done. If he only talks about the Sabbath, the Jews might disagree, but they may have tolerated Him. There are many opinions about the Sabbath among Jews at the time. The Pharisees' view is not the only one, and even among the Pharisees there are different opinions. If Jesus comes and starts a nice little discussion about Sabbath-keeping, everything is fine. But when Jesus starts doing things on the Sabbath, then the Pharisees get very upset.

He often heals people on the Sabbath. Many of the Pharisees believed that it is lawful to help someone who is about to die on the Sabbath. If someone is bleeding on the side of the road, a Pharisee will not think it is breaking the Sabbath to help him. But Jesus heals people who are not in any danger at all—and He does it on the Sabbath. A man who has been blind since birth can wait one more day before He gets healed (Jn. 9:1–13). A man with a withered arm is

not about to die; heal him on the day after the Sabbath, the
Pharisees would say (Mk. 3:1–6). Jesus does not wait. He
keeps healing on the Sabbath, and He knows that this will
keep making the Pharisees angry.

Jesus' whole point is to provoke the Jews. He is not only
teaching them that they are misusing the law. He does
things that make it obvious that they are abusing the law.
He provokes them to bring them to repentance. He provokes
them also because He is trying to break the power that the
Pharisees have over the people. Although the Pharisees are
a minority within Israel, they are the watchdogs, the community police, of the Torah. They are the ones who prowl
around making sure that everyone is keeping the law their
way. They make sure that everyone stays "Purity Correct."
But Jesus keeps breaking the Pharisees' rules and then defends Himself when the Pharisees attack Him. He becomes
a folk hero. He is the bold rebel who stands up to the oppressive authorities, and gets away with it. By doing this, He
is freeing the ordinary Jews from their fear of the Pharisees.
When they see Jesus defying the Pharisees, they are inspired
to defy the Pharisees too. Jesus takes the heat, and ordinary
Jews can keep the law faithfully without the Pharisees looking over their shoulders.

Jesus does something similar with regard to table fellowship. Table fellowship is very, very important for the
Pharisees. They believe it is very important to eat the right
food with the right people. Eating the right food means eating only the foods that the law permits, and avoiding any
contamination from unclean foods. The right people are
the clean, pure Jews, Jews like the Pharisees who kept the
dietary laws, are scrupulous about cleanness, and avoid any
sort of pollution. Eating with Gentiles is prohibited. Eating
with Jews who spend too much time with Gentiles causes
defilement. Eating with Jews who are not serious about the

laws of cleanness is dangerous. For the Pharisees, this is not a small issue. Their hope for Israel depends on forming a clean, pure Israel within the nation of Israel. They can form pure Israel only if they keep the boundaries between clean and unclean very clear. When two people sit to eat, boundaries become messy. A clean Jew might eat the same food as an unclean Gentile, and that is dangerous. Pure table fellowship is one of the main ways the Pharisees use to clean up Israel. When Israel gets clean enough, the Lord will come to deliver them from the Romans and keep all the rest of His promises to Israel.

Jesus' choices about table companions are, like His Sabbath-keeping, deliberately designed to provoke the Pharisees. He knows that when He goes to the home of a tax collector for dinner, the Pharisees will be livid. He knows they will object to Him eating with tax collectors and sinners. But Jesus wants to challenge the Pharisees' practice of table fellowship because it is a violation of the demands of Torah, not because Jesus is opposed to Torah. He feeds four thousand, and then five thousand, in the wilderness. He is setting up an alternative table, an alternative temple, where the multitudes of Israel can eat and drink and rejoice. He is gathering a people in the wilderness, and feeding them the bread of heaven, preparing them for a new conquest of the land.

Jesus' table fellowship, just as much as the Pharisees', pictures His entire plan for the future of Israel. For the Pharisees, the future of Israel depends on Israel becoming a holy people. For them, holiness means separation, and so the true pure Jews have to keep away from Gentiles and impure Jews if they want the Lord to deliver them. Jesus also teaches Israel to be holy, to keep the Torah. And He also believes that Israel's future depends on holiness. But for Jesus, holiness, perfection, and being like the Father do not involve separation primarily. For Jesus, holiness is compassion, kindness, love of neighbor and love of enemy.[10]

Jesus embodies this future for Israel in His ministry of healing as well. He spends much of His time healing the blind, the lame, the deaf and mute, cleansing lepers, raising up paralytics from their beds and in a few instances raising the dead from their tombs. This not only shows Jesus' compassion and the compassion He expects of His disciples. It also shows the character of Jesus' ministry, what He comes to do. All of the illnesses He heals are ultimately the result of sin and God's curse and judgment on sin. Jesus enters a fallen world full of broken people, and He starts putting them back together again. His whole purpose is to put them back together again. He comes to restore the world, and especially the human race, to glory and beauty.

Many of Jesus' healings also have to do with holiness and cleanliness. Leprosy in the New Testament is not the leprosy we know, a debilitating disease that causes noses, ears, fingers, and limbs to decay. It is a form of skin disease, which does not make the person sick but unclean. A leper can function fairly normally in daily life, but cannot fulfill any function as a worshiper of God or a member of the people of God. He cannot serve as a priest. In cleansing lepers, Jesus restores them to the worshiping community of Israel. Many of the other ailments that Jesus heals are sicknesses that disqualified a man from serving as a priest (see Lev. 21–22). Jesus restores human beings to full humanity by making them priests.

Jesus' healings, in short, are not just displays of power. They do show God's power, power to overcome sickness, uncleanness, even death. They show that God intends to

---

10. See Marcus Borg, *Conflict, Holiness, and Politics in the Teaching of Jesus* (Harrisburg: Trinity Press International, 1998).

use His power to heal and help. But they also show the form
that God's help takes. They display the character of Jesus'
ministry, a ministry to restore Israel, and through Israel to
restore humanity, to the role given to Adam. Jesus comes
to advance humanity to heights that Adam never attained.
He comes not only to "restore" but to "glorify" us, to "lead
many sons to glory" (Heb. 2:10).

Many Things in Parables

Jesus' teaching provokes the Jews. More seriously, His activities provoke the Jews. They worry that He eats and drinks
with the wrong sorts of people. They think He is too loose
in His Sabbath-keeping. They also notice the large crowds
that come to hear Jesus and hang on His every word. The
Jewish leaders begin to worry that Jesus will lead the whole
nation of Israel astray. If Jesus' teaching and practice catch
on, then the redemption the Jewish leaders hope for will
never come. If Jesus has His way, Israel will stay unclean,
too defiled to be saved.

Very early in Jesus ministry, the Pharisees and others begin challenging Him. At first, they keep their questions and
hostility to Jesus quiet. They know that Jesus is popular, and
that opposing Him might endanger their own standing with
the people. When they hear Jesus forgive sins, they think it is
blasphemy, but they say nothing (Mt. 9:3). Eventually, they
begin voicing their criticisms of Jesus. They are typically
Pharisaical concerns: Why don't your disciples fast? Why
don't Jesus' disciples wash before eating? How can Jesus let
them "work" on the Sabbath by gathering some grains from
the wheat fields?

Their attacks become more intense after Jesus sends the
Twelve disciples out to minister throughout Israel. He gives
them authority to do just what He has been doing. They

preach the good news of the kingdom, heal diseases, raise the dead, cleanse lepers (Mt. 10:7–8). They have great success. The demons submit to them, the dead are raised, many of the Jews respond gladly to their ministry. That frightens the Jewish leaders even more. Jesus is no longer simply a nuisance. He poses a mortal danger to Israel, at least to Israel as the Pharisees conceive it.

Eventually, their criticisms and attacks reach a climax. When Jesus casts out a demon, the Pharisees say that He casts out demons only by the power of Beelzebub, the chief of the demons (Mt. 12:22–32). Jesus says that even if he is casting out demons by the power of the devil, His work is still a sign that Satan's kingdom is being torn down, since it has become divided against itself. But in fact Jesus comes in the power of the Spirit's storm to blow away the demons. That is a sign that God's kingdom has come, the kingdom that fulfills all of Israel's hopes and restores all of humanity's brokenness. Jesus is greater than Moses, a "stronger man" come to deliver mankind from slavery to the "strong man" and to plunder the strong man's house. He is greater than David, conquering Israel's greatest enemies. The Jews have gone over the line. They have not simply raised questions and criticisms of Jesus' ministry. They reject it wholesale, attributing the power of Jesus' ministry to Satan rather than to the Spirit. The Jews have become a "wicked and adulterous generation" (Mt. 12:39, 41–42), like the generation of Israel that comes out of Egypt and resists Moses. Like that generation, they will be destroyed.

Early in His ministry, Jesus withdraws when Herod kills John. When the Jewish leaders become increasingly hostile to Jesus, Jesus "withdraws" in a more subtle way. Instead of teaching straightforwardly, He begins to teach in parables. In the Bible, "parables" are often short stories, but they can also be proverbs, striking comparisons, and one-liners.

Jesus' parables are not just moral stories that illustrate Jesus' teaching. Parables are a weapon Jesus wields against His enemies and a tool He uses to build His kingdom.

His parables almost always deal with the situation in front of Jesus at the time. He does not tell parables to explain general truths. He doesn't tell parables primarily to teach things like "God is good" or "God forgives sins." His parables assume those truths, but the stories are about the events of His ministry. When He tells the parable of the vineyard (Mt. 21:33–44), it is obvious that the Jewish leaders who oppose Jesus are the tenants who want to kill the Son and seize the vineyard. The parable of the wedding (Mt. 22:1–14) is about Jesus' invitation to the Jewish leaders to join the wedding feast, and their hostile reaction. Some of Jesus' parables reach back to Israel's return from exile, and bring the story of Israel to Jesus' time. The parables of the sowing and harvest (Mt. 13:1–9, 24–30) take up a picture that the prophets used to describe the return from exile. The sower is Yahweh, and the seed is Israel, replanted in the land after exile (e.g., Jer. 31:27). Yahweh plants Israel in the land, but Israel springs up and soon withers; Yahweh sows the land with people, but the devil plants weeds among the wheat. Jesus comes at the end of that story to sow the seed that will produce a harvest and to separate the wheat from the weeds.

Because Jesus is telling stories about His own ministry, Jesus puts His enemies in the stories. The tenants are the Pharisees and scribes who keep the vineyard of Israel, the "older brother" of the parable of the prodigal son are the Jews who complain about the feast that Jesus has begun (Lk. 15:11–32), the weeds in the field are the Jewish leaders who hate and oppose Jesus (Mt. 13:24–30). Jesus puts the Pharisees and scribes in His stories and gives them the role of the villain. He is still calling them to repentance. If they can see just how evil and vicious they are, maybe they will turn from their sins and honor Jesus as the one who is anointed with the Spirit. If they see themselves in the "mirror" of Jesus' stories, they might still be saved.

Putting His enemies in His stories has another effect too. It damages the reputation of the Pharisees and scribes. They like to think of themselves as the heroes of Israel. They are the pious and faithful. They are the ones that are going to lead Israel to glory. But Jesus says they are wicked, opposed to God's purposes for Israel. This makes the Pharisees angry, so angry that they want to make Jesus shut up once and for all. Their honor is at stake, and Jesus is making them look foolish, ignorant, and evil. Like His debates with the Pharisees, Jesus' stories also embolden the people who listen to Him. Many Jews have been faithfully living in covenant with Yahweh, hoping for the restoration of Israel. They suspect that the Pharisees are not as pious as they claim to be, but they keep quiet out of fear. Faithful Jews criticize the Pharisees in whispers and back alleys. But here is Jesus, openly telling stories that make the Pharisees look like idiots. Jesus is a hero to the faithful poor of Israel, the powerless Jews who know that their leaders are evil. Samson made up funny poems about the Philistines, songs that children sang in the street. It made the Philistines furious. Jesus is the greater Samson.

Parables also hide the real story. Jesus' parables are about the Jewish leaders, Jesus' ministry, and the coming of the kingdom. But they look like they are simple stories about farmers and farm life.[11] If you do not have the setting for the parable of the sower, it looks like a simple story about the way different seeds can have different effects. If you take it out of the context of Jesus' ministry, it looks like a general story

11. Many traditional interpreters have been taken in, and comment on how "rustic" and "quaint" Jesus' stories are. That's true in many cases, but it misses the main point of the parables.

about how different people respond to the word of God. In Jesus' ministry, it has a hidden meaning about Israel's return from exile, the failure of earlier "sowings," and the coming harvest of Jesus. Only people "in the know" realize what Jesus is really talking about.

When Jesus' disciples ask why He is teaching in parables, He says that He wants to hide the truth of the kingdom from those who have decided they do not want to hear it:

> In their case the prophecy of Isaiah is being fulfilled, which says "You will keep on hearing, but will not understand; you will keep on seeing, but will not perceive; for the heart of his people has become dull, with their ears they scarcely hear, and they have closed their eyes, otherwise they will see with their eyes, hear with their ears, and understand with their heart and return, and I will heal them." (Mt. 13:14–15)

Jesus' parables veil the truth from the Pharisees and scribes who refuse to hear Him, but they also reveal truth about the kingdom to the disciples, those to whom "it has been granted to know the mysteries of the kingdom of heaven" (Mt. 13:11).

Jesus' parables divide Israel in two. On one side are the scribes and Pharisees who hate Jesus and refuse to listen to Him. Parables make them even more hostile to Jesus and divide them further from Jesus' kingdom. On the other side are the disciples and the crowds who eagerly listen to Jesus. Through His parables, Jesus is acting like Elisha, forming a "new Israel" within the old Israel.

Jesus' ministry is a potent mix. He announces the kingdom of heaven, the fulfillment of all of Israel's hopes. He embodies that kingdom in His ministry of healing and casting out demons, and He teaches Israel the way they ought to keep the law fully. In order to call Israel to repentance, He deliberately "disobeys" the rules that the Pharisees and scribes have added to the law. He wants to challenge the leaders of Israel, and He wants to provoke conflict. When the Jewish leaders react by accusing Jesus of being in league with Satan and plot to silence and even kill Him, Jesus withdraws out of harm's way and begins to teach in code—in parables. The faithful gather around Him, forming a new Israel within Israel.

But Jesus is not finished. He has come to confront Israel at the heart of Israel. His most provocative actions and words are still to come.

Review Questions

1. How is Jesus like Elisha?

2. Describe the work of the Spirit in Jesus' ministry.

3. What does Jesus teach about the law?

4. Does Jesus break the Sabbath? Why does He do what He does on the Sabbath?

5. Summarize the Pharisees' views on table fellowship. How does that help explain Jesus' own meals?

6. What are Jesus' parables about?

7. How are parables "weapons" for Jesus?

Thought Questions

1. Read Nathan's parable in 2 Samuel 12. How is it like Jesus' parables?

2. Write a parable of your own about a situation in today's political world, in your home town, or at your school.

3. How can we follow Jesus' example of fellowship with "sinners" today?

In Jerusalem

The disciples do not understand much about what Jesus is doing, but they do get one basic thing right. When Jesus asks during a visit to Caesarea Philippi who His disciples think He is, Peter pipes up with the answer: "You are the Christ, the Son of the living God" (Mt. 16:16). They have seen Jesus' healings, and know that He is fulfilling the prophecies of Isaiah. They have seen Jesus triumphing over demons, and know that He has come as the conquering new David to deliver Israel from bondage to Satan. They believe Jesus' teaching and are trying to follow His commandments. Jesus has proven to their satisfaction that He is the anointed one from Yahweh come to redeem Israel and the nations.

As soon as Peter makes that confession, Jesus says He must go to Jerusalem. It is never Jesus' intention to remain in Galilee throughout His ministry. His ministry starts in Galilee, far from the center of Israel. But He intends from the beginning to move from the outside to the center. He knows that He has to go to Jerusalem. He has been contending with Pharisees and scribes, but He knows that He has to take on the priests and elders in Jerusalem. It is time to set His face toward Jerusalem.

He also knows that the priests and elders at Jerusalem will not accept Him. Throughout His ministry in Galilee, Jesus has been provoking the Jews, and word has gotten to the capital city. When He gets to Jerusalem, He tells His disciples, He will have to suffer:

> From that time Jesus began to show His disciples that He must go to Jerusalem, and suffer many things from the elders and chief priests and scribes, and be killed, and be raised up on the third day. (Mt. 16:21)

After this, Jesus again and again reminds His disciples of what is coming. He is going to Jerusalem, as the prophets say the Messiah will. He is going to receive His kingdom and to receive glory, as the prophets say He will. But the path to glory and the kingdom is the path of the cross. That too the prophets foretell.

To the Temple

Centuries before Jesus, Zechariah prophesied of a conquering king who will enter Jerusalem (Zech. 9:1–9). The king will come from the far north, make his way down the coast toward Jerusalem, conquering as he goes. Finally, he will enter Jerusalem, not in a great triumph, with war horses and captured slaves, but instead as a king of peace, a king who came to free slaves rather than make them. He will ride into the city on a donkey, as a king of peace, rather than as a war hero.

Jesus knows of this prophecy, and He knows what it means to the Jews. They understand that when a king comes riding into Jerusalem on a donkey, then the redemption of Israel is near. Jesus wants to announce His arrival in the capital city and send the people of the city the message that He is the king they await. So He sends His disciples into a village to get a donkey, and stages his entry to remind everyone of the prophecy of Zechariah 9. He not only tells everyone He is the promised king. He also makes sure He looks like the promised king.

No wonder the crowds are excited. They know the prophecy too, and they know what Jesus is telling them by entering the city in this way. They take their garments and cast them on the ground, making a carpet for Jesus' donkey to walk on. Some find palm branches and lay them on the road, celebrating Jesus' coming to Jerusalem as a great Feast of Booths. They sing Jesus' praises, as the crowds once sang the praises of David: "Hosanna to the Son of David! Blessed is He who comes in the Name of Yahweh" (Mt. 21:9).

Not everyone in Jerusalem is excited about Jesus' coming. When the magi come to Jerusalem seeking a king, Herod and all Jerusalem tremble about it. They are frightened that a new king is born. When Jesus returns to Jerusalem on a donkey, and the people acclaim Him as the king, the powerful leaders of Jerusalem and Israel are frightened again. The city trembles. The leaders in Jerusalem have heard about Jesus, but they have never seen Him. They have never seen crowds singing His praises and almost worshiping Him. When they do see it, they don't like it. This Jesus is dangerous, and He attracts a crowd. He has to be watched and has to be stopped.

If Jesus' entry into Jerusalem frightens the Jewish leaders, Jesus' next action angers them. Jesus enters the capital city as the Son of David, the king, the new and greater Solomon. Because He is the new Solomon, His first stop is the temple. He keeps traveling through the city, straight up to the temple. There He overturns the tables of the money-changers in the temple, drives out the people buying and selling, and chases away the animals (Mt. 21:12–17). Quoting Isaiah (56:7) and Jeremiah (7:11), He announces that the temple is supposed to be a house of prayer for the nations, but that the Jews have made it a den of thieves (Mt. 21:13).

Buying and selling in the temple is not the issue. Sacrificial animals need to be pure, without any marks or blemishes. If an Israelite lives a hundred miles from Jerusalem, he will have a hard time bringing an animal and keeping it in good enough shape to sacrifice. So Yahweh permits the Jews to sell animals in their hometown, and take the money to the temple to buy a pre-approved 100 percent blemishless sacrificial animal (Deut. 14:22–27). Over time, a market in sacrificial animals develops around the temple.

Jesus condemns the temple for the same reason Jeremiah does: Israel has turned the temple into a safe haven for thieves, murderers, wicked men who oppress other Jews.

Thieves do not steal and pillage in their own dens. They steal and pillage elsewhere, and then retreat to their dens to be safe. That's how the Jews are using the temple. Outside the temple, powerful Jews abuse the weak, the rich abuse the poor, the Pharisees turn the good law into a weapon to beat people, zealots look for opportunities to attack Romans and compromised Jews. Israel is not seeking the peace of the city where they have been sent. But then they run back to the temple, offer their sacrifices, keep their feasts, and think everything is fine. It isn't. In Isaiah's time, Yahweh told Israel that He abhorred the sacrifices they offered with bloody hands (Is. 1:10–15). Yahweh hasn't changed His mind. In Jesus' time, He still hates them.

Jesus is telling the Jews that their temple has become as wicked as the temple in the time of Jeremiah. Overturning the tables and driving out the animals are visual predictions of what the Lord is going to do to the temple. When Solomon's temple turns into a den of thieves, the Lord destroys it. He sends the Babylonians under Nebuchadnezzar to overturn the altars and tables, to drive out the animals, and to end the sacrifice. Within a generation after Jesus' death and resurrection, the Romans will do the same to Herod's temple. Jesus is showing the Jews what they can expect. Jesus overturns the tables for only a few minutes; soon the Romans will come to overturn them for good. When Jesus drives out the animals, the sellers get them back into their pens; when the Romans come to Jerusalem, they are going to put an end to sacrifice. A few days later, Jesus leaves the temple for the last time, climbs the Mount of Olives with His disciples, and tells them that the temple is doomed (Mt. 24; Mk. 13; Lk. 21). It is a prophecy in action.

This is the most provocative of all Jesus' provocative actions. Pharisees already hate Jesus for eating with tax collectors and sinners, for telling stories about them, for telling them they are hypocrites and blasphemers. But the temple is the center of Jewish life. All of Israel's hopes are centered on the temple. As long as Yahweh is in His house, Israel will be safe. When the temple is finally finished, the Lord will move in, and He will defend the city against every attacker. All of Israel's history is symbolized by the temple. Now, Jesus is saying that the temple is going to be destroyed. It will be as if a prophet showed up in the Capitol or the White House in Washington, and announced that these great symbols of America are going to be destroyed. The Secret Service would be on him in a minute. Eventually, he would be on trial and would be locked up. So is Jesus.

As if that is not enough, Jesus spends the next several days in the temple carrying on His ministry. He doesn't just drive out the thieves. He also shows the Jews what the temple is actually for. It is for healing and restoration, a place of teaching the law, a house of prayer, worship, and service. "Who gives you authority to do these things?" the Jewish leaders demand. "Who told you you can take over the temple?" Jesus responds with parables. These are some of the most obvious parables in the gospels. More clearly than ever before, Jesus is telling everyone that the Jewish leaders are unfaithful tenants who are willing to plot Jesus' murder.

The Jewish leaders have to do something. Perhaps they can trap Jesus. Perhaps they can make Him say something that will make the crowds lose respect for Him. Perhaps they can trick Him into saying something that will draw the attention of the Romans. One after another, Pharisees, Sadducees, Herodians, lawyers, scribes try to trap Jesus. They ask him controversial questions, and pretend to seek His advice on disputed subjects in the law. Instead of trapping Jesus, they find themselves trapped. They fall into the pit of their own making. And they get madder and madder. Jesus is right: He has come to Jerusalem to be handed over to the Jewish leaders, tortured, and killed.

Passover

Jesus arrives in Jerusalem at the time of the Passover feast. Thousands of Jews and Gentile God-fearers are gathered in Jerusalem for the event. It is a time when Jesus' actions will have the most dramatic impact. It is also the feast that celebrates Israel's redemption from slavery in Egypt. Jesus has started His ministry announcing that He comes to liberate His people, and He ends His ministry at the feast that celebrates Israel's original liberation from slavery.

Jesus is in Jerusalem with His disciples, and so he arranges for them to celebrate the Passover meal together. They get an upper room in a house in the city, and recline for the meal. During the meal, Jesus speaks to them about His coming departure (Jn. 13–16), warning them that they will be persecuted and hated as He has been and promising to send His Spirit to be with them in His absence. He prays that the disciples will grow in unity, so that they can share in the unity that Jesus has with His Father, and display that unity before the world (Jn. 17). When the meal is over, Jesus takes off his robe, puts on the clothing of a servant, and pours a basin of water. He moves from one disciple to another, washing their feet. He says it is a lesson, teaching them how they should serve one another.

At the end of the meal, Jesus takes some of the bread of the Passover meal, offers a prayer of thanks, breaks the bread, and hands it out to the disciples. It is not a strange gesture. Jews always pray before meals. What is strange is what Jesus says about the bread: "This is my body, which is given for you." Jesus equates Himself with the Passover lamb, which Israel ate in celebration of her deliverance from Egypt. Then He takes a cup of wine, gives thanks, and offers the cup to His disciples, with similar words: "This cup is the new covenant in my blood, which is shed for you and for many for the forgiveness of sins. All of you drink it." This is something new. Jews are strictly forbidden to eat blood (Lev. 17). At the first Passover, the Israelites spread the blood on the doorposts of their houses, so that the angel of death will see it and pass by. In all the Passovers after the first, and in Israel's sacrifices at the temple, blood is always splashed on the altar. Here, Jesus is saying that His disciples should drink the blood of the new Passover. Just as surprising, Jesus uses the phrase "This is the new covenant." He is echoing the words of Moses, when he mediated the covenant with Israel at Sinai (Exod. 24:8). But He is saying that a new order is coming to replace the order established by Moses. With a new Passover comes a new covenant.

Long before Jesus' time, David complained to the Lord that his close and trusted friend, who ate bread with him, has lifted up his heel against him (Ps. 41:9). Jesus has the same complaint. Among His table companions is one who has become an enemy. Seeking to catch Jesus, the Jewish leaders promise to pay Judas Iscariot thirty pieces of silver to betray Jesus to them. Jesus knows it, and during the meal He tells His disciples that one of them will betray Him to the Jews. The disciples are astonished, and ask Jesus who it is. Finally, Jesus dipped a piece of bread into a cup of wine, and handed the sop to Judas, saying "What you do, do quickly." Still the disciples are confused. Some of them think Judas is going to distribute some money to the poor. But Judas knows otherwise. He leaves the upper room, and walks out into the night.

With Judas' departure, the drama of the life of Jesus entered its final act.

Review Questions

1. What prophet predicted a king's arrival in Jerusalem?
2. What message does Jesus send by arranging His entry to Jerusalem as He does?

3. What prophets does Jesus quote when He "cleanses" the temple?

4. Why does He cleanse the temple? What is He attacking?

5. What does Jesus mean when He offers His disciples bread and wine during the Passover meal?

Thought Questions

1. Looking at a concordance, explain the significance of Jesus' arrival in Jerusalem on a donkey.

2. Read 2 Kings 9–10, and think about Palm Sunday. What are the crowds saying when they lay branches and clothing on the road?

3. Read Psalm 118. How does that Psalm shed light on Jesus' actions in the last week of His life?

Lifted Up

After the meal, Jesus and His disciples sing a hymn, and then go out of the city of Jerusalem to the east, climbing down the steep slope that goes down to the Kidron brook, and then up the other side onto the Mount of Olives. On the Mount of Olives is a garden that Jesus and His disciples frequently visit, called Gethsemane. Jesus leaves eight of His disciples, takes His three closest friends—Peter, James, and John—and goes further on into the garden to pray.

From the beginning of His journey toward Jerusalem, Jesus knows that He will be arrested, tried, and put to death in Jerusalem. Now the hour is almost come. Judas is meeting with the Jewish leaders to lead them to Gethsemane to arrest Jesus. The Jews are preparing for a "trial" that they know will convict Jesus. Jesus knows that a horrible death is ahead of Him. And He knows that in His suffering, He will be drinking down all the wrath that the Father is going to pour out on Israel (Jer. 25). He will suffer Israel's fate in His own person, and He is frightened. So He prays three times that His Father will remove the cup from Him. After praying, He comes to His three disciples and finds them sleeping.

They are awakened by the clash of armor and weapons and the light of torches. Judas has led members of the temple guard and some Roman soldiers to the garden to find Jesus. "Whom do you seek?" Jesus asks. When the soldiers tell Him they are seeking "Jesus of Nazareth," Jesus spoke "I am He." At those words, which contain the Name of Israel's God—"I am"—the soldiers fall back on the ground. When they recover, He tells them again that He is the man they are looking for, the Jesus they seek.

Peter leaps into action. Now is the time to protect his Lord. He draws a sword and attacks one of the servants who is with the priests' guard, a man named Malchus, and cuts off his ear. Jesus turns and rebukes Peter. The sword is not the solution. The sword is the power of Jews and Romans. It is not the power that Jesus will use. Jesus has to die. That is what He has come to do. That will be His great victory.

Jesus willingly goes with the soldiers, who take Him to the high priest's palace for a late-night trial before the Jewish "Senate," the Sanhedrin. The Jewish leaders have organized a case against Jesus. At the center of their case is Jesus' action against the temple. "He says He will destroy the temple and raise it in three days," some of the witnesses say. Other witnesses bring other evidence, but the witnesses contradict each other. Some of the witnesses are paid by the Jewish leaders to testify, so that Jesus will be convicted. Throughout all this testimony, Jesus remains silent. This is unusual. Throughout His ministry, Jesus has responded to criticisms and attacks, refuting false accusations and silencing the Jews who attacked him. Now, Jesus is silent. Finally, the high priest puts Him under an oath and demands to know if Jesus claims to be the Messiah, the son of God.

Jesus answers, "It is as you say," and goes on to warn that the high priest will someday see the Son of Man enthroned in heaven. This is enough for the high priest. He tears his priestly robes and cries out, "He has blasphemed." There is no reason for the trial to go on: "He is deserving of death," the Jewish leaders conclude.

Meanwhile, Peter has come to the court of the high priest, following along behind Jesus to find out what will happen. The apostle John has connections at the high priest's court, and is able to get into the courtyard along with Peter. Peter goes over to the fire to warm himself, when a servant girl spots him. "You're a disciple of this Jesus, aren't you?" she asks. Peter denies it. Two more times people ask whether he is Jesus' disciple, and every time Peter denies even knowing Jesus. Finally, a cock crows, and Peter remembers a prediction that Jesus had made at supper just a few hours before: "Before the cock crows, you will deny Me three times." Desperate at his betrayal, Peter goes out of the court to find a place to mourn and weep. The last of His disciples has abandoned Jesus. He faces the cross alone. When the Shepherd is struck, the sheep flee.

The Jewish leaders have found Jesus guilty of blasphemy, a capital crime in Israel's law. Because the Jews are under the authority of Rome, however, they do not have the authority to carry out the death penalty on their own. They have to involve the Romans. In the morning, when the Roman court in Jerusalem opens, they send Jesus in chains to Pontius Pilate, the governor assigned to Judea at the time. While the Jews are concerned about Jesus' violations of Jewish law, Pilate is only concerned about order. Like most Roman provincial governors, he makes his decisions based on what he thinks will keep things calm and peaceful. If he has to kill an innocent man to keep things peaceful, he is willing to do that. Being a Roman, Pilate is also concerned with the political dimension of Jesus' ministry. Whether or not Jesus blasphemed the God of Israel, he does not care. But if Jesus claims to be a king, that is a different matter. Pilate knows that a Jew who claims to be a king will arouse all the hopes and passions of the Jews, and possibly stir them up to rebel against Rome. Rome can handle it, but it will be messy. If Pilate lets things get too out of control, he could lose his post. He wants to avoid the problem if he can.

So Pilate's questions to Jesus all focus on His claims to be a king. "Are you king of the Jews?" Pilate asks. Jesus tells him He is. Pilate wonders why Jesus does not respond to any of the Jews' accusations, but Jesus says nothing. Pilate quickly discerns what is going on. So far as Pilate is concerned, Jesus is harmless. He might claim to be a king, but He is not starting a rebellion against Rome. Pilate sees that the Jewish leaders dislike Jesus because Jesus is more popular with the people of Judea than they are. He sees that they have brought Jesus to him because they envy Him.

Pilate thinks that he can satisfy the Jews by having Jesus tortured and beaten. His soldiers whip Jesus, spit on Him, and pull his beard. They dress him like a king, in a purple robe and crown, and then they bow to the "king of the Jews." It is all mockery. They are mocking not only Jesus, but the Jews: "This is the kind of king you deserve," the Romans say, "one who wears a crown of thorns. This is the kind of king you Jews should have, a pathetic peasant prophet." The Jews are not satisfied with torturing Jesus. They want Jesus dead.

Pilate hears that Jesus comes from Galilee, which at the time is under the jurisdiction of Herod Antipas, the son of Herod the Great. That might be a solution for Pilate's dilemma. He can pass responsibility off to Herod. So he sends Jesus over to Herod, who is also in Jerusalem for the feast. Herod has heard all about Jesus, and is curious to meet the Galilean prophet and miracle-worker. But Jesus does not respond to Herod either, and Herod soon passes Jesus back to Pilate.

Pilate thinks of another, final solution. At the Passover, it is customary for the Roman governors to release one Jewish prisoner. The custom sends a message that Rome is benevolent and kind. Since Passover is a celebration of Jewish liberty from Egypt, releasing a prisoner showed that the Romans understood something about Passover. Pilate has two prisoners now, Jesus and Bar-Abbas, a revolutionary who has been stirring up trouble in Judea and Galilee. He decides to let the Jews decide which one they want him to release. It is more than a choice of two men. The Jews are choosing two paths for their future—the path of Jesus that involves love of enemies and submission to Rome, or the path of Bar-Abbas, which will lead eventually to armed war with the Romans.

The Jews have already made their choice. When Pilate presents the choice to them, they shout that they want Bar-Abbas released. "What shall I do with Jesus?" Pilate asks. The Jews cry "Crucify Him! Crucify Him!" Crucifixion is an appropriate punishment in their minds. Usually, slaves are crucified when they rebel. Lifting up a slave rebel on the cross mocks the slave's pretensions. "You want to lift yourself up," the Romans say when they put someone on a cross, "You want people to look up to you. Well, they will look up to you, on a cross." The Jews are thinking the same about Jesus: He has "lifted Himself" as the Messiah and Son of God; they want Him to be punished by "lifting him" up.[12]

Crucifixion is a gruesome public form of execution, as much an effort to shame the crucified as to torture him. Most of those executed by crucifixion are completely naked,

---

12. Joel Marcus, "Crucifixion as Parodic Exaltation," *Journal of Biblical Literature* 125:1 (2006), 73–87.

lacking even the small loin cloth that Jesus usually wears in paintings. Hanging from nails driven into the wrist and ankle, or by ropes tied to the arms and legs, the victim slowly suffocates. Added to Jesus' pain and shame are the jeers and mockery that the Jewish leaders throw at Him. He's such a great miracle-worker, they joke, why can't He bring Himself down from the cross? Where is His God? When Jesus cries out to the Father, the Jews, who certainly know better, says that He is crying out for Elijah.

Few of His disciples are at the cross. Most of them scatter at the time of His arrest and are in hiding. It is common for the Romans to suppress Jewish rebellions by executing not only the leader of the rebellion but his followers as well. The disciples fear that the Jews will come after them as they come after Jesus. Only John is at the cross, along with Jesus' mother, Mary. As they weep at the foot of the cross, Jesus tells John to care for His mother when He is gone.

After hours of torture, Jesus cries out with a loud voice, "It is finished." Then he dies. The Jews insist that Pilate set up a guard around His tomb. They have heard and understand Jesus' prediction that He will die and rise from the dead, and they suspect that the disciples will try to steal His body and then claim that He has been raised. Pilate agrees.

Early on the morning of the day after the Sabbath, an angel comes to the tomb, frightening the soldiers who are stationed there so that they become as dead men. The angel moves the stone away, revealing an empty tomb. Later on the same morning, some of the women who have followed Jesus to Jerusalem and ministered to Him come to the tomb to dress His body. They find the tomb empty, and an angel sitting on the rock telling them that Jesus is no longer in the tomb but has been raised from the dead. They run to tell the disciples, and Peter and John dash to the tomb and find things just as the women say.

Jesus remains on earth for another forty days after His resurrection. He appears to the remaining apostles several times. He teaches them about the meaning of His death and resurrection, and about their ministry. After forty days, Jesus takes the disciples onto a mountain, and rises from earth to heaven until a cloud covers Him. Jesus, the crucified and risen Jesus, has been exalted to the throne at the right hand of His Father. He has been installed as King, and He is reigning until His enemies are placed beneath His feet.

Finally, the disciples believe the great Good News: Jesus is risen. He is risen indeed.

It is a strange story, the story of Jesus. To the Jews, it is not the story of Israel's redemption but some odd detour. For Christians, though, the story of Jesus is the final chapter of the story of Israel. For Christians, all that Israel hopes for—redemption from enemies, forgiveness of sins, triumph and exaltation, a restoration of Eden, the conversion of the nations, the earth filled with the glory of Israel's God—all of it comes to pass through Jesus. Not through the sword of Zealots, or the rigid purity of the Pharisees, or the political compromises of the Sadducees, or the withdrawal of the Essenes. Israel's story is carried to its conclusion by a different sort of Jew entirely, a different sort of holiness, a different story-line, a story-line of compassion, service, suffering, death. And, over all and transforming all, resurrection.

For Jesus is risen. He is risen indeed.

Review Questions

1. Why do the Jews want to kill Jesus?

2. Discuss Pilate's calculations and his efforts to avoid making a decision about Jesus.

3. What happens to the disciples when Jesus is arrested?

4. How are the Roman soldiers mocking the Jews?

5. How do people die when they are crucified? What is the message of crucifixion?

6. How does Jesus fulfill the hopes of Israel?

Thought Questions

1. What does the name "Bar-Abbas" mean? Why is that significant?

2. Looking at a Bible dictionary, summarize the history of crucifixion.

3. How would you defend the fact of Jesus' resurrection to an unbeliever?

CHAPTER 3

FOUR GOSPELS [1]

The so-called "synoptic problem" is one of the most complicated issues that Bible scholars deal with. The word "synoptic" refers here to the first three gospels, Matthew, Mark, and Luke. The questions posed by the "synoptic problem" are, Where do the gospels come from? Which gospel comes first? Do any of the evangelists use the writings of other evangelists? These questions arise from a fairly simple observation: The synoptic gospels are very similar in their basic structure and in many of their incidents, but they are not identical. They differ in their wording even when they are telling about the same event; they differ in the arrangement of the events of the life of Jesus; and they sometimes include different events. The synoptic problem is to explain the similarities, and the differences.

For example, Matthew tells the story of Jesus' healing of a leper this way:

> When Jesus came down from the mountain, large crowds followed Him. And a leper came to Him and bowed down before Him, and said, "Lord, if You are willing, You can make me clean." Jesus stretched out His hand and touched him, saying, "I am willing; be cleansed." And immediately

1. This is the most technical chapter in this book, and teachers may want to instruct students to skip it. The material, though, is important, and should be at least summarized to students studying the gospels.

his leprosy was cleansed. And Jesus said to him, "See that you tell no one; but go, show yourself to the priest and present the offering that Moses commanded, as a testimony to them." (Mt. 8:1–4)

Mark tells the same story this way:

And a leper came to Jesus, beseeching Him and falling on his knees before Him, and saying, "If You are willing, You can make me clean." Moved with compassion, Jesus stretched out His hand and touched him, and said to him, "I am willing; be cleansed." Immediately the leprosy left him and he was cleansed. And He sternly warned him and immediately sent him away, and He said to him, "See that you say nothing to anyone; but go, show yourself to the priest and offer for your cleansing what Moses commanded, as a testimony to them." (Mk. 1:40–44)

Luke also tells this incident:

While He was in one of the cities, behold, there was a man covered with leprosy; and when he saw Jesus, he fell on his face and implored Him, saying, "Lord, if You are willing, You can make me clean." And He stretched out His hand and touched him, saying, "I am willing; be cleansed." And immediately the leprosy left him. And He ordered him to tell no one, "But go and show yourself to the priest and make an offering for your cleansing, just as Moses commanded, as a testimony to them." (Lk. 5:12–14)

There are some minor differences. Mark mentions Jesus' compassion, and in both Matthew and Luke (but not in Mark) the leper addresses Jesus as "Lord." Overall, though, these are very close, both in the facts of the story and the words used to tell it.

Scholars want to understand how three books from different authors, writing at different times and in different places, can be so similar. But they also want to know why the three books are different. Though the three gospels tell this story in very similar ways, the placement of this incident differs from one gospel to the next. In Matthew, this incident occurs after Matthew's long account of the sermon on the mount, in chapter 8; in Mark, the story appears in the *first* chapter; in Luke, the incident is recorded *before* Luke's account of the sermon of Jesus, the sermon on the plain. This raises a question about chronology: When exactly does this incident happen in the life of Jesus? Scholars who think about the synoptic problem, though, are more interested in the history of the gospel books themselves: How do these books come to be what they are, and why?

For many, the problem is more precise. Many modern scholars believe that Mark is the first gospel written. Their reasons are not very strong. It's the shortest gospel, and for some, apparently, short means early. The church fathers, by contrast, said that Mark is short because he is writing an abridgement of Matthew. Modern scholars don't see it that way. Believing that Mark is the first gospel, they also think that both Matthew and Luke rely on Mark as a source for their own gospel. About 41 percent of Luke overlaps with Mark, and 45 percent of Matthew. That makes sense if the two have Mark's gospel open in front of them. But the other part of the problem is that Matthew and Luke often agree with one another, in factual details and wording, when they record incidents that are not found in Mark at all. About 25 percent of Matthew is shared with Luke, but not with Mark, and 23 percent of Luke's gospel is similar to Matthew but not to Mark.

For instance, all three synoptic gospels record Jesus' prophecy about the destruction of Jerusalem (Mt. 24–25; Mk. 13; Lk. 21), but Matthew and Luke include things that Mark does not. Matthew writes,

But be sure of this, that if the head of the house had known at what time of the night the thief was coming, he would have been on the alert and would not have allowed his house to be broken into. For this reason you also must be ready; for the Son of Man is coming at an hour when you do not think He will. Who then is the faithful and sensible slave whom his master put in charge of his household to give them their food at the proper time? Blessed is that slave whom his master finds so doing when he comes. Truly I say to you that he will put him in charge of all his possessions. But if that evil slave says in his heart, "My master is not coming for a long time," and begins to beat his fellow slaves and eat and drink with drunkards; the master of that slave will come on a day when he does not expect him and at an hour which he does not know, and will cut him in pieces and assign him a place with the hypocrites; in that place there will be weeping and gnashing of teeth. (Mt. 24:43–51)

Luke has a very similar passage:

But be sure of this, that if the head of the house had known at what hour the thief was coming, he would not have allowed his house to be broken into. You too, be ready; for the Son of Man is coming at an hour that you do not expect. . . . Who then is the faithful and sensible steward, whom his master will put in charge of his servants, to give them their rations at the proper time? Blessed is that slave whom his master finds so doing when he comes. Truly I say to you that he will put him in charge of all his possessions. But if that slave says in his heart, "My master will be a long time in coming," and begins to beat the slaves, both men and women, and to eat and drink and get drunk; the master of that slave will come on a day when he does not expect him and at an hour he does not know, and will cut him in pieces, and assign him a place with the unbelievers.

These passages are not identical, but they are very close, and there is nothing similar in Mark. One of the intriguing details, though, is that Luke includes this discussion and parable in chapter 12 (vv. 39–46) of his gospel, not in his account of the Olivet Discourse, and in Luke's account Peter interrupts Jesus with a question. Even when Luke and Matthew are very similar, there are still differences.

Matthew and Luke cannot have gotten this passage from Mark, because Mark doesn't include it. But the two passages are so similar that scholars find it difficult to believe that Matthew and Luke write their stories separately. Many scholars in recent decades believe that Matthew and Luke must have been relying on another written source besides Mark. They label this document "Q," which stands for the German word Quelle, "source." Using Mark and Q, Matthew and Luke come up with gospels that resemble Mark at many points, but also resemble each other.

What is in Q? Scholars say that Q contains all the parts of the gospel story that Matthew and Luke share, but are not found in Mark. Put as a fairly accurate mathematical formula, Q = Matthew + Luke − Mark. No one has ever found a copy of Q. But some scholars are so certain that Q exists that they have written commentaries and other books on it. They believe that Q gives us the earliest gospel story, a gospel story very different from the gospel story that we find in the New Testament. They want to revise our understanding of Jesus by looking at Q rather than at Matthew, Mark, Luke, and John.

All this would be funny, except for the fact that many people are misled from faith in Christ by believing this nonsense. Q has never been found, and there is no reason at all to believe that it ever existed. Let's suppose that the gospels are what they say they are, and what the early church believed they were: Eyewitness accounts of the life of Jesus, or books based on eyewitness accounts. For the church fathers, Matthew writes the first gospel. He is one of the Twelve, and therefore writes down things he himself saw and words he himself heard. Being a tax collector, Matthew can read and write. Even during Jesus' life, Matthew may have written down things Jesus says and does. A few days after the sermon on the mount, we can imagine, copies of Matthew's "sermon notes" begin circulating among Jesus' followers.[2]

Mark isn't one of the twelve, but according to the church fathers, he knows Peter, and Mark's gospel has long been seen as Peter's version of the gospel. So, both Matthew and Mark were based on eyewitness accounts. According to the church fathers, Mark is trying to summarize the gospel in a shorter book than Matthew's. He has Matthew with him as he writes. That explains why Mark and Matthew can have so many passages in common. Luke isn't one of the Twelve either, but by the time he is writing his gospel, Matthew and Mark have written their gospels, and Luke can rely on them. Luke says he does research (Lk. 1:1–4). He apparently talks with Mary (the most obvious source for the narratives of Luke 1–2) and he also is an associate of Paul. John, the Beloved Disciple, is one of the Twelve, John the son of Zebedee and the brother of James, a fisherman of Galilee. So, his gospel comes from an eyewitness, as John himself says.

If we accept the view of the church fathers, we can make sense of the gospels. Why are the first three gospels so similar? Because they are based on eyewitness accounts of things that actually happened.[3] Matthew sees Jesus heal a leper, and so does Peter; Matthew writes down the story himself,

2. This is not fanciful. Disciples of other rabbis definitely took notes. Why not Jesus' disciples?

3. Richard Bauckham's recent *Jesus and the Eyewitnesses* (Grand Rapids: Eerdmans, 2008), is a very sophisticated defense of the traditional view that the gospels depend on eyewitness testimony.

and Peter tells Mark. They are also similar because they were using each other's gospels. Mark knows Matthew's gospel, and in some cases simply repeats Matthew's story in Matthew's words; Luke does the same. Why would they differ at all? Sometimes, they differ because the eyewitnesses have different recollections of the event. Matthew remembers the leper saying "Lord," while Peter (perhaps) doesn't. They also differ because, as we shall see throughout this book, they want to emphasize different things about Jesus. John is very different from the synoptic gospels, but that might be an argument for saying that he is an eyewitness. If he is not an eyewitness, then would he have risked telling the story of Jesus so differently from Matthew, Mark, and Luke? Wouldn't he try to make his gospel as similar to the others as he could?

If the view of the church fathers explains the gospels, and does so fairly simply, why do scholars have to invent a complicated "synoptic problem" and resolve it with a mythical document called "Q"?

There are many answers to that question, but at base the answer is that much of modern New Testament scholarship is a Satanic attack on the truth and reliability of the gospel of Jesus. Many New Testament scholars today treat the New Testament as a merely historical document, not a word from our Creator and Lord, and the effect of much New Testament scholarship is to raise doubts about whether we really can know Jesus through the gospels. This is not to say that New Testament scholars themselves are demonic. They aren't. But New Testament scholarship is an arena of spiritual battle, where we fight not against flesh and blood but against principalities and powers and rulers of wickedness.

Review Questions

1. What are the "synoptic gospels"?
2. What is the synoptic problem?
3. What gospel do modern scholars think came first?
4. What is "Q"?
5. According to the church fathers, in what order were the gospels written?
6. How can we explain the similarities and differences among the gospels?

Thought Questions

1. Compare Matthew 5 and Luke 6. How do the two passages differ? How are they the same? How do you explain the similarities and differences?
2. Who is Matthew? How do we know? Use a concordance if you need to.
3. Who is Mark? Again, use a concordance if necessary.
4. Summarize the career of Luke. Again, use a concordance if necessary.

Dating the Gospels

One aspect of the "synoptic problem" is the effort to date the gospels, at least in relation to one another. This may seem like a highly technical question, but, as with the synoptic problem as a whole, the issue of dating is ultimately a spiritual battle. Consider: If the gospels are written shortly after Jesus dies and rises again, by eyewitnesses, are you inclined to believe them? What if they are written fifty years after Jesus, by people who never knew Jesus Himself? Are you as likely to believe the gospels then? The further away the gospels are from the events of Jesus' life, death, and resurrection, the less reliable they seem.

Today, most New Testament scholars, both "conservative" and "liberal," believe that the gospels were written sometime between the A.D. 50s and A.D. 100.[4] According to this view, both are written decades after Jesus lives and dies and rises again. How do they arrive at these dates?

Let's use Matthew as an example. Most scholars today believe that Matthew is written (not by Matthew) sometime between A.D. 80 and 100. Mark, on which Matthew relies, is written between A.D. 55 and 70, and since Matthew uses Mark, Matthew must have come later. The church fathers also help. Ignatius, who writes in the early second century, refers to Jesus' birth, the star of Bethlehem, and quotes Jesus' exhortation to "be wise as serpents and harmless as doves." Those words appear only in Matthew's gospel, and so these quotations are evidence that, at least by the time of Ignatius, the gospel of Matthew is available to a bishop in Antioch. At the latest, then, Matthew must have been written by the end of the first century.

Scholars try to get more specific by looking at the details of the gospels themselves. Some think that Matthew uses terminology that is not used early in the first century. Twice (16:18; 18:17), Matthew uses the Greek word *ekklesia,* translated as "church." In both passages, moreover, the "church" that he refers to is an organization with rulers and leaders and structures. Peter is the rock on which Jesus builds the church, and in Matthew 18 the "church" has disciplinary authority over its members. Before the late first century, many believe, the Christian community is not this highly organized. The early communities are not "churches" but free-form cell groups. Matthew also writes a lot about conflicts

---

4. The following discussion summarizes some of the arguments of the evangelical *Introduction to the New Testament* (Grand Rapids: Zondervan, 2005), written by D. A. Carson and Douglas Moo.

between Jesus and the Jews, and according to many scholars this reflects the circumstances of the writer rather than the actual life of Jesus. Late in the first century, the Jewish Council of Jamnia formulates a Jewish canon of Scripture and formally expels Christians from the synagogues. Prior to that Christians and Jews are much closer. Because Matthew records intense conflicts between Jews and Christians, he must be writing after the Council takes place.

None of these is a very good argument. If Mark writes the first gospel, then we have to date Matthew after Mark. But not everyone believes that Mark writes first. The church fathers don't, and the arguments for Mark as the first gospel are questionable. Besides, the date of Mark is just as much in dispute as the date of Matthew. Even if Matthew does write after Mark, that does not help us much in deciding a date for Matthew, since using one questionable date (Mark's) to establish another date (Matthew's) isn't very convincing. The notion that an organized "church" is a late development is false. Paul writes sometime in the middle of the first century, yet he freely uses the word "church" (Rom. 16:1; 1 Cor. 1:2; 16:19; Gal.1:2),[5] assumes that the churches will discipline members who fall into flagrant sin (1 Cor. 5–6), and writes to "overseers and deacons" at Philippi (1:1).[6] As for the Council of Jamnia, there are doubts as to whether it really happened, or, if it did, what effect it had. Even if the Council of Jamnia was very important, why do we use that council to set the context for Matthew? To interpret Matthew in the light of that Council assumes already that Matthew is writing more about his own time than about

5. Paul uses the word "church" nearly seventy times in his letters. Even if we exclude the disputed letters, the number is near forty.

6. The references to church "officers" are of course much more abundant if one believes, as I do, that the Pastoral Epistles are Pauline. See 1 Timothy 3:8-13; 5:17-19; Titus 1.

the times of Jesus. Maybe, just maybe, Matthew includes disputes with the Jews in his gospel because *Jesus* got into disputes with Jews, and Matthew sees some of them with his own eyes.

In short, there are no good reasons to think that the gospels are written as late as A.D. 80. In fact, there are good reasons for thinking they were written much earlier.

Re-Dating the Gospels

How much earlier? John Wenham has recently argued that the synoptic gospels are written sometime between A.D. 40 and 60.[7] He believes that the gospel of Matthew is written first, around 40, Mark around 45, Luke around 54, and Acts around 62. One of the reasons for finding these early dates is that the gospels give no hint that they are written after the fall of Jerusalem in A.D. 70. Liberals argue that the prophecies about the destruction of Jerusalem in the synoptics are put in Jesus' mouth after the fact. Matthew writes so accurately about the fall of Jerusalem because it already happened. This argument assumes that the gospels are not reliable, and also ignores the fact that the descriptions in Jesus' prophecies are drawn from Old Testament descriptions of the fall of Jerusalem to Nebuchadnezzar, rather than specifically describing the historical events of A.D. 70. We would expect an after-the-fact description to be much more precise. Moreover, since the fall of Jerusalem proves that Jesus is a prophet, we would expect the writers of the New Testament to mention that event to defend themselves and their Master. The church fathers often mention the fall of Jerusalem in their arguments with Jews. But the apostles

---

7. *Redating Matthew, Mark and Luke: A Fresh Assault on the Synoptic Problem* (Downers Grove: IVP, 1992).

never do. Why not? The most likely reason is that Jerusalem was still standing. Wenham argues that the entire New Testament is finished before the fall of the temple.[8] I agree.

But Wenham tries to be more specific, and he starts with Acts. The latter part of Acts is all about Paul's journey toward Rome. The story builds toward the climax of Paul's trial before Caesar, but it never arrives there. Wenham sensibly argues that Acts does not include the trial and death of Paul because Paul is still alive when Luke ends the story. He also thinks that Luke finishes Acts prior to the events leading up to the Jewish wars that begin in the mid 60s. There is no reference to Roman-Jewish war in Acts. Besides, throughout Acts, the relations between the church and Rome are still good. There is no hint of the persecutions during Nero's reign in the mid-60s. The Sadducees have a role in Acts that they do not have after A.D. 70. Finally, James the Elder of the Jerusalem church is killed around 62, but there is no mention of this in Acts. All this leads the conclusion that Acts is completed around 62.

Working backward, Luke must be before Acts. Luke begins Acts with a reference to his earlier work, his gospel. How much earlier does Luke write his gospel? Second Corinthians 8:18 may help. Paul mentions a "brother whose praise is in the gospel," and there is an ancient tradition that Paul is talking about Luke.[9] How does Luke have "praise in the gospel"? Perhaps he is well known throughout the churches because he has written a gospel book. Paul says that his fame is in *all* the churches, and this is unlikely if Paul is referring to preaching. A book, though, could spread Luke's fame all over the church. Since Corinthians is written when Paul is in Macedonia around A.D. 56, Luke must

---

8. This is the argument of J. A. T. Robinson, *Redating the New Testament* (Eugene: Wipf & Stock, 2000), on which Wenham relies.

9. Origen, Eusebius, Ephrem, Chrysostom, and Jerome all say this.

write before 56, and long enough before that date to give the book time to circulate throughout the churches. Wenham concludes that Luke's gospel was written around 54.

Tradition says that Mark and Peter were together in Rome from 42 to 44, and there is strong evidence that Luke used Mark. Mark could have been written anytime from 44 to the early fifties. Wenham argues that Matthew rather than Mark was written first, and then, relying on the church fathers, dates Matthew in the early 40s. One early witness even says that Matthew is written during the persecution that followed the martyrdom of Stephen, very soon after Pentecost.

Wenham's arguments are strong, and he has studied the question for a long time. He may be right. But I suspect that the gospels are written even earlier than Wenham thinks. I don't see any reason why Matthew could not have written his gospel in the 30s. For millennia Jews were people of the book: All the major events of Israel's history were written, and those written accounts were the basis of Israel's entire national life. Many of them were written soon after the event. Before Moses dies, Genesis and the Books of the Law are compiled into a Bible, and Joshua is added soon after. Probably in the early monarchy period, someone writes Judges, Ruth, the history of David's rise in the book of Samuel. First and Second Kings are written while Israel is in exile, and Chronicles shortly after the return. Are we to believe that now that the climactic event of Israel's history has occurred, they decide to wait several decades to write it all down? What reason do they have for waiting at all?

Several New Testament passages imply that the New Testament writings are already considered Scripture very early on. In 2 Peter 1, Peter says that his teaching is no fable. It is confirmed by the transfiguration of Jesus. He says that the transfiguration confirms the "prophetic word," and so does the fact that no Scripture is of one's own interpretation (or unraveling). Peter's argument doesn't work unless the prophetic word that Peter is talking about is in Scripture. But the prophetic word he writes about is the prophecy of the "power and coming of Jesus" (cf. Mt. 16:27–28). Where is this in Scripture? He must be talking about the gospels. At the end of 2 Peter, Peter explicitly refers to Paul's writings "and other Scriptures" (3:16), so Paul is also considered Scripture by that time.[10]

Another example appears in 1 Timothy 5:18: "The laborer is worthy of his wages." There is some Old Testament background to this comment (Lev. 19:13; Deut. 24:15), but these passages do not match exactly. Matthew 10:10 and Luke 10:7 match much better. So, Paul quotes from the gospels, and cites them *as Scripture,* when he writes the pastorals.[11] Second Timothy 3:16–17 may also be relevant. In that well-known passage, Paul urges Timothy to continue in Scriptures that he has known since childhood, and these are Scriptures that lead to salvation through faith in Christ Jesus. This might be said of the Old Testament Scriptures, but saying that the Old Testament teaches faith in *Jesus* is a pretty strong statement. This passage may imply that Timothy has known the Scriptures of the *New* Testament since childhood. If Paul is writing in the 50s or early 60s, and Timothy is 30 at the time (a youth), that means he grows up during the time shortly after the crucifixion and resurrection of Jesus. Even at that early time, there are "writings" available that teach about Jesus.

The specifics of these arguments are not tremendously important, but I do want to at least point out a reasonable alternative to the modern view of the gospels.

---

10. The reference to Pauline Scripture is one of the reasons for the late dates assigned to 2 Peter. But the letter's appeal to "eyewitness" testimony (1:16-17) is crucial, and the letter collapses completely unless the author was on the Mount of Transfiguration.

11. Obviously, this argument depends on the assumption that the Pastorals are Pauline. Which they are.

Review Questions

1. What are the accepted dates for the gospels in modern scholarship?

2. What are the arguments for saying that Matthew is written in the late first century?

3. Discuss the weaknesses of the arguments for a late date for Matthew.

4. Summarize Wenham's arguments for dating the gospels when he does.

5. Why should we probably date the gospels even earlier than Wenham?

Thought Questions

1. A recent introduction to the New Testament says that Mark is probably written in the 60s. He emphasizes the "way of the cross" and so must have written his gospel when Christians are being persecuted. Evaluate that argument.

2. Using the Internet, find the church father who wrote that Matthew composed his gospel "in the Hebrew dialect." Who is he? What is he talking about?

Why Four Gospels?

For well over a century, New Testament scholars have obsessed over the synoptic problem. They miss the whole question, I think, because they put Mark before Matthew and because they date the gospels far too late. An equally serious problem is that they leave John out of the picture.[12] The synoptic problem leaves us with a ¾ Jesus.

---

12. This is a flaw in N. T. Wright's magnificent *Jesus and the Victory of God*. For strategic reasons, Wright wants to make his case to the New Testament academic world on the basis of the synoptics, but in doing so he leaves out, or misemphasizes some things. He is eloquent, for example, on the "surprising" character of Jesus' ministry, but John's gospel makes it clear that Jesus *expected* the Jews to recognize Him. They should have known that He was Messiah from their own Scriptures.

But that raises a different question. We have four gospels. The first three are very similar. We hear the same stories over and over again. Then the last one seems to go off in a very different direction. Why? Why do we have three gospels that are virtually the same? Why is John so different? Most of the rest of this book tries to answer these questions. Here, I answer a more basic one: Why do we have four gospels in the first place?

The church father Irenaeus offers one answer in *Against Heresies:*

> Since there are four zones of the world in which we live, and four principal winds, while the Church is scattered throughout all the world, and the 'pillar and ground' of the church is the Gospel and the Spirit of life; it is fitting that she should have four pillars, breathing out immortality on every side, and vivifying men afresh. From which fact, it is evident that the Word, the artificer of all, he that sitteth upon the cherubim, and contains all things, He who was manifested to men, has given the gospel under four aspects, but bound together by one Spirit . . . For the cherubim too were fourfaced, and their faces were images of the dispensation of the Son of God. For, as the Scripture says, 'The first living creature was like a lion,' symbolizing His effectual working, His leadership, and royal power; the second was like a calf, signifying His sacrificial and sacerdotal order; but the third had, as it were, the face of a man—an evident description of His advent as a human being; the fourth was like a flying eagle, pointing out the gift of the Spirit hovering with His wings over the Church: Matthew shows him as a man, Mark as an eagle; Luke is the calf; John is the eagle. (3.11–8.9)

Irenaeus also sees in the four gospels an overview of the history of the Old Testament. "The Word of God Himself used to converse with the ante-Mosaic patriarchs, in accordance with His divinity and glory," he writes, "but for those

under the law he instituted a sacerdotal and liturgical service. Afterwards, being made man for us, He sent the gift
of His celestial Spirit over all the earth, protecting us with
His wings." These match up to the four principal covenants:
"one, prior to the deluge, under Adam; the second, that after
the deluge, under Noah; the third, the giving of the law,
under Moses; the fourth, that which renovates man, and
sums up all things in itself by means of the Gospel, raising
and bearing men upon its wings into the heavenly kingdom."
Because the form of the gospel is so wise, "all who destroy
the form of the Gospel are vain, unlearned, and also auda-
cious." This is an argument against Marcion, who accepted
only Luke, and in a shortened version.

Irenaeus' explanation is not a bad start: The gospels correspond to different covenants or ages of the Old Testament.
Let's push that a bit further. There is a progression in the
four gospels. They trace out the history of Israel.[13]

Matthew emphasizes Jesus' relation to the law. We see this
in the Sermon on the Mount (Mt. 5–7), in instructions about
discipleship in two chapters (Mt. 10, 18), and many allusions
to the Old Testament that connect Jesus with Moses.[14] Mark
presents Jesus as a man of action. He is constantly on the
move, always acting "immediately." He battles with demons
and shows that He is the Stronger Man. In Mark, Jesus is
the Davidic king, the son of the Father. Luke emphasizes the
poor of the land and Jesus' ministry to outcasts. Luke dates
events by reference to Roman rulers, so that the whole story
is placed in Roman history. If we include Acts, Luke's writing moves toward Rome. For Luke, Jesus' ministry is thus

13. In much of the following, I am summarizing things I've learned
from lectures from, conversations with, and writings of James Jordan
and Jeffrey Meyers.

14. See Dale Allison, *The New Moses: A Matthean Typology* (Minneapolis: Fortress, 1994).

in the midst of the Gentiles, just as Israel was during the time of the "latter days" (see chapter 1 previously). John's gospel breaks out of this, and goes into the New Covenant proper. John refers to the Old Testament, and links Jesus with Moses and other figures from Israel's history. But John starts his gospel by showing us that Jesus is greater than anything that came before. Moses delivered Yahweh's word, but Jesus *is* that Word; the law came through Moses, but grace and truth through Jesus. John emphasizes that with Jesus the world begins anew. He doesn't just start a new cycle of Israel's history. He concludes that history and starts a new one.

We can summarize these links this way:

Gospel	Old Testament Period
Matthew	Mosaic/Priestly
Mark	Davidic/Kingly
Luke	Exilic/Prophetic
John	New Covenant: Combines all three

New Testament history runs through four periods as well. Different elders or apostles take center stage at different points during the first century. Early on, James the son of Zebedee is the chief leader of the church at Jerusalem (cf. Acts 12:2), Peter follows as a key leader in Jerusalem and then moves on (Acts 1–7), Paul leads the mission to the Gentiles (Acts 13–28), and finally John completes the entire canon in the book of Revelation. Each of these phases of the apostolic age matches a gospel. Matthew is a very Jewish gospel, and was probably written in Jerusalem. It has many similarities with the epistle of James, and is located in the history recorded in the early chapters of Acts. Both Matthew and James heavily emphasize the goodness of the law. Mark fits with the Petrine period. Tradition says that Mark works with Peter, and Mark's gospel moves, as we shall see, from a Jewish to a Gentile setting. In Acts, Peter bridges this gap (Acts 10–11), as we see in the letters of Peter. Luke travels with Paul, and as noted above, Luke emphasizes the ministry to the Gentiles, especially in the second volume of his work, Acts itself. Taken together, Luke and Acts move from the temple to Rome, from the heart of Judaism to the capital city of the Roman Empire. John fits the period following the end of Acts, leading up to the destruction of Jerusalem. John's gospel is connected, of course, with the other writings of John in the New Testament—not only Revelation but his three brief epistles. We can chart these correspondences like this:

Gospel	Old Testament History	New Testament History
Matthew	Mosaic/Priestly	Jacobin
Mark	Davidic/Kingly	Petrine
Luke	Exilic/Prophetic	Pauline
John	Combines all three	Johannine

Irenaeus makes connections with the four faces of the cherubim as well, and that is possible. The four faces are: ox, lion, eagle, man. The ox is a "priestly" animal, associated with sacrifice and especially with the priests' sacrifices (cf. Lev. 4). The lion is a symbol of the Davidic dynasty, the "lion of the tribe of Judah" (Gen. 49:9; Rev. 5:5), a kingly beast. The eagle is an unclean animal, representing Gentiles, and in some prophetic passages the eagle symbolizes swift invaders (Jer. 48:40; 49:22; Lam. 4:19). Thus:

Gospel	Old Testament History	New Testament History	Face of Cherubim
Matthew	Mosaic/Priestly	Jacobin	Ox
Mark	Davidic/Kingly	Petrine	Lion
Luke	Exilic/Prophetic	Pauline	Eagle
John	Combines all three	Johannine	Man

So far, we have been looking at the gospels separately, but they also form a large "symphony" in four parts. Each gospel prepares for the next. Matthew ends with a command to "go," and Mark opens by talking about the "way." Mark focuses on the way of Jesus, so Mark fills out the command "go" by answering the question "How?" Matthew ends with the Gentile centurion confessing the "son of God," and Mark begins by identifying Jesus as the Son. Some ancient manuscripts of Mark end at Mark 16:8: "they said nothing to anyone, for they were afraid." If this is Mark's abrupt ending, he poses a question: If everyone is fearful and uncertain, what will happen? Will the disciples ever get started on the mission Jesus gives them? Luke–Acts narrates the story of the church, telling the story of disciples who regain their courage what happened following the women. Luke ends with Jesus teaching about Himself in all the Scripture, and John shows how Jesus fulfills all of Scripture.[15] When we read the gospels as a symphony in four movements, we see a growth and maturation: Jesus is the Jewish Messiah; and yet more, Jesus is the Crucified Messiah; and yet more, Jesus is the universal savior; and more, Jesus is the Word made flesh.

That, not some ¾ or harmonized or edited gospel, is the four-dimensional portrait of Jesus that God wants us to have. That is the fourfold Jesus whose gospel conquers from the river to the seas, and to the four corners of the world.

---

15. Another approach could be to see in the four gospels that Jesus sums up the four ages of human history, or the four types of human civilization. Ancient humanity had four types of civilization: tribal cultures, temple cultures devoted to sky gods, Israelite civilization oriented to the future, and Greco-Roman civilization organized into the democratic city-state. Matthew is associated with tribal civilization, Mark with the temple, Luke with Greco-Roman, and John is Israelite and future-oriented. This is developed in a provocative way in Eugen Rosenstock-Huessy's neglected classic, *Fruit of Lips: or Why Four Gospels* (Pittsburgh: Pickwick Press, 2004).

Review Questions

1. Why is John's gospel neglected by modern scholars?

2. According to Irenaeus, why are there four gospels?

3. How do the four gospels match four periods of biblical history?

4. What are the phases of apostolic history? How do the gospels fit in?

5. Explain how the gospels are linked together like a "symphony in four movements."

Thought Questions

1. How do we know that cherubim have four faces? Use a concordance if necessary.

2. Besides the passage given above, where does the Bible link together oxen/bulls with priests? Lions with kings?

3. Find three parallels between the gospel of Matthew and the letter of James.

CHAPTER 4

MATTHEW

righteousness that
surpasses the scribes

The first gospel has traditionally been attributed to Matthew or Levi, the tax collector who becomes the disciple of Jesus (Mt. 9:9; 10:3; Mk. 2:14). As a tax collector, he is able to read and write. He is ideally suited to write a gospel.

Matthew knows the Old Testament well. Matthew writes for a Jewish or Jewish-Christian audience. He assumes that his readers know a good bit of the Bible and something about Jewish customs. When He records Jesus' condemnation of the Pharisees and scribes for "broadening phylacteries" and "lengthening the tassels of their garments" (23:5), he does not stop to explain what he's talking about. He assumes that his readers know what phylacteries and tassels are. Numbers 15 requires Israelites to have tassels on the corners of their garments, and many first-century Jews wear Torah-boxes or phylacteries on their foreheads or wrists to fulfill the command of Deuteronomy 6. As recorded by Matthew, Jesus' words make sense only to an audience that knows Jewish customs.

We find another example in Matthew 15. The Pharisees and scribes rebuke Jesus and His disciples for failing to wash their hands before eating. Washing is very important to the hyper-pure Judaism of the Pharisees (see chapter 2). Matthew does not explain why the Pharisees are worried about washing hands. Mark, by contrast, explains the Pharisees' customs at great length (7:3–4). Matthew assumes his readers will know about washings; Mark does not. Matthew is writing to an audience that knows Judaism, while Mark writes to a Gentile audience.

This Jewish background is important to understanding the way the book is put together. Matthew writes to a Jewish audience, and he writes a very Jewish gospel. He writes the gospel of the ox, the Mosaic gospel, the gospel to the Jew first.

Beginning and End

Matthew begins with a quotation from Genesis: He writes the "book of generations" of Jesus. In Greek, the phrase is *biblos geneseos,* and the second word is a form of the word "genesis" or "beginning." He begins his book by referring to the first book of the Bible. He is writing a "new Genesis," the story of a new creation. The very same phrase "book of the generations" is found in Genesis 2:4 and 5:1. Matthew wants us to know that he is writing a new book of Genesis, a "book of new beginnings."

The opening phrase is not Matthew's only allusion to Genesis. He gives Jesus' genealogy, which reminds us of the numerous genealogies of Genesis (Gen. 4:16–26; 5:1–32; 10:1–32; 11:10–32; 36:1–43). He tells about a miraculous birth, like the births of Isaac, Jacob, and Joseph. Jesus' father has dreams, and his name is Joseph. He is like the Joseph of Genesis, who was also a dreamer. As Matthew moves into chapter 2, he continues the story of Israel but moves to the book of Exodus. In Matthew's view, Israel has become an Egypt. Instead of Pharaoh, Herod the Edomite oppresses Israel and kills small children. Jesus has to escape "by night" (cf. Exod. 12:30) to safety, an event that Matthew sees as a fulfillment of a passage from Hosea that speaks of the exodus (Mt. 2:15; Hos. 11:1). His water-crossing in baptism

(3:13–17) is like the exodus of Israel through the sea. Immediately after He goes through the water, Jesus is tempted in the wilderness for forty days, as Israel was tempted for forty years in the wilderness. During His temptations, Jesus quotes from passages referring to Israel's forty-year sojourn (4:1–11). He ascends a mountain, where He instructs His disciples in the righteousness that surpasses that of the scribes and Pharisees (chs. 5–7). He lays before Israel the choice between life and prosperity, death and disaster, a choice between maintaining their "house" and seeing it dismantled by a "river" rising from Rome.

Matthew begins where Israel's history begins, with creation and exodus. He ends his gospel where Israel's history ends. At the conclusion of his gospel, Jesus gives the "great commission" to His disciples. Jesus has all authority in heaven and on earth and commands His disciples to "Go" to the Gentiles. This is similar to the decree of Cyrus, recorded in 2 Chronicles and Ezra:

> Now in the first year of Cyrus king of Persia—in order to fulfill the word of Yahweh by the mouth of Jeremiah—Yahweh stirred up the spirit of Cyrus king of Persia, so that he sent a proclamation throughout his kingdom, and also put it in writing, saying, Thus says Cyrus king of Persia, "Yahweh, the God of heaven, has given me all the kingdoms of the earth, and He has appointed me to build Him a house in Jerusalem, which is in Judah. Whoever there is among you of all His people, may Yahweh his God be with him, and let him go up!" (2 Chr. 36:22–23)

Cyrus has received "all the kingdoms of the earth" from Yahweh, God of heaven. With this authority, he commissions Israel to "go up" to Jerusalem to rebuild the temple (2 Chr. 36:23). In both Matthew 28:18–20 and 2 Chronicles 36:23, we have the following sequence:

    A. Statement regarding universal authority
      B. Statement regarding the source of authority
        C. Commission to "go"

Jesus the Anointed ("Christ") is greater than Cyrus (also anointed: Is. 44:28; 45:1), because He has authority in *heaven* as well as earth. Cyrus sends the Jews home. Jesus sends His disciples to new places where they have never been. Jesus is greater than Cyrus, but He is a new Cyrus. He is the new emperor of creation, ruling the "heaven and earth" that God created (Gen. 1:1).

In our English Bibles, Malachi is the last book of the Old Testament. But the Hebrew Bible is different. The last book of the Hebrew Bible is 2 Chronicles, and the words of Cyrus are the very last words. Matthew, in other words, ends his gospel with a commission that reminds us of the last words of the Old Testament.

When we put the beginning and end of the first gospel together, we realize that Matthew covers the whole story of the Old Testament. He begins with a genealogy, and even uses the word "Genesis" in the first verse. He ends with a commission to go to the Gentiles. He begins with an allusion to Genesis, and ends with a commission like the decree of Cyrus. He tells the story of Jesus by moving from the Alpha to the Omega of the Old Testament, from A to Z, from creation to restoration. At the beginning and end, Matthew gives us a hint that Jesus is Israel, and that the story of Jesus is the story of Israel re-told. Jesus is the "Son" who is called out of Egypt (cf. Exod. 4:23), and He remains that Son until the end of the gospel. Matthew tells the story of Jesus as a re-telling of the story of Israel.[1]

---

1. This supports the view of Irenaeus that Jesus recapitulates human history.

Pillars of Matthew

Between the beginning and end of the gospel, Matthew fills out this story-line. One of the most obvious things about Matthew is that is includes five large sections of teaching. Look at a red-letter copy of Matthew, and you'll see long sections where Jesus speaks without any, or much, interruption (chs. 5–7, 10, 13, 18, 23–25). Jesus' five discourses hint that He is a new Moses, since Moses also wrote five books.[2] Each of these sections ends with basically the same words: "when Jesus finished these words" (7:28; 11:1; 13:53; 19:1; 26:1). This sentence reminds us of the conclusion of the creation story (Gen. 2:2: "God completed His work," work done by speaking). It also alludes to the end of Moses' building the tabernacle (Exod. 40:33). God spoke to create, and then finished; Jesus speaks to re-make, and then finishes His words. These five discourses are like five pillars that hold up the book of Matthew, set between the "book of Genesis" and the new "Decree of Cyrus."

The first (the Sermon on the Mount, chapters 5–7) and the last (the Olivet Discourse, chapters 23–25) are similar in many respects. Both cover three entire chapters. Both begin with a list of promises or threats. Jesus begins the Sermon with eight "Beatitudes" or blessings (5:1–11), and He begins the Olivet Discourse with eight "woes" or curses (23:13–39). At several points, the woes recap the blessings.

To the poor in spirit, Jesus says, "theirs is the kingdom of heaven" (5:3) and the first woe to the scribes and Pharisees is "because you shut off the kingdom of heaven from people; for you do not enter in yourselves, nor do you allow those who are entering to go in" (23:13). The final Beatitude promises

2. The Discourses do not match the books of the Pentateuch in detail, however. Matthew 13 has nothing to do with Leviticus, and there is not much of a connection between Matthew 18 and Numbers. The numerical link is the only apparent connection with Moses.

blessing to the persecuted, and compares them to the prophets who suffered in a similar fashion (5:10–12). The final woe condemns the Pharisees and scribes because they are the sons of those who persecuted the prophets:

> Woe to you, scribes and Pharisees, hypocrites! For you build the tombs of the prophets and adorn the monuments of the righteous, and say, "If we had been living in the days of our fathers, we would not have been partners with them in shedding the blood of the prophets." So you testify against yourselves, that you are sons of those who murdered the prophets. Fill up, then, the measure of the guilt of your fathers. (Mt. 23:29–32)

The second Beatitude blesses those who mourn, while the second woe condemns the Pharisees' treatment of widows, who are among the mourners (5:4; 23:14). The sixth Beatitude and the sixth woe both concern purity (5:8; 23:25–26). The chart summarizes the similarities:

Beatitudes-Blessings	Woes
poor in spirit-kingdom	shut up kingdom
mourn-comfort	devour widows
meek-earth	travel to make proselytes
hunger and thirst-filled	blind guides: swear by temple
merciful-mercy	tithes
pure in heart-see God	clean outside
peace-sons of God	whitewashed tombs: lawlessness
persecuted (prophets)-kingdom	prophets

Both of these discourses also ends with parables. The Sermon on the Mount ends with the parable of the wise and foolish builders (7:24–27) and Jesus closes the discourse on chapter 24 with parables warning His disciples to be prepared for His coming (24:45–25:30).

These two discourses are the most important pillars that hold up the gospel of Matthew. At the beginning, Jesus goes on a mountain to offer blessings and a way of life to Israel, a way of peace and national survival, a way of life and salvation and communion with the God of Israel. By the end of the gospel, Jesus pronounces judgment against the scribes and Pharisees for rejecting Him and His kingdom. Jesus warns the Jews at the beginning that their "house" will fall if they do not keep His words (7:24–27). By the time we get to chapter 23, the Jews have made it clear that they are not going to keep Jesus' words. So He predicts that the "house" in Jerusalem will fall, and there will not be one stone upon another (24:1–2).

Review Questions

1. What phrase begins Matthew's gospel? Why?

2. What Old Testament passage matches the "Great Commission"? Why is that significant?

3. How many large discourses are there in Matthew? What chapters are they in?

4. How is the sermon on the mount similar to the "Olivet Discourse"?

5. How are the Beatitudes and woes similar?

6. What happens between the first and last of Jesus' discourses?

Thought Questions

1. Compare the genealogy in Matthew 1 to that in Luke 3. How are they similar? How different? Why are they different?

2. Where is Jesus when He delivers the woes in chapter 23? Where is he when He preaches against Jerusalem in chapter 24? Why has He changed places?

3. Look at Matthew 7:15–23 and the parable in Matthew 25:1–13. How are these passages similar?

Five Discourses

The first discourse, the Sermon on the Mount, is clearly modeled on the revelation at Sinai. Jesus is on a mountain, after having passed through the Jordan and spent forty days in the wilderness. From the mountain, He quotes from the law, and teaches His disciples that they must produce a righteousness that surpasses that of the scribes and Pharisees. He is Moses on the mountain, or Yahweh delivering the law to His people.

Remember that the whole gospel of Matthew moves from "Genesis" to "2 Chronicles." The first discourse fits snugly in that context. So do the rest of the five discourses. The close of the Sermon on the Mount is similar to various passages from Deuteronomy.[3] The phrase "Jesus finished these words" links to Deuteronomy 31:1–24 and 32:45.[4] His second discourse (Mt. 10) begins with references to the twelve spies of Numbers 13 and the commissioning of Joshua as Moses' successor. Jesus observes that Israel is "distressed and downcast like sheep without a shepherd" (Mt. 9:36). That phrase comes from Numbers 27:18, where Moses decides to commission Joshua. Like Moses, Jesus instructs the heads of a new Israel about their duties when they enter the land. Matthew 10:1–3 brings together Numbers 27:18 with Numbers 13:1. From the latter it borrows "sending" (*apostelon* in both the Greek Old Testament and Matthew), while from the former it borrows conferral of authority (Septuagint, *doxa;* Matthew, *exousia*).

This means that when we come to the end of the Sermon on the Mount, we come to the end of the "Mosaic" or "Pentateuch" phase of Matthew's gospel. From that point, Matthew is borrowing more from the time of Joshua and the conquest.[5]

---

3. Allison, *New Moses,* 190–191.
4. Allison, *New Moses,* 192–194.
5. See Allison, *New Moses,* 23–28, and most commentaries on the book of Joshua. Given the fact that Joshua is himself typologically

Jesus treats the mission of the Twelve as a quasi-military operation. The apostles are "sheep in the midst of wolves" (10:16), and should expect to face persecution and rejection (10:17, 23). Their ministry will create turmoil among their hearers, turning brother against brother and children against parents (10:21, 35–36). To fulfill their mission, the Twelve need to act with courage, trusting their Father and fearing God rather than man (10:28–29). Jesus announces that he has come to bring a "sword" rather than peace (10:34), and demands a total commitment from His disciples, including a willingness to die for His sake (10:37–39). In exhorting His apostles "Do not fear," Jesus is repeating the words of Moses and Joshua to Israel before the conquest (Num. 14:9; 21:34; Deut. 1:21; 3:2, 22; 31:8; Josh. 8:1; 10:8, 25). The discourse anticipates that some will receive the Twelve, and promises that those who do will, like Rahab, receive a reward (10:40–42). Of course, this conquest is quite different from the original conquest. It is a conquest of liberation and life-giving—the sick healed, dead raised, lepers cleansed, demons conquered (10:8). If this is holy war, it is directed not against Canaanites, but against Satan and His demons. Like Moses, Jesus instructs and sends the Twelve into the land but does not accompany them (11:1).

The third discourse has multiple links to the wisdom literature and to Solomon in particular. Jesus begins to speak in "parables," a word first used in 13:3, and used twelve times in the chapter.[6] The Septuagint employs *parabole* to translate the Hebrew *mashal*, a wisdom term that can be

---

compared to Moses, it is not surprising that traces of Mosaic typology continue into chapter 10, but these traces become faint because Matthew has brought another typology to the forefront and allowed the Mosaic typology to recede to the background.

6. The only other uses of the word are in Matthew 15:15; 21:33, 45; 22:1; 24:32. Chapter 13 is, at least in terms of the distribution of the term, the chapter of parables.

used both of pithy two-line proverbs and extended allegorical narratives.[7] In this chapter above all Jesus uses a wisdom style associated with Solomon. Immediately after Jesus finishes his parabolic teaching, he goes to His home country to teach, and the people are astonished at His "wisdom" (13:54). Apart from this reference, "wisdom" is used only in 11:19 and 12:42, the latter a reference to the wisdom of Solomon that so impressed the queen of Sheba. The content of Jesus' teaching in Matthew 13 is associated with Solomon. Jesus speaks about a kingdom, and says that the kingdom comes in paradoxical, puzzling ways. Jesus' parables reveal, for those with ears to hear, the mysteries of the "kingdom of heaven" (13:11), and many of the parables are metaphors of the kingdom (13:24, 31, 33, 44, 45, 47). Though the terminology of the kingdom is widely distributed throughout the gospel, chapter 13 most thoroughly describes the dynamics, future, and demands of the kingdom of heaven.[8]

Skipping Matthew 18 for the moment, we turn to the fifth discourse, which includes both Jesus' attack on the scribes and Pharisees and His discourse concerning the temple and Jerusalem (Mt. 23–25). Jesus acts as a prophet in the tradition of Jeremiah and Ezekiel, so that this discourse corresponds to the prophecies that come in the latter days of the kingdom of Judah. Jesus, like Jeremiah, engages in verbal combat with the priests and leaders, and gives an extended prophecy concerning the destruction of the temple by the Romans.[9] Jesus' style is very similar to the style of Old Testament prophets. Chapter 23 contains Jesus' most

7. See Friedrich Hauck, "*Parabole*," in *Theological Dictionary of the New Testament*, vol. 5, eds. Gerhard Kittel and Gerhard Friedrich, trans. Geoffrey W. Bromiley (Grand Rapids: Eerdmans, 1967), 747–751.

8. Michael Goulder (*Midrash and Lection in Matthew* [Eugene: Wipf & Stock, 2004], 364, 388) links Matthew 13 with the harvest feast of tabernacles, which was the setting for the temple dedication in 1 Kings 8.

9. See Wright, *Victory of God*, 339–368.

extended and intense condemnation of scribes, Pharisees, and hypocrites. No setting is explicit, but the narrative indicates that this speech takes place in the temple: Jesus arrives in the temple in 21:23, tells parables and engages in debate, but never changes location until the beginning of chapter 24. The temple setting reminds us of the temple sermons of Jeremiah 7 and 26. Like Jeremiah, Jesus charges that the scribes and Pharisees have become a "den of robbers" condemnation (Jer. 7:11; Mt. 21:13). Like the "weeping prophet," Jesus laments the rebellion of the city he condemns (Mt. 23:37–38), and warns Jerusalem she will be left to desolation (23:38; cf. Jer. 22:5). Matthew 24:1 records Jesus' final departure from the temple, reminiscent of the departure of the glory of Yahweh from the temple in Ezekiel 8–11.

From this sketch, we discover the following sequence:

Matthew	Old Testament
Sermon on Mount, 5–7	Sinai revelation
Mission of Twelve, 10	Deuteronomy: preparation for conquest
Parables of Kingdom, 13	Wisdom of Solomon
Eschatological doom, 23–25	End of Judah; Babylonian exile

If this is correct, Matthew 18 should have some relation to the divided kingdom period of Israel's history. In this chapter, Jesus emphasizes that His disciples will be characterized by childlike humility and faith (18:1–3) and warns the community to avoid causing little ones to stumble (18:5–14). Verses 15–20 sketch out the procedures for dealing with sin among the brothers, and Jesus' final parable describes the spirit of forgiveness that must characterize the church (18:21–35). Jesus assumes that His disciples will be separated from Israel as a whole. The word "church" (Greek, *ekklesia*) is virtually unique to this chapter. In 16:18, the word refers to Jesus' own temple-community that He intends to build on the rock of Peter, and the word has the same connotation in 18:17. It is used in the Greek Old Testament to refer to the "assembly" of Israel (cf. Deut. 4:10), and Jesus uses the word to refer to the "new Israel" of His disciples, in contrast to the "Gentiles" outside. Matthew 18:17 goes beyond 16:18, however, in indicating that the new *ekklesia* will have its own structures of authority to enforce the community's standards. In short, Jesus is forming an Israel in the midst of Israel, just as Elijah and Elisha had done during the Omride dynasty.[10]

Israel's God

Jesus is Israel, but Jesus is more than Israel. He is also Israel's God. We can go back to the opening verse of the gospel to see this. As I've said, two passages in Genesis use precisely the same phrase—"book of generations"—as Matthew does here. They are Genesis 2:4 and 5:1, and they describe the "genealogies" of the "heavens and earth" and of "Adam." But Genesis seems to use the phrase in a different sense. In Genesis, the phrase does not, as in Matthew 1:1, introduce a genealogy. Rather, *biblos geneseos* in Genesis 5:1 introduces a list of *descendants* (not ancestors) and in 2:4 does not seem to introduce any sort of ancestry or genealogy at all.

Let's assume Matthew knows what he is doing, and he expects his readers to go back to Genesis 2:4 and 5:1 to see what the phrase means. To see his point, we need to recognize that Genesis normally uses the phrase to introduce "descendants." Genesis 10:1, for instance, introduces the "generations of Shem, Ham, and Japheth," and then goes on to list those who are born from them, and the events generated by those generations. Genesis 2:4 also introduces a series of "generations." In 2:4, the "heavens and earth" are the "parents" who

10. For more on the typological dimensions of the Elijah–Elisha narratives, see my *1 & 2 Kings*.

generate (though God's work) plants, mist, a garden, a man, etc. Adam's "mother" is the earth, as his father is the God of heaven. He is taken from mother dust, and his heavenly Father breathes life into Him. Genesis 5:1 also begins a list of descendants, those who are "generated" by Adam. In both places where Genesis uses the same phrase as Matthew, the text lists those things that come *from* the one named. Genesis is talking not about those who come before the person named but those who come after him—not about the ancestors of heaven and earth, but their progeny; not about the fathers of Adam, but his sons.

If Matthew is using the phrase this way, then the first verse of the gospel names Jesus as the *ancestor* of Israel. Jesus is Israel's *father,* and all the names Matthew lists are "sons," the "generations" of Jesus. Israel's history climaxes in Jesus, but Matthew is hinting at something more surprising: Israel's history *begins* with Jesus. This is neatly captured by the chiastic structure of Matthew's genealogy. The genealogy begins with Jesus-David-Abraham (1:1) in that order. The rest of the genealogy goes through those generations, but in that order, Abraham (v. 2) to David (v. 6) to Jesus (v. 16). Jesus is the first Man and the Last Man, the beginning Israelite and the final Israelite. He is not only the Omega, the climax of Israel's history, He is the Alpha.

This means that the history of the gospel is not only a retelling of the history of Israel, but a retelling of *God's* history. As Yahweh in human flesh, Jesus relives Yahweh's history, His history in His dealings with Israel. The parable of the vineyard (Mt. 21:33–46) highlights this. The owner of the vineyard cares for the vineyard. He provides a wall and builds a tower, and put in a wine press. Then he rents the vineyard to servants and goes on a long journey, leaving the tenants in charge of the vineyard. But the tenants don't honor the owner of the vineyard. When he sends servants to collect rent, the tenants beat them and chase them away. Finally, the owner sends his son, and instead of honoring the son, the tenants kill him, in hopes that they can seize the vineyard for themselves.

This is the story of Matthew's gospel in a nutshell, and it is the story of Israel. Jesus is Israel, and He also comes in the guise of all those servants and prophets that Yahweh sends to Israel to call her to follow the covenant. Jesus is Moses (Mt. 5–7), Joshua (Mt. 10), Solomon (Mt. 13), Elisha (Mt. 18), Jeremiah (Mt. 23–25). When Jesus comes to Israel, all these leaders of Israel come back again, perfected. But by emphasizing that Jesus is the beginning of Israel's history, Matthew shows us that God comes whenever these servants come in His name.

Matthew is also showing us that the story of Israel is the story of her rejection of Yahweh. Each time God comes, Israel turns from Him. God comes to Israel in Moses, and is rejected. God comes to Israel through priests and kings and prophets, yet Israel refuses to listen to her Lord. God comes to Israel through Moses and Joshua, through Solomon, through Elisha and Jeremiah, and yet Israel rejects the servants of Yahweh. Now, in Jesus, Yahweh comes in flesh. Yahweh comes in person, as the Son. And Israel still rejects him.

That's not very good news. But that's not the end of Matthew's story. The God of Israel doesn't stop coming. After His servants have been rejected again and again, after *He* has been rejected time without number, He still keeps coming, and will not give up coming. As Matthew tells the story, Israel's history is a story of a spurned husband who is rejected by a scornful wife. But it's a story of a spurned husband who refuses to give up on His bride. His bride spurns Him and finds other husbands, but He woos her back. He is the relentless, pursuing Hound of Heaven.

That is the message of the final act of this romantic comedy. Yahweh comes in flesh; Israel's Father comes as Israel's Son, and He is rejected yet again. He is rejected more thoroughly than ever. Persecuting prophets is bad; killing God Himself is worse. But the resurrection shows that Israel's God will not let Israel have the final word. He will not let Israel's rejection stand. He keeps coming back, even after Israel thinks they have killed Him. Israel does her worst: Yahweh comes as man, and Israel kills Him. If this were not a gospel, it would be a horror story, because this God cannot be stopped, cannot be buried. He comes back, and back again, even from the grave.

This is great good news, the unsettling gospel of God. Matthew's gospel reveals that God is Love, and Matthew's gospel shows us what kind of love God is: He is relentless, faithful, persistent Love.

Review Questions

1. What are the connections between Matthew 10 and the conquest under Joshua?

2. How does Matthew 13 remind us of the life and teaching of Solomon?

3. How is Matthew 23–25 like the prophecy of Jeremiah?

4. Explain the connections between Matthew 18 and the ministry of Elisha.

5. What does the phrase "book of genealogy" mean in Genesis 2:4 and 5:1? How is Matthew using the phrase?

6. What does the order of Matthew's genealogy tell us about Jesus?

7. How does Matthew tell the story of Yahweh's dealings with Israel?

Thought Questions

1. How is God's love as described in Matthew different from ideas of love that you find in popular songs and movies? How is it similar?

2. Why does Jesus teach from a boat in Matthew 13? How does that fit with the idea that He is taking on the role of Solomon?

3. If the five discourses match different periods of Israel's history, what period of Israel's history matches Matthew 26–27, the crucifixion and resurrection of Jesus?

Sermon on the Mount

Matthew has a unique version of the Sermon on the Mount. Portions of this sermon appear in the other gospels, particularly in Luke 6, but only Matthew records a sermon of this length and with this focus. Jesus "sits," taking the posture of a rabbi teaching in the synagogue, but this is no ordinary rabbi (cf. 7:28). The sermon presents Jesus as the new and true Moses, delivering the law to the people from a mountain. It also presents Him as Yahweh, the Lord of Israel, who does not receive the law from angels (Acts 7:53) but delivers the word of the Lord from His own mouth. The structure of the sermon appears roughly chiastic:

A. Multitudes: goes onto mountain, 5:1
  B. Beatitudes: blessings: framed by blessing of the kingdom, 5:3, 10
    C. Not abolishing law and prophets, 5:17–20
      D. "You have heard," 5:21–48
        E. Righteousness before God, 6:1–18
      D. Miscellaneous: Possessions, judging prayer
    C. Summary of law and prophets, 7:12
  B. Warnings: kingdom of heaven, 7:21
A. Multitudes: coming down, 7:28–8:1

This structure puts three Jewish acts of piety at the center: alms, prayer, fasting. That helps us see the audience Jesus addresses. He is speaking specifically to His followers in first-century Palestine. He contrasts this with the "hypocrites," (Mt. 6:2, 5, 16), the Pharisees, and Jesus is telling His disciples how their righteousness is to surpass that of the scribes and Pharisees. They must do their acts of piety, but do them before God in secret rather than to gain a reputation for piety among men. The key is to seek honor from God, not from men.

The sermon has been interpreted in a number of ways. Some think that Jesus is challenging the harsh requirements of the Mosaic Torah. He contrasts what the people have "heard" with what He is teaching them. When He speaks of what they have heard, He quotes directly from the Old Testament, not from Jewish interpreters (5:21, 27, 31, 33, 38). This has led many Christians to conclude that Jesus is tossing out the Old Testament law. The Old Testament law, according to some, is concerned with external obedience, but Jesus comes preaching heart obedience and internal purity. While Jesus does quote from the Old Testament in the sermon, however, He makes it clear that He is not overturning the Old Testament (5:17). Jesus is not rejecting the Old Testament law or prophets.

Others have thought that Jesus' teaching applies specifically and only to the Jews of His day, who live under Roman overlords. The way of life Jesus describes is a way of life for a subject people. When you are powerless, the best thing to do is to turn the other cheek and give your coat to the one who asks for your tunic (5:39–40). In other circumstances, this would not be necessary. If the Jews had power, they could fight for their rights. If the Jews had power, they could punch back twice as hard. As it is, they go along to get along. Others believe Jesus is preaching the end of the world. He thinks that the whole world is about to collapse and come to an end. So Jesus gives His disciples instructions about how to live during the brief time before the end comes. They don't have to worry about how to exercise power as disciples of Jesus, because there is no time for them to gain power. Neither of these interpretations works. Jesus tells His disciples at the end of the gospel to go to the nations "teaching them everything I have commanded you" (Mt. 28:18–20). This includes more than the Sermon on the Mount, but it clearly includes the Sermon on the Mount. The apostles are commissioned to teach the nations to turn the other cheek, give to him who asks, love their enemies. This is not a temporary ethic. It is part of Jesus' teaching for the nations. It is a way of life for the powerful as well as the powerless.

Many believe that Jesus is only correcting Pharisaical misinterpretations of the law and reinforcing all that the law taught. He is not changing anything, but coming to confirm the law. This interpretation of the sermon makes sense of Jesus' opening words, which demand from His disciples a righteousness that exceeds the righteousness of the scribes and Pharisees.

> Do not think that I came to abolish the Law or the Prophets; I did not come to abolish but to fulfill. For truly I say to you, until heaven and earth pass away, not the smallest letter or stroke shall pass from the Law until all is accomplished. Whoever then annuls one of the least of these commandments, and teaches others to do the same, shall be called least in the kingdom of heaven; but whoever keeps and teaches them, he shall be called great in the kingdom of heaven. For I say to you that unless your righteousness surpasses that of the scribes and Pharisees, you will not enter the kingdom of heaven. (Mt. 5:17–20)

Jesus says that even the smallest details of the law will stand "until heaven and earth pass away," and He says that anyone who ignores the "least of these commandments" is least in the kingdom. They may be in the kingdom, but only those who keep and teach the law will be great in the kingdom.

This is a powerful theory, but it doesn't quite fit what Jesus says. The issue turns on the meaning of Jesus' word "fulfill." What does it mean for Jesus to "fulfill" the law and the prophets? Does it mean that He confirms the law, and changes nothing? Or is there something more?

We can get an idea of what Jesus means by looking at the way Matthew uses the word "fulfill" in the first four chapters of his gospel. Several times, he quotes from the Old Testament and tells us that something Jesus did "fulfills" the Old Testament (1:22; 2:15, 17, 23; 4:14). By the time we get to Jesus' statement in 5:17, we should have some idea of what the word "fulfill" means in Matthew. Two things stand out. First, in all the previous uses in Matthew 1–4, Matthew points to Jesus Himself as the fulfillment of Old Testament. That is part of what Jesus means when He says that He comes to fulfill the law and the prophets. He's talking about His own life and work as the fulfillment of the law and prophets. He fulfills the law and prophets because the things that happen to Him fulfill Old Testament types and shadows. He doesn't choose to go to Egypt as a baby, but it happens as a fulfillment of Hosea 11:1 (Mt. 2:15). He doesn't choose to live in Nazareth, but when Joseph moves there it fulfills prophecy.

Jesus also fulfills the law and the prophets because He obeys the law perfectly. He does what the law requires at every point. He is the one who keeps the jots and tittles of the law and teaches men to do so, and so He is the greatest of the great in the kingdom of heaven. When He teaches on the righteousness that surpasses the righteousness of the scribes and Pharisees, He is also talking about the way *He* keeps the law. Of course, the Pharisees and scribes who consider themselves experts on the law think Jesus is breaking the commandments of God. He is not. He is fulfilling the law in its depths. As we saw in chapter 2, Jesus' Sabbath keeping is a good example of this. Jesus' obedience to the Sabbath laws looks very different from the apparent obedience of the scribes and Pharisees. Jesus keeps the Sabbath with an eye to the "weightier matters of the law," which are justice, mercy, and truth. Jesus keeps the Sabbath as an adult. Children are very worried about keeping the rules, and forcing other people to keep the rules. But children might keep rules so rigidly that they actually violate the rules. That's how the Pharisees keep the law. They are childish law keepers. Jesus is a mature law-keeper, and He calls His disciples to keep the law in the same way.

But the word "fulfill" has another connotation in Matthew 1–4. In every passage where Matthew uses the phrase, the event that fulfills the prophets is surprising. Matthew 2:15 says that Jesus' flight from Israel fulfills Hosea 11:1, "Out of Egypt I called My Son." Everything is backwards here. Jesus is not leaving Egypt, but Israel. The king who attacks the children is not Pharaoh, but Herod. Jesus finds safety in Egypt, not in an exodus from Egypt. Yet, Jesus' upside-down exodus "fulfills" the prophecy of Hosea. Throughout Jesus' ministry, His fulfillments of the law and prophets have this same surprising quality. The righteousness that Jesus requires of His disciples has this same quality. If you slapped my cheek and I slapped back, there would be pain but no surprise. Slapping back is the response you expect. But if you slap me, and I turn to let you slap again, that is surprising. That is a "fulfilled" keeping of the law. That is *mature* law-keeping, a law-keeping of those who have outgrown childhood.

To get the sermon right, we also have to understand the structure of Jesus' teaching.[11] Typically, Jesus' sermon—

11. I rely here on the superb article of Glen Stassen, "The Fourteen Triads of the Sermon on the Mount," *Journal of Biblical Literature* 122 (2003).

especially in chapter 5—is understood as a series of "antitheses" or contrasts. Jesus quotes from the Old Testament, or some Jewish interpretation of the Old Testament, and then corrects that teaching. Jesus says, "The ancients said, 'Do not murder'"; but then tells His disciples His own teaching, "Do not be angry." The Old Testament says, "Do not commit adultery," but Jesus says "Do not lust." Jesus states a thesis, and then contradicts it with an anti-thesis.[12]

In fact, much of the Sermon on the Mount is organized more by "triads" than by contrasts. First, Jesus states the traditional teaching, and this sometimes in triadic form. Then Jesus describes a "vicious cycle plus judgment" associated with the commandment, and this section is not an imperative but begins with "I say to you." Finally, Jesus gives an actual commandment that presents a "transforming initiative" that not only avoids the sin but acts positively, redemptively, to break the vicious cycle of sin.

For example, in 5:21–26, Jesus first gives the traditional teaching: "You have heard it was said; don't murder; whoever murders will be judged." Jesus goes on to describe how anger and insults can lead to murder and to punishment: "Anger leads to judgment; uttering *raka* leads to council; uttering fool leads to hell." So far, Jesus hasn't given any commandments. He has not told His disciples, "Never be

12. Stassen believes that the typical antithetical interpretation misses the central thrust of the sermon. When we interpret the sermon in this way, it seems that Jesus is teaching "impossible ideals rather than positive ways of deliverance." Can anyone completely avoid lust, or anger, or vengeful feelings? No. If we think Jesus is prohibiting these emotions, then we begin to think of "Jesus' good news as high ideals, hard teachings, impossible demands." But none of the "prohibitions" of anger, lust, or vengeance are stated in the imperative. Jesus' sermon includes many imperatives, but on the usual interpretation these imperatives appear as "illustrations" rather than as "prohibitions." Finally, "emphasizing the prohibition of anger, lust, and so on, places the importance on the hard human effort not to be angry rather than on the good news of the gracious deliverance of the reign of God."

angry." He is simply telling His disciples that obeying the prohibition against murder requires them to keep anger under control. He hasn't told them *how* to keep anger under control. That comes in the last section (vv. 23–26), when He finally gives commands: "Leave gifts and be reconciled; make peace with your accuser; in this way escape judgment." If His disciples obey His commands, they will defuse anger before it flames up into murder. If they obey this commandment, they will transform their enemies and help to bring in the kingdom.

The section on lust (5:27–30) works the same way. First, Jesus repeats the traditional teaching from the Ten Commandments: "Do not commit adultery." Then He tells His disciples that they cannot obey that commandment in depth without controlling sexual desire. Looking at a woman to stoke up sexual desire—that is, "checking her out"—is already adultery.[13] Again, Jesus has not yet given a command. He's describing the kind of attitudes and looks that are, and will lead to, adultery. Then He gives the command: "Therefore, pluck eye, cut off hand; in this way escape judgment." Jesus' commandment is not about intention or internal desire, but about *action*. Jesus says we must *do* something to avoid the judgment pronounced against sexual sinners. The specific act is a radical removal of the cause of lust. Jesus doesn't say, Change your mind. He says, *Do* something that radically alters your stance and attitudes toward women and sex.

13. Jesus is absolutely not prohibiting sexual desire as such. If Christians have to renounce sexual desire, Christianity is a one-generation wonder. The world must be peopled, and it's peopled by people who have sexual desires for others. As Stassen shows, Jesus emphasizes the purpose clause: Looking at a woman *in order to* lust is adultery; looking at pornography in order to arouse desire is heart adultery. Noticing a woman's beauty and desiring to unite with her sexually is not, by itself, heart adultery.

Jesus and the Jews

We can go some way to a deeper understanding of Jesus' mature law-keeping by noting how Jesus' commandments address issues in first-century Judaism.

Jesus is criticizing the various programs for Israel's renewal that were available in first-century Judaism. Pharisees, Essenes, Sadducees, as well as the "Zealots" all have a political, not just a religious, orientation. As we saw in chapter 2, many Jews want to fight back against Rome. Jesus doesn't tell them to forget politics, or to ignore the fact that Rome dominates Israel. It is hard to imagine a Jewish teacher who isn't interested in politics. After all, God is God of nations, and Israel is the light to the nations, so politics is inherent in the Jewish worldview. Jesus isn't rejecting the political orientation of Judaism, but he is teaching a different sort of political stance. He is a new Jeremiah, condemning zealotry and revolutionary violence, urging peaceableness and a generosity and love that is so excessive that it resembles God's own superabundant love.

Matthew 5:39 is usually translated, "do not resist evil." It is better to translate as "Do not resist *by evil means*." The usual translation doesn't make much sense of Jesus' work. Jesus resists the devil in the wilderness, He resists the Pharisees and scribes, He resists all the evil of the world in His death and resurrection. Jesus' entire ministry is about resisting evil. He wants His disciples to follow Him and His example, and so He cannot be forbidding them to resist evil. Jesus resists evil, but He resists evil by doing good. He calls us to the same kind of resistance. He calls us to resist evil by doing good, rather than by returning evil for evil.

The word for "resist" here is almost a technical term for revolutionary resistance.[14] Jesus is telling His disciples,

14. Wright, *Victory of God.*

"Don't join the Zealots; don't act like the Jews at the time of Nebuchadnezzar." But Jesus is also teaching His disciples to resist, and to resist actively. But they are to resist by acts of charity and generosity, not by vengefulness and anger. Roman soldiers have the right to force Jewish citizens to carry their gear for one mile. Jesus tells His disciples that instead of refusing, they should carry the gear two miles (5:41). It is possible that verse 40 also refers to practices of the occupation troops: If a Roman soldier wants your clothes, Jesus tells His disciples not to stop at the outer garment but also offer the inner garment. Strip yourself to the skin. Jesus says that His disciples should not insist on their own rights, but be willing to suffer loss, trusting in God alone to supply their needs (cf. 6:26–34). Jesus teaches that rather than being judges ourselves, we ought to entrust ourselves to the God who judges rightly.

Similarly, in verses 43–48 the enemy is not merely a personal enemy. The word is used for both personal and national enemies in the New Testament (e.g., Lk. 1:71, in the Song of Zechariah), and Jesus is talking in the charged context of occupied first-century occupied Israel. Jesus' disciples are supposed to love those who hate them, because that's what God does. "If you want to distinguish yourself from tax collectors and Gentiles," Jesus says, "show yourselves the true Israel, show it in love even for enemies, and not love restricted to those who love us." Israel was the son of Yahweh (Exod. 4:23), but Jesus says that the true sons of the Father are those who do good to their enemies. That is the radical, revolutionary path that Jesus teaches His disciples in the first century.

Verse 48 sums it all up: "You therefore must be perfect, as your heavenly father is perfect." There is an echo here of Leviticus 19:2: "Be holy as Yahweh your God is holy." That is the theme verse of Leviticus, and it is a theme verse for many of the Jews of Jesus' day. The Pharisees' program, for example, is altogether a holiness program. Their goal is to establish a holiness that will eventually encompass all Israel, but a holiness that means essentially separation from the unclean. Jesus, by his explicit echo of Leviticus 19:2, is setting out His own version of the "holiness program." His disciples are to be perfect as the Father is perfect, but holiness is understood here as love of enemies, meekness in the face of persecution, truthful speech, strict sexual faithfulness, and refraining from vengeance. This is the way of "perfection." It is "holiness" or "perfection" defined in terms of the Father's unlimited generosity to the just and the unjust.

So far, we've been looking at how Jesus' words are applied in the first century, among the Jews who are Jesus' disciples. But what are the more permanent principles of justice in these laws? How do the commands "do not resist evil" and "turn the other cheek" fulfill the law? How is this a righteousness that surpasses the righteousness of the scribes?

Redemptive Righteousness[15]

In 5:38, Jesus quotes from the Old Testament *lex talionis*, the "law of retribution" (cf. Exod. 21:24; Lev. 24:20). This is the principle summarized as "eye for eye, tooth for tooth," and it is a principle of civil justice in the Old Testament. If someone damages person or property, he has to restore what he damages or suffer a similar damage to himself. Jesus doesn't deny the justice of this principle, and in some places uses it as a principle of justice. For example, Jesus says, "Whoever is ashamed of the Son of man, of him shall the Son of man be ashamed" (Mk. 8:38; Lk. 9:26). Paul says whoever destroys

---

15. Here again, I borrow from Stassen, who uses the phrase "redemptive righteousness."

the temple of God will be destroyed (1 Cor. 3:17). So, the principle stands.

Originally, the law of retribution is designed to limit violence. Lamech says he would take seventy-sevenfold vengeance on anyone who mistreated him. Yahweh tells Israel not to follow the example of Lamech. They cannot take seventy-sevenfold vengeance, but only the limited vengeance the law permits. If someone strikes out one tooth, you can't take out seventy-seven of his teeth, even if he has that many. But this principle can be applied in ways that perpetuate violence rather than arrest it. Jesus warns that applying this principle in many settings leads to cycles of violence, of insult and return insult, of vengeance and counter vengeance. An insult leads to a response that is twice as bad, and that leads to a response and that leads to a response that doubles the insult again. A cycle of vengeance, of eye for eye for eye for eye for eye, goes on forever until no one has any eyes left. As in *Hamlet,* it's life for life for life for life, and it ends only when everyone is dead on the floor or too exhausted to go on.

Eternal vendettas like this are still common—gang warfare in our inner cities, the Middle East, Kosovo during the late 1990s. These examples show that Jesus' words are not confined to the first century. These examples also show that Jesus' teaching is not only for personal life and decisions. How many wars are the result of defenses of honor, attempts to apply some version of eye-for-eye? For Serbs and Croats, for Tutsis and Hutus, all the evil that's been done over centuries has to be avenged, but when the vengeance has happened, it just initiates a new cycle.[16]

---

16. If we think that we're free from these primitive instincts and patterns, we're fooling ourselves. Don't think, *I've never been involved in a family feud. I've never been tempted to be a vigilante. So this doesn't apply to me.* We still act the same way, in our marriages, in our friendships,

Jesus is telling His disciples not to get caught up in those cycles of honor and violence. Don't even step into that circle, He warns, because it won't stop. But He doesn't dismiss the *lex talionis* so much as suggest a surprising fulfillment of the principle. He describes a paradoxical, surprising fulfillment of the law, a fulfillment that surpasses the fulfillment of the law by the scribes and Pharisees, a fulfillment that participates in the coming of the kingdom of God that restores harmony and peace and justice in the world.

Jesus' first example—the slapping example—illustrates His point. He is not describing a situation in which our lives are imperiled. He's not denying the legitimacy of self-defense. He's not talking about an adversary coming at you with deadly force. The law provides for self-defense and defense of your house, family, and property if someone is breaking in. Jesus is not eliminating that. He's talking about honor and dishonor, insult and shame. If I receive a slap on the right cheek, either the slapper has slapped me with his left hand or he is slapping me with his backhand. Either way, it's insulting. In Israel, the left hand is reserved for dirty work—using the bathroom and such. So, getting slapped with the left hand is insulting. But a slap on the *right* cheek with the *right* hand is a backhanded slap, an insulting slap rather than a danger to life and limb. The person who slaps you with the back of his hand is treating you as a slave, as an underling. He's not treating you as an equal. He's sweeping you away like a flea.

How does Jesus tell us to respond? Instead of returning evil for evil, a slap for a slap, insult for insult, Jesus calls His

---

in our dealings with difficult people at work or difficult leaders in the church. We receive an insult, and we want to pay it back. Someone makes us look stupid in class, and we want to do something to humble him. Our husband or wife does something embarrassing, and we look for a chance for payback.

disciples to bear the burden of retribution and offer to receive a second slap. If you applied the *lex talionis* as normally understood, the slapper would be slapped, perhaps twice. Jesus says, apply the *lex talionis* in this redemptive, surprising, way: *Accept* the second slap rather than *giving* it. The "double restitution" comes back on the disciple, who bears not only the original insult, but bears the punishment on behalf of the one who assaults him. That "fulfills" the law.

Jesus is forbidding us to enter into the cycle of vengeance and counter-strike, but He's also forbidding us to do nothing. Jesus doesn't want us simply to accept evil and not resist at all. Jesus is not telling us to "take it," glowering and seething as we get beat to a pulp. Jesus is not talking about a situation where you grudgingly trudge along beside the Roman soldier, burning inside the whole time. He's not talking about passively living with it when someone takes your cloak from you. Scribes and Pharisees could do that; often they had no choice.

That's not redemptive righteousness. That's not righteousness at all. That's just realism, Stoicism, accepting oppression and evil, and doing nothing because you can't do anything about it. Doing nothing is not redemptive righteousness. Jesus says we *can* do something about oppression. We can act, and act in ways that stop abuse, injustice, and oppression, and even undo it. Jesus is teaching a form of resistance, but a form of resistance in which good triumphs over evil.

How does this happen? How does this kind of response work? Instead of perpetuating insults and blows, Jesus teaches His disciples to act in a surprising way that brings an end to the cycle. Instead of a series of slaps and return slaps, there are at most two slaps, both on the cheeks of the disciple, and then it's over. Instead of a cycle of vengeance and retribution, it's all over after two miles, after the disciple strips down to nothing. No more to be done. It breaks the cycle in that obvious way.

Following these instructions also, subtly, restores the dignity of the person who gets slapped. The slapper wants to treat the slappee as a victim, the object of his oppression. The slappee has no choice, no dignity. When I slap someone, he's nothing more than the thing my hand lands on. But then he turns and offers his other check, and I'm suddenly put on the spot. I've got to decide whether to slap him again. He's wrested initiative out of my hands. Instead of suffering the shame of being a victim, the disciple takes initiative into his own hands—he offers his cheek, he removes his undershirt, he goes a second mile, he gives to whoever demands (5:40–42). In doing so, the disciple also exposes the bully for the brute that he is, turning the tables in a way brings shame on the oppressor. Slapping may make the slapper look virile, manly, in control. Slapping someone who's willing to be slapped makes the slapper look cruel (think of the attack dogs of the Civil Rights Movement).

Jesus says much the same when He describes our response to enemies. In verse 43, the quotation is not from the Old Testament, but summarizes a view that was held by some Jews, for instance at Qumran. The Old Testament doesn't endorse the view that we are free to hate enemies. The law tells us that we are to do good even to enemies—caring for his animals, for example (Exod. 23:4). Proverbs tells us to feed and give a drink to our enemy (Prov. 25:21–22). The stories of the Bible include many examples of people doing good to those who are persecuting them: Joseph doesn't take vengeance on his brothers, but feeds them and robes them in glory. David has opportunity to pay Saul back, but refuses. The prophets suffer for doing good, and don't strike out in vengeance. Jesus particularly challenges the perversion of loving only those who love you (vv. 46–47). We are to love those near to us (cf. Gal. 6:10), but if our love is restricted by blood, race, kinship, church membership, or whatever, it is no better than the love of Gentiles and tax-collectors. It is not the righteous love that surpasses that of the scribes and Pharisees. And notice again that Jesus doesn't tell us to leave our enemies alone. He's not talking about non-resistance or non-intervention. He's talking about resistance that takes the form of doing good.

Instead of doing nothing when our enemies persecute us, we are to pray for them. And Paul goes further in Romans 12:

> Bless those who persecute you; bless and do not curse. Rejoice with those who rejoice, and weep with those who weep. Be of the same mind toward one another. Do not set your mind on high things, but associate with the humble. Do not be wise in your own opinion. Repay no one evil for evil. Have regard for good things in the sight of all men. If it is possible, as much as depends on you, live peaceably with all men. Beloved, do not avenge yourselves, but rather give place to wrath; for it is written, "Vengeance is Mine, I will repay," says the Lord. But if your enemy is hungry, feed him, and if he is thirsty, give him a drink; for in so doing you will heap burning coals on his head." Do not be overcome by evil, but overcome evil with good. (vv. 14–21)

These instructions have been read as shrewd tactics for an oppressed people. They are that, but Jesus doesn't justify them in a pragmatic way. When He instructs us to love enemies, He appeals instead of the example of our Father, who gives sunshine and rain to His enemies (Mt. 5:45). Ultimately, Jesus is not endorsing this kind of conduct because it works. It does work, and works because it advances the kingdom by undoing cycles of violence and anger and revenge and moving toward restoration.

In the end Jesus teaches His disciples to act this way because it's the way He acts. It's the way we follow Him. There are a number of parallels between this passage and the description of the suffering servant in Isaiah 50:4–7.

> The Lord GOD has given Me the tongue of the learned, that I should know how to speak a word in season to him who is weary. He awakens Me morning by morning, he awakens My ear to hear as the learned. The Lord GOD has opened My ear; and I was not rebellious, nor did I turn away. I gave My back to those who struck Me, and My cheeks to those who plucked out the beard; I did not hide My face from shame and spitting. For the Lord GOD will help Me; therefore I will not be disgraced; therefore I have set My face like a flint, and I know that I will not be ashamed.

Nearly everything that Jesus mentions here happens to Him in His passion: "Jesus Himself was struck and slapped (26:67), and his garments (27:35) were taken from him. If his followers then turn the other cheek and let the enemy have their clothes, will they not be remembering their Lord, especially in his passion?"[17] Jesus is the Suffering Servant, and so are we. In Him, and in imitation of Him, we offer our cheeks to the smiter, our beards to those who pluck them. That is the mature, redemptive righteousness that surpasses the righteousness of the scribes.

Review Questions

1. Describe the structure of the Sermon on the Mount.

2. Summarize two of the popular interpretations of the sermon. Do you agree with them? Why or why not?

3. Is the sermon organized by "antitheses"? Why or why not?

---

17. W. D. Davies and Dale C. Allison, *Matthew 1–7* (New York: T&T Clark, 2004).

4. Explain how Jesus' teaching regarding carrying a burden applies to the first-century Jews.

5. What is the *lex talionis?* How does Jesus want His disciples to fulfill that law?

6. Does Jesus teach us a way of non-resistance to evil? Why or why not?

Thought Questions

1. What would Jesus say about all the wars that Israel fought in the Old Testament? Is He anti-war?

2. Discuss the "triadic" structure of Matthew 6:1–17.

3. Give two illustrations from your own life where you had an opportunity to "turn the other cheek," whether you did it or not.

CHAPTER 5

MARK

the way of the
Son of Man

Mark's is the shortest gospel, and Mark writes at a break-neck pace. In contrast to Matthew, he includes only two larger blocks of teaching material, in chapters 4 and 13, but neither of these is as long as Matthew's longer blocks, and they don't have the same structuring role in the gospel. Mark has no infancy narrative. John the Baptist simply bursts on the scene (like Elijah, 1 Kgs. 17:1), and then Jesus bursts on the scene right after him. Matthew's account of John's preaching takes up twelve verses in chapter 3, but Mark summarizes the same ministry in seven verses; Matthew takes five verses for the baptism scene, but Mark uses three; most strikingly, the temptation scene in Matthew 4 takes up eleven verses, and in Mark only two. Matthew's gospel moves in a leisurely fashion from a genealogy to the beginning of Jesus' ministry in four chapters; Mark has Jesus born, baptized, tempted, and calling disciples before he is half-way through the first chapter. It is no accident that one of Mark's favorite words is "immediately." If Matthew presents Jesus as a new Moses, as a Rabbi or Teacher, Mark presents Him as a man of action, always on the move, a new David, the Warrior.[1] Matthew is like a slow-moving, talky art film;

1. In several cases, Mark's account of an event is considerably longer than Matthew's. The story of the Gadarene demoniac is much longer in Mark (cf. Mt. 8:28–34 with Mk. 5:1–20).

Mark is an action movie. For Matthew, Jesus is what He teaches; for Mark, Jesus is what He *does*. This also makes a difference for their conception of discipleship. For Matthew, being a disciple means holding to all the words that Jesus speaks (Mt. 7:24–27); for Mark, discipleship involves following Jesus, doing what He *does*.

With its fast pace and its emphasis on action, Mark looks simple. It isn't. One of the things that makes Mark subtle and complicated is his use of irony. Irony depends on a difference between the meaning on the surface and the real meaning. If I say to a midget, "You are very tall," I'm using a (lame) form of irony. In literature, irony often depends on the readers or audience knowing something that characters don't know. When Oedipus sets out to find out who murdered his father, the audience already knows that the criminal is Oedipus himself, and part of our enjoyment of the play is watching Oedipus catch up with us. We know throughout *Othello* that Iago is a manipulative villain, but Othello doesn't know that, and neither does Desdemona, his accused wife.

Mark uses irony to make the Pharisees and scribes look bad. He doesn't put up flashing neon lights. He tells his stories so that the Pharisees condemn themselves without realizing it. Chapter 3 is a good example of this ironic technique. Jesus enters a synagogue on the Sabbath and heals a man with a withered hand. In Matthew's version (12:9–14), Jesus asks the assembled Jews if it is lawful to heal on the Sabbath (the Old Testament answer is, of course, yes). In Matthew, Jesus asks the kind of question a rabbi might ask. Mark includes another part of Jesus' question: "Is it lawful to heal *or to kill?*" That sets up the ending of the story. The Pharisees oppose Jesus for doing good on the Sabbath, but immediately afterward they go out to make plans to kill Him (v. 6). They don't say a word to Jesus, but they answer

His question with their actions: For them, it *is* lawful to kill on the Sabbath.

Mark also makes abundant use of intercalation, or "sandwich stories." He begins one story, interrupts it with a completely different story, and then returns to complete the original story. All three synoptic gospels tell the story of Jairus' daughter as a sandwich story. First we hear of the sick girl, then the story is interrupted for Jesus to heal the woman with the hemorrhage, then He returns to the task of healing the sick (now dead) girl. Matthew 9:18–26 contains a fairly brief rendition of the story, but Mark has some additional details that help us see the purpose of this structure. Mark tells us, for instance, that the woman has had a hemorrhage for twelve years. This means that the woman has been in a state of uncleanness for more than a decade, cut off from the temple worship, and having some inconveniences in daily life. Uncleanness is ceremonial death, and this woman has been effectively dead for a long time (cf. Lev. 15). When we get to the end of the story, the number twelve is repeated with reference to the girl: She is twelve years old (Mk. 5:42). The woman and the girl are linked by the number, and thus they are interlaced in Mark's telling. Mark implies that the woman's uncleanness parallels the girl's death. Uncleanness is a form of death, and Jesus has come to cleanse as much as to raise the dead. The emphasis on the number twelve here is not accidental, since it associates both the woman and the girl with Israel, God's now unclean bride, God's dead daughter. Jesus has come to raise up dead *Israel*. The sandwich story links the two women, and shows that Jesus' ministry is both to the outcasts, and to the dead; and Mark shows us that the outcasts are dead, and the dead, outcasts.

Mark uses sandwich stories when Matthew and Luke do not. In Mark 6:14–29, we read about John the Baptist's martyrdom. In Matthew 14:3–12, the story is told as a digression after Matthew mentions that Herod believes that Jesus is John raised from the dead. In Matthew, it is not a sandwich story at all. In Luke 9, it is technically a sandwich story, but it's very short, only three verses, and many of the details that Mark gives are not there. In Mark 6, it's a long story sandwiched in the midst of the account of Jesus sending out the Twelve to preach repentance, cast out demons, and heal the sick. In 6:30, after the account of John's death, the disciples return and they go out by themselves for a rest. Placing the story of John's death in the middle of a story of mission teaches us something about the disciples' work. When Jesus sends you on a mission, you might end up like John. This also foreshadows Jesus' death, who is sent to proclaim the kingdom and will suffer like John. Also, Mark tells the story in a way that captures the contrast between Jesus and Herod as "king of the Jews." Jesus as the true king, worried about sheep without a shepherd. Herod is a false shepherd who devours the prophets, while Jesus is the true shepherd-king who feeds His people.

Son of God

The phrase "son of God" marks a frame or *inclusio* around the entire gospel, and provides another large example of Mark's use of irony. Mark 1:1 tells us that Jesus is God's son. In the course of the gospel, demons recognize Him as the "son of God" (3:11; 5:7; cf. 1:34), but as soon as they say it, Jesus silences them. The disciples don't confess that Jesus is Son of God, not even Peter, who says only that Jesus is the "Christ" (8:29). As readers, we know from the first verse that Jesus is the "Son of God"; we see that the demons know who Jesus is. As we read along, we hope that one of the disciples will catch on. Finally, just as Jesus *dies,* and because of the way He dies, the person confessing Jesus as the Son is not a disciple, but a Roman centurion (15:33–39).

Though no other human being confesses Jesus as the "son of God," God the Father uses this title in a few places. The first is at the beginning of the gospel in the baptism scene. Jesus is baptized and called the "beloved Son." In the same passage, Mark tells us that the heavens are "opened." The Greek word here is *schizo,* and the use of this word to describe the opening of the heavens at the baptism is unique to Mark. It is used regularly in the Old Testament to describe the Lord's coming by rending the heavens (Is. 64:1; Ps. 18:9). At the baptism, the Father shows that He has torn open the sky to come to deliver His people. Jesus' arrival is the sign that the heavens have been opened. Later, Mark uses the same verb for the rending of the temple veil (15:38), just before the centurion confesses Jesus. Heavens rent, and the Father identifies His Son; the temple curtain is divided, and a Gentile echoes the Father's words.

The Father speaks again in the middle of the book at the Mount of Transfiguration (Mk. 9:1). Jesus' baptism and His transfiguration are closely linked. In both events, there is a voice from heaven; in both places, the Father says, "This is My beloved Son." In both there is a reference to "Elijah." In chapter 1, John is dressed like an Elijah (2 Kgs. 1), and in chapter 9, Elijah himself appears and shortly after Jesus tells His disciples that John is "Elijah" (9:12–13). After the Transfiguration, Jesus goes down from the mountain, and immediately encounters a boy possessed with an unclean spirit, just as Jesus encounters the devil right after His baptism. In Mark, these two events are at the beginning of the two phases of Jesus' ministry. Each of these passages discusses the connection of Jesus with John (1:6; 8:28). When we put the parallels between the baptism and the transfiguration together with Mark's use of the phrase "son of God," we get this sketch of the book as a whole:

1:1–8:21	8:22–16:7 (or 20)
A. "Son of God," 1:1	"Christ," 8:29
Baptism	Transfiguration
schizo	
John	"Elijah"
Beloved Son	Beloved Son
Encounter with demon	Encounter with demon
Befuddlement of disciples	Centurion confesses the "son of God"
	schizo

The book divides almost exactly in half. Each half begins with the Father telling us what we've known since verse 1: Jesus is God's Son.

The two halves of the book are linked in various ways. Jesus' Galilean ministry starts in 1:14, but after 8:27, Jesus begins to head toward Jerusalem. After the "prologue" culminates with the call of four disciples in 1:16–20, Jesus begins His ministry with a confrontation with demons in a synagogue, and does a series of healings that provoke the Herodians to plan to kill him (3:6). Similarly, in the second section, we see Jesus enter the temple and denounce it (11:15ff.), and this provokes a plot against his life (12:12). The first half of the book climaxes with Jesus' predictions about His death; the book climaxes with His death.

The *inclusio* also suggests that there might be a chiasm in the book as a whole:

  A. Baptism: splitting heavens and "You are My Son"
    B. Jesus tested in wilderness, 1:12–13
      C. Sower parable, 4:1–9
        D. Stilling of storm, 6:45–52
          E. Peter's confession, 8:27–30
            F. Prediction concerning passion, 8:31–33

> E'. Transfiguration, 9:2–10
> D'. Exorcism of possessed boy, 9:14–29
> C'. Vineyard Parable, 12:1–11 (key words are parable and fruit)
> B'. Jesus tested in temple, 12:13–17 (Jesus sees this as a "test": same as the word for "tempt" in chapter 1)
> A'. Death: splitting veil and "This is the Son"

The "B" sections connect the wilderness with the corrupted temple, and also connect the tempting scribes, Pharisees, and priests to Satan. The parables in the "C" sections provide a "bread" and "wine" pair. Stilling the chaos of the storm (D) is connected with stilling the chaos of demonic possession (D'), and the confession of Peter that Jesus is the Christ (E) is confirmed by the transfiguration (E'). At the center of the whole book is Jesus' first prediction of His death.

In both of the structure outlines we have suggested, the passage in 8:31–33 stands at or near the center, where Jesus predicts His own suffering and death as a way of explaining what it means to be the "Christ." What is Mark telling us?

Review Questions

1. How is Mark's gospel different from Matthew's?

2. What is irony? How does Mark 3 illustrate Mark's use of this device?

3. What is a sandwich story? Why does Mark use sandwich stories?

4. How are the beginning and end of Mark's gospel similar?

5. How is Jesus' baptism like His transfiguration?

6. What is at the center of the chiasm of Mark's gospel?

Thought Questions

1. Mark 3:20–35 is a kind of sandwich story. Explain.

2. In some manuscripts of Mark, the book ends at 16:8. Is that a good place to end the book? Why or why not?

3. Compare Matthew 16:16 with Mark 8:29. What's different? Why?

God's Messenger

Mark begins his gospel with a quotation from Isaiah 40: "The voice of one crying in the wilderness, make ready the way of the Lord, make his paths straight" (Mk. 1:2–3). This comes from the opening verses of a section where Isaiah prophesies about the coming redemption of Israel from Babylonian exile.[2] It is the only direct quotation that Mark gives (though Jesus quotes the Old Testament a lot). Return from exile the big theme of Isaiah 40–66, and Mark is saying that Jesus is the one who comes to fulfill that hope. The gospel is the good news of deliverance from exile. In this passage, Isaiah promises not only return from exile, but also promises the coming of the Divine Warrior. As He did in Egypt, Yahweh will again arm Himself and fight for His people to bring them from bondage (Is. 40:10; see also 42:13–15). In 49:24ff., Isaiah talks about taking the prey of the mighty man. By starting with this quotation, Mark is putting Jesus in the place of the "Divine Warrior" and the mighty man. In short, "Just as Yahweh had promised to deliver Israel from the strong man Babylon (Is. 49:24–25), to lead his blind people along a path that they did not know (Is. 42:16), and to return them finally through the suffering of his servant to Jerusalem (Is. 52–54)," so Mark tells us that Jesus comes to deliver "Israel from the strong man Beelzebul . . . , leading

2. Joel Marcus' study of Mark's use of Scripture (*The Way of the Lord* [Louisville: Westminster/John Knox, 1992] provides a helpful discussion of this passage. See also Rikk E. Watts, *Isaiah's New Exodus in Mark* (Grand Rapids: Baker, 1997).

his blind followers along a way . . . that they do not understand . . . , and arriving finally in Jerusalem."[3]

Mark's opening quotation not only links the ministry of
Jesus to the prophecies of Isaiah, but highlights the crucial
theme of the "way of the Lord" (1:3). Mark commonly refers to the "way," especially in the second half of the book.
Often, "way" refers merely to the road on which Jesus and
His disciples are traveling. The crowds will faint on the
"way" if Jesus sends them home without food (8:3), and Peter
confesses Jesus as He questions them "on the way" (8:28).
Along the way to Jerusalem, Jesus overhears the disciples
discussing which is the greatest and asks, "What were you
discussing on the way?" (9:33–34). At other times, the "way"
is an image of a way of teaching or a way of life. Jewish leaders flatter Jesus by saying that He teaches people the "way
of God" in truth (12:14). By using the phrase "way of the
Lord" at the beginning of the gospel, Mark fills the phrase
with symbolic content. The "way" that the Lord travels in
Isaiah is the way of return from exile, the way of the exodus,
the way through the wilderness, the way toward the promised land, the way of conquest behind the Divine Warrior.
When readers of Mark's gospel find themselves following in
the "way of Jesus," they "perceive, that their journey up to
Jerusalem was a victory march of the divine warrior, casting
down every obstacle as he made his triumphant way to Zion,
causing the blind to see and the desert to bloom."[4]

Mark's quotation is not, however, entirely from Isaiah.
Mark begins his quotation with "I send My Messenger before your face," quoting from Malachi 3:1: "Behold I am going to send My Messenger, and he will clear the way before

3. Rikk E. Watts, "Mark," in Greg Beale and D. A. Carson, *Commentary on the New Testament Use of the Old Testament* (Grand Rapids: Baker, 2007), 119.

4. Marcus, *Way.*

Me." Malachi goes on to warn that the messenger of the covenant will "suddenly come into His temple" and will refine Judah and especially the sons of Levi as silver and gold are refined in the fire (Mal. 3:2–3). With this quotation, Mark signals the central importance of the temple, and shows that Jesus comes to purify and judge Israel in order to save her.[5] Behind Malachi 3:1 stands Exodus 23, which warns Israel to obey the "angel" or "messenger" of Yahweh.[6] Yahweh sends the angel to lead them to the promised land, at which point Yahweh Himself will take over to conquer the land and drive out the Canaanites. For Mark, the messenger is John, who leads the people to a new land but who then gives way to Jesus, the new Joshua, Yahweh Himself, who conquers the land and brings His people in.[7]

The reference to Exodus 23 highlights Israel's hope for a second exodus, and a new conquest, but this hope is given an ironic twist in Malachi 3. Like Exodus 23, Malachi 3 is about Israel's faith*less*ness, but the two passages diverge from that point: Exodus 23 promises that the Lord will lead Israel to the land in spite of her sin, so long as she follows His messenger. Malachi 3 warns that the Lord's coming to judge and purge will result in a judgment and purgation of Israel herself. Thus, when "Israel accuses [Yahweh] of dereliction of duty since he has not dealt with evildoers . . . Yahweh's response is that, after sending a messenger to prepare his way, he will indeed come but his coming may not inaugurate the blessing his people expect since they themselves may well be the ones who are purged in the judgment."[8] Malachi turns the promise of Exodus 23 into a threat against Israel.

---

5. Watts, *New Exodus.*
6. In Hebrew, both "messenger" and "angel" translate the word *malach,* which is the name of the final book of our Old Testament.
7. Watts, *New Exodus.*
8. Watts, *New Exodus.*

Overall, Mark's opening quotation sets up the themes and emphases of the gospel as a whole: Conquest, hope for return, judgment, threat, and the coming of the Messiah. The quotation also identifies that Messiah. Malachi talks about a "messenger," Isaiah about a "servant," and when Jesus is baptized the Father describes Jesus as His "Son." Isaiah uses "servant" to describe the Davidic king who is coming to lead the people from exile, and the Father's words at the baptism refer to Psalm 2, which also identify a Davidic prince. References to Psalm 2 continue through the rest of the first chapter, as Mark shapes his story according to the plot of the Psalm. "The enemy forces, concretizations of primeval chaos, array themselves against the Lord and against his anointed, shouting in defiance, 'What have you to do with us?' (see Mk. 1:24) and throwing against them all their hostile might (see Ps. 2:1–3). The one enthroned in heaven, however, shrugs off this display of impotent rage and majestically brings forth his earthly executive, an executive whose purpose and power are so deeply congruent with his own that he can be called his son, and that the revelation of his kingship can simultaneously represent the earthly manifestation of the kingly power of God (see Ps. 2:4–7). In the continuation of Mark's story, and beyond its end, this figure will shatter God's enemies and be given worldwide dominion, receiving the nations for his inheritance and setting them on the road toward trust in God (see Ps. 2:8–11)."[9]

Stronger Man

The opening verses of the gospel identify Jesus with the conquering, delivering servant of Yahweh, leading Israel back from slavery. Jesus is the "stronger man" especially in His combat with demons. In some of the other gospels, Jesus'

9. Marcus, *Way.*

contests are largely with the scribes and Pharisees and leaders of the Jews, that is to say, with humans. In John, Jesus
says that the Jewish leaders are sons of their father the devil,
but in John's gospel we never see Jesus directly confront a
demon. Mark, however, is an "apocalyptic" gospel. Mark
draws back the curtain on the events of history, showing the
conflicts behind the conflicts.[10] Even when Jesus deals with
human opponents, Mark brings out the demonic influence
behind the scenes. When Jesus imposes silence on His disciples after Peter's confession, the verb He uses is the same
verb used to describe the silence imposed on demons earlier
in the gospel (8:33; cf. 1:25).[11] In the chiasm sketched above,
there is a structural parallel between the Parable of the Sower
and the Parable of the Vineyard. Drawing out this parallel,
we see also a parallel between the enemies of the word, who
are unclean spirits, and the caretakers of the vineyard. In
Mark, Jesus is still in conflict with the scribes and Pharisees
and other Jewish leaders, but beyond this He is confronting
Satan and demons. Once the Lord has rent the heavens at
the baptism, the veil is torn away and we see Jesus, the Great
Warrior, making war on principalities and powers.

John says that Jesus' miracle of turning water to wine at
Cana in Galilee was the first of His signs. Mark highlights
something else at the beginning of His gospel. After calling
His disciples, Jesus enters a synagogue and is met by a man
with an unclean spirit (1:21–28). Jesus rebukes the spirit,
which throws the man into convulsions before leaving. Jesus'
first sign is not a transformation of water into wine, but a
battle with a demon. Significantly, the demon is found in
the synagogue. Jesus comes to cast out the demons, and
particularly to cast them from the religious centers in Israel.

10. Wright, *People of God*, 392–393.
11. Mark is the only gospel writer to use this verb.

No wonder John comes to announce that the Lord is coming into His house to purge it with fire. In Mark 3:20–35, Jesus is accused of being in league with Satan. He replies that instead He is the stronger man who comes to overthrow the strong man and plunder his house (v. 27).

Jesus' greatest battle with demons comes in Mark 5, when Jesus confronts the Gadarene demoniac. The passage is organized as a chiasm:

A. To the other side, sea; out of boat, vv. 1–2a
   B. Man from tombs, vv. 2b–5
      C. Runs and speaks to Jesus, vv. 6–8
         D. Name: Legion, v. 9
            E. Swine, vv. 10–14
         D'. Man who was legion, vv. 15–16
            E'. Jesus depart, v. 17
      C'. Speaks to Jesus, vv. 18–19
   B'. Man proclaims in Decapolis, v. 20
A'. Boat, other side, multitude, sea, v. 21

Jesus gets off the boat in the country of the Gadarenes, and immediately meets a man who is possessed of unclean spirits. The man lives among the tombs, in a state of living death. When Jesus casts out the demon, He releases Him from the graves at the same time. Jesus' deliverance is also a resurrection. These demons are so strong in him that he cannot be subdued. No one is strong enough (v. 4). When Jesus addresses the demons, at the very center of the passage, they say their name is "Legion," a Roman military term, and there other terms that also are used in military contexts: "herd" and "rush down." Jesus subdues the legion. Jesus is the stronger man. He is a one-man army, confronting a whole regiment.

On the Way

Jesus is the stronger man, leading His people out of Babylon after defeating the strong man. Like the Lord in Isaiah, He leads a company of the blind and lame. Mainly, this is a description of the disciples, who are more befuddled and confused in Mark than in any other gospel. At the very center of the gospel, Jesus addressees the problem with the disciples, which is the problem of hardened hearts. Hardening of hearts is reminiscent, of course, of Pharaoh in Egypt, so the disciples here are Egyptians. Mark has already charged the disciples with having hardened hearts because they don't learn anything from the miracle of the loaves (6:52). In 8:18, Jesus uses the phrase "eyes but not seeing, ears but not hearing," which echoes 4:12, where Jesus teaches in parables so that "seeing they may not see." The parables are a judgment against an Israel that refuses to see and hear, but the disciples are no better. Jesus' statement in 8:18 also alludes back to Psalm 135, where idols and idolaters have eyes but cannot see, ears but cannot hear. Jesus essentially compares His disciples to pagans.

But there is hope for the disciples. They follow a master who can heal the blind. When Jesus challenges His disciples, He has just healed a deaf and dumb man, and He's about to heal a blind man. These are emblematic of the condition of the disciples. The healing of the blind man at Jericho is also related to the disciples. Bartimaeus calls to Jesus and asks for His mercy, to which Jesus replies, "What do you want Me to do?" (10:51). This is the same question Jesus has asked in verse 36. There, Jesus asks this question of James and John, who want to sit on the right and on the left when Christ comes into his kingdom. They are still blind and deaf and dumb, while Bartimaeus has the right idea. He knows enough to know that he's blind. The disciples, so close to Jesus, who hear so much of His teaching and see His miracles, don't even know that they can't see. Mark's irony here is at the expense of the disciples.

The disciples are especially blind to the direction that Jesus is heading. That's not surprising. When they first join Him, He is the stronger man, taking on legions of demons in super-hero combat. As soon as Peter confesses that Jesus is the Christ, Jesus suddenly changes direction and begins talking about His coming death in Jerusalem. Mark is extremely fond of groupings of three, and in 8:27–10:45, there are three episodes, each of which has a triple structure:

8:27–30: *suffering*	9:30–32: *suffering*	10:32–34: *suffering*
8:31–33: *disciples want glory*	9:33–34: *disciples want glory*	10:35–40: *disciples want glory*
8:34–9:1: *call to discipleship*	9:35–40: *call to discipleship*	10:42–45: *call to discipleship*

Jesus' teaching takes a turn here. He begins to teach His disciples about His coming rejection in Jerusalem. He must suffer. As He teaches the disciples this, He is summoning them to Himself and summoning them to a self-sacrificing type of discipleship. They must take up their crosses, ready not only to suffer but to die, ready not merely to die but to die the death of a rebel against Rome. That is the "way" on which Jesus leads them. That is the ironic "way" of the strong man, the Divine Warrior.

The emphasis on the suffering of Jesus and the need for disciples to suffer with Him is also brought out in the *inclusio* of "son of God." Ironically, the disciples are with Jesus throughout His ministry, but they are constantly misconstruing what He's doing, consistently blind and deaf to His teaching and miracles. They don't recognize Him as divine Son. When the centurion sees Him die, he knows that he is the Son of God. Jesus reveals His divine Sonship most fully in His suffering and death, not in His exercises of power.

The fact that it is a Roman who recognizes Jesus also plays into Mark's themes. Gospel means "good news of victory," one of the Latinisms in the gospel. Mark begins his book talking about the "gospel," the good news of victory. That word puts the work of Jesus in a Roman political context. Ironically again, it is a Roman, a soldier devoted to the exertion of force, who sees Jesus as truly divine in His suffering. It takes a Roman to see the real power that the disciples cannot see, that Jesus dies like a Son of God.

Early on in the gospel, Jesus warns the disciples, demons, and everybody else not to reveal His identity. This is the famous "Markan Messianic secret." Why doesn't Jesus want His disciples and the people who benefit from His ministry talking about Him? The reason is that Jesus has not yet revealed Himself for who He is, the true Son of God who cannot be recognized until the cross. He cannot be seen as Son of God until He is seen as the dying Son of God. He does not want people to recognize Him as the Son of God because of His power. He wants them to see that the Son of God gives Himself for the disciples.

Review Questions

1. What passage of Isaiah does Mark quote at the beginning of his gospel? What is that passage about?

2. What passage of Malachi is he quoting in the opening verses?

3. Explain the connection between Malachi 3 and Exodus 23.

4. How is Mark's gospel an "apocalyptic gospel"?

5. How does Jesus show Himself to be the stronger man?

6. Why don't the disciples understand the "way" of Jesus?

Thought Questions

1. Mark mentions that there are "wild beasts" in the wilderness where Jesus is tempted (1:13). Why?

2. What are the disciples supposed to learn from Jesus' feeding of the four thousand and five thousand? See Mark 8:14–21.

3. Other than the centurion at the foot of the cross, how does Mark depict Romans? Roman soldiers? Use a concordance if necessary.

In the Temple

Strangely to us, Jesus does not march into Jerusalem and make His way toward the palace. Instead, He arrives in Jerusalem and makes a beeline for the temple. He comes as a king, but heads straight for the priestly center of Israel, not the political center.

According to Mark's account, Jesus first enters the temple and inspects it on Palm Sunday itself (11:11), but then He withdraws to Bethany for the night. The next day He returns to the temple and begins to throw out the money changers and overturns the tables. As we saw in chapter 2, Jesus is not condemning trading, buying, and selling in the temple area as such. The law encouraged the development of a market in sacrificial animals around the temple. According to Deuteronomy 14:24–26,

> If the distance is so great for you that you are not able to bring the tithe, since the place where Yahweh your God chooses to set His name is too far away from you when Yahweh your God blesses you, then you shall exchange it for money, and bind the money in your hand and go to the place which Yahweh your God chooses. You may spend the money for whatever your heart desires: for oxen, or sheep, or wine, or strong drink, or whatever your heart

desires; and there you shall eat in the presence of Yahweh your God and rejoice, you and your household."

It was natural that a market would develop in the temple area where Jews could buy blemishless sacrificial animals.

Nor is Jesus objecting to cheating and shifty dealing going on at the temple. He accuses the Jews of making the temple, the "house of prayer for all nations," into a "robbers' den" (11:17), but robbers do not cheat in their den. Robbers cheat and steal and do their violence elsewhere, and then retreat to the den for safety. This is how the Jews are treating the temple, as a safe haven where they can escape from the consequences of their sins. That Jesus means this is clear from the context of Jeremiah 7, the passage He is quoting:

> Thus says Yahweh of hosts, the God of Israel, "Amend your ways and your deeds, and I will let you dwell in this place. Do not trust in deceptive words, saying, 'This is the temple of the LORD, the temple of the LORD, the temple of the LORD.' For if you truly amend your ways and your deeds, if you truly practice justice between a man and his neighbor, if you do not oppress the alien, the orphan, or the widow, and do not shed innocent blood in this place, nor walk after other gods to your own ruin, then I will let you dwell in this place, in the land that I gave to your fathers forever and ever. Behold, you are trusting in deceptive words to no avail. Will you steal, murder, and commit adultery and swear falsely, and offer sacrifices to Baal and walk after other gods that you have not known, then come and stand before Me in this house, which is called by My name, and say, 'We are delivered!'—that you may do all these abominations? Has this house, which is called by My name, become a den of robbers in your sight? Behold, I, even I, have seen it," declares Yahweh. (vv. 3–11)

Jesus symbolically enacts the coming destruction of the temple, when the sacrifices and operations of the temple will cease forever.

More specifically, Jesus condemns the Jews of His day for their violent opposition to the Romans. The word for "robber" means "brigand" or even "revolutionary."[12] As in Jeremiah's time, the Jews in Jesus' day foolishly and disobediently chafe under Gentile rule, plot revolutionary violence, and think that they can escape from the consequences of their actions by winning Yahweh's favor in the temple. Jesus warns that these hopes are futile, and that the Jews will ultimately fall precisely because of their false confidence in the temple of the Lord, the temple of the Lord.

Once Jesus pronounces His condemnation of the temple and its worshipers, He sets up shop in the temple, in the heart of Judaism. Over the course of the last week of His life, He wages a battle in the temple. He is not attempting to reform the temple. Things are too far gone already for that. He is announcing the temple's destruction in both veiled and open ways, and He is acting in a way that provokes further response from the Jewish leaders. But He is showing the Jews, one last time, what the temple is for: It is to be a place of teaching, healing, salvation. Not a safe-house for brigands.

He leaves the temple in the evening after His demonstration, but then He is back (11:27), and is challenged by the chief priests, scribes, and elders about His authority to do "these things" (v. 28), the things He has been doing in the temple. Jesus claims that His authority comes from John's baptism, where the Father announces that He is the beloved Son. He has authority to take over the house of Yahweh because He is the heir, the Son. The parables and debates in Mark 12 also take place in the temple (11:27; 12:35; 12:41; 13:1). In the temple, surrounded by the jostling crowds gathering for Passover, He tells the tale of wicked vineyard tenants

12. Wright, *Victory of God.*

who are trying to seize the vineyard; He responds to the challenge concerning the poll-tax to Caesar; He responds to the Sadducees' unbelief; and He poses a conundrum from Psalm 110. The fact that Jesus speaks in parables is itself a sign of judgment, for it ensures that "seeing they shall not see" and "hearing they shall not understand." In the temple where scribes and chief priests walk and work, He warns about "scribes who like to walk around in long robes" and who seek "respectful greetings in the market places" and who seek "places of honor at banquets," but who meanwhile are preying on widows (12:38–40).

Jesus spends the week making the temple a place of teaching and healing, a house of prayer for all nations, demonstrating what the temple could be, but also condemning the Jewish leaders for their sacrileges. Those leaders spend the week attempting to trap Jesus, trying to publicly humiliate Him, and finally plotting to kill Him. Throughout these debates and conflicts, Jesus emerges victorious, publicly embarrasses the scribes and priests, leads His opponents to fall into the traps that they set for Him, and earns their murderous hatred. Throughout, their response confirms His evaluation: They have turned the temple into a den of robbers, and Jesus' actions provoke them to attempt one climactic act of violence: the murder of Jesus.

Though it may seem strange to us that Jesus would come as a King and then head to the temple, in Scripture it is not strange at all. The temple is Yahweh's palace, the seat of His throne. Jesus comes as the anointed of Yahweh, as Yahweh incarnate, and He comes to His Father's house to challenge the stewards of His house to give an account of their actions. Further, the king of Israel was responsible for the upkeep and oversight of the temple; it was the king's job to ensure that the temple was kept in good repair and was maintained properly. The battle in the temple is a battle about Jesus' kingship, about Yahweh's kingship. In resisting and rejecting Jesus, the Jewish leaders are resisting and rejecting the One who has been set up as judge and ruler over them. Instead of subjecting themselves to Jesus' trial, they put Him on trial. Instead of repenting of their violence, they plot to kill Jesus.

In Mark 14:62, Jesus refers to Daniel 7, and that passage is lurking behind the trial narrative as a whole.[13] Daniel 7 tells about judgment against the bestial empires in favor of the people of the saints of the most high. Dominion is taken from the empires and given to the saints. Mark ironically turns this upside down by alluding to this passage in the midst of a scene where Jesus is on trial, and where the bestial empires look healthy as can be. Yet, "Mark's use of Daniel implies that in the long run it is Jesus' judges who will be judged; they, who today are scandalized by him and his words, will be condemned by him when they see him coming with the clouds at the eschaton."

The Temple and the Cross

The Olivet Discourse in Mark 13 thus does not come out of the blue. Jesus passes initial judgment on the temple by calling it a den of thieves. After a week of conflict and debate, He pronounces a more definitive judgment on the temple: It is doomed. Jesus has predicted this in various ways through riddles and stories and parables and ripostes. But in 13:1 we have the most dramatic sign that the temple is doomed: Jesus leaves it, and never returns. As in Ezekiel 8–11, the glory of God, incarnate glory, departs from the temple, leaving it empty and vulnerable to desolation.

13. Marcus, *Way.*

Though Mark 13 is often interpreted as a prediction of the end of the world, Jesus is talking about something else. It comes at the end of a series of conflicts between Jesus and the Jewish leaders, and it is about the temple in Jerusalem. This sermon is Jesus' answer to the question of the disciples about the timing and signs of the destruction of the "wonderful buildings" that made up the temple (13:1–4). He describes a series of events that will take place before "this generation" passes away (v. 30).

Everything in the sermon is about events that occur within the generation of the apostles. The disciples will be delivered to the courts, flogged in the synagogues, and taken before governors and kings (v. 9). Jesus promises the apostles that the Spirit will give them utterance when they are forced to testify (v. 11). Families will divide over Jesus during the first generation of the church (v. 12), and people will hate the apostles because of Jesus (v. 13). The warnings of verses 14–15 are specific to the first century context: Jesus speaks of "those who are in Judea," and assumes people will be on their "housetops." While many of the Jews will flee to the city and temple for protection, Jesus urges His disciples to flee *from* the city. The whole passage deals with events within the lives of the apostles.

Verses 24–27 are often seen as a problem for this interpretation of the passage. We know that the sky did not collapse in the generation of the apostles. When seen in biblical context, these verses pose no problem at all. In verses 24–25, Jesus is quoting from Isaiah 13 and 34, both of which are prophecies about the end of an empire. Jesus is not talking about the end of the whole universe, but about the end of a particular earthly and historical order. Mark 13:27 contains a quotation from Daniel 7, which speaks of the Son of Man ascending to heaven on the clouds. Jesus says that the destruction of the temple will enable the Jews to "see" or perceive that the Son of Man, Jesus, has been given all authority and power and dominion. The destruction of Jerusalem will prove that He was a prophet, and more than a prophet.

But there is another crucial dimension to Jesus' prophecy, one that helps us to see the depth of what Jesus is predicting. Jesus is talking about the destruction of the temple, but Jesus Himself is the temple. Jesus' prediction of the destruction of the temple thus foreshadows His own arrest, sufferings, and death.[14] Jesus predicts that the Jews will deliver the apostles to the courts (13:9); but first Jesus is delivered to the courts. Jesus predicts that the apostles will be "flogged in the synagogues" (13:9); but first Jesus is flogged (15:15). Jesus warns the disciples that they will stand before governors and kings to testify (13:9); but first Jesus stands before Pilate the governor (cf. Mt. 27:2, 11, 14–15, 21, 27) and before King Herod (cf. Lk. 23:7ff.). Jesus tells the apostles to leave their cloaks behind them when they flee from the city (13:16); in Gethsemane, a young man flees without his cloak (14:51–52). Jesus predicts tribulation (13:19), and suffers tribulation, sorrow, and pain.

Most dramatically, the apocalyptic imagery of 13:24–27 is literally fulfilled in the cross. After the days of tribulation, "the sun will be darkened and the moon will not give its light" (13:24). At the cross, "when the sixth hour had come, darkness fell over the whole land until the ninth hour" (15:33). In the coming generation, "the powers that are in the heavens will be shaken" (13:25); at the death of Jesus, the temple veil, which symbolizes the veil of the firmament dividing heaven and earth, is torn in two, rent like the heavens at Jesus' baptism. When the temple falls, all will perceive

14. Mark Horne, *The Victory According to Mark* (Moscow: Canon Press, 2003).

that the Son of Man has received dominion from His Father (13:26). As Jesus dies, as the temple of His body is destroyed, a Gentile centurion confesses that Jesus was the Son of God (15:39). The gospel is preached to the ends of the earth. Even the Jews who mock Jesus on the cross recognize a connection with His temple predictions: "Ha! You who are going to destroy the temple and rebuild it in three days, save Yourself, and come down from the cross!" (15:29).

In short, Jesus' sufferings and death are a first fulfillment of the prophecy about the destruction of the temple. In this we see the purpose of Jesus' work, His substitutionary sacrifice for the people of God. Israel has made the temple of God into a den of robbers, and that temple is going to be destroyed. But there is still hope, since Jesus offers Himself to destruction as a substitute temple, a temple destroyed and raised on the third day. Should the leaders of Israel respond in faith, they might yet be saved, and the vineyard might not be taken from them.

Jesus predicts that this will not happen. If they hate the Master, they will hate the disciples; if they flog and arrest and kill Jesus, they will flog and arrest and kill the disciples. Because they resist and reject the gospel as it comes through Jesus' disciples, the vineyard of God is taken from the tenants, the chief priests and scribes, and given to another, to the Son and His apostolic patriarchs. Because the harlot Jerusalem drinks the blood of Jesus' disciples, she becomes unclean, and will be burned. Because they trust in their temple of stone, rather than in the destroyed and raised temple of Jesus' body, "not one stone shall be left upon another which will not be torn down."

The most obvious Markan irony in the trial and crucifixion of Jesus is the fact that the Roman soldiers mock Jesus for being king of the Jews when He in fact is the king of the Jews. God has the last laugh; God is not mocked, even when

He's mocked. But there are more subtle ironies at work. The Jews are seeking help from the Roman authorities to put Jesus to death. To make the charge stick, they have to translate their religious objections to Jesus into political terms: Jesus is fomenting revolution. Of course, this is precisely what many of the Jewish leaders have been doing for some time, and they show their hand when they choose to welcome Barabbas rather than Jesus. The internal contradictions of the Jewish leaders are neatly exposed: They kowtow to Roman power, but at the same time prefer the way of revolution to Jesus' "revolutionary way of being revolutionary."[15] Mark exposes the inner continuity between Jewish and Roman programs: Jewish anti-imperialism is just as much an idolatry of power as Roman imperialism. Jesus, the dying Son of God, offers a way different from both.

Mark treats the Pharisees ironically to expose their wickedness. He points out the ironies in the disciples behavior, hoping for rewards on the way while Jesus talks about nothing but the way of the cross. He highlights the irony of both Jews and Romans during Jesus' trial and crucifixion. But the deepest irony is an irony at the expense of the reader. There is a large-scale irony overarching the book that is worthy of Sophocles. We readers know from the first verse of the gospel that Jesus is the Son of God, and that title is used periodically through the gospel by the Father and by demons. There is the ironic distance between our knowledge and the knowledge of the characters in the story. But that irony is eventually doubled back on the reader: Are we not as blind as the disciples about Jesus, the Stronger Man? Would we recognize Jesus as Son of God while He's dying in anguish? Can we join the centurion in confessing faith in

15. The phrase comes from N. T. Wright's *New Testament and the People of God.*

a crucified Messiah? Are we bold enough to follow Jesus on the way that is the way of the cross?

Review Questions

1. Why does Jesus condemn the people in the temple? Why does He overturn the tables of the moneychangers?

2. What does Jesus do during the week after He enters Jerusalem?

3. What is Mark 13 about?

4. How is Mark 13 a prophecy of the cross?

5. What are some of the ironies of the trial scene?

6. How does Mark's irony turn back on us readers?

Thought Questions

1. Examine Genesis 1:14–16. How does that help us interpret Mark 13:24?

2. How does Jesus answer the Pharisees question about paying taxes? What does He mean by His answer?

3. Discuss Peter's actions in Mark 14. What is his role in the story?

CHAPTER 6

LUKE

a table for
the poor

Luke and Acts function as a single book, and should be interpreted and studied as one. This is evident from the introduction to the book of Acts in 1:1–2, where Luke addresses Theophilus, the same person whom he addresses in the opening verses of the Gospel of Luke. In Acts 1, Luke refers to the "first account" about the things that "Jesus began to do and to teach." This suggests that Acts also, just as much as Luke, is a book about the works of Jesus; Acts is the continuation of what Jesus began to do and teach. There are other indications of a single unified book, and suggestions that Luke intended the books to be read together, and, while writing his gospel, intended to complete it with a second book.

Luke delays certain themes and events until he gets to Acts. For example, the accusation that Jesus had threatened to destroy the temple is included in Mark's account of Jesus' trial (14:58), but in Luke's writings this accusation doesn't come up until the Stephen episode (Acts 6:14). Mark 7's account of cleansing of meats is not in Luke's gospel, but the idea is picked up in Acts 10–11, with the story of Cornelius and Peter's dream. Luke gives a partial quotation from Isaiah 6 in Luke 8:10 (compare Mk. 4:12), but a fuller quotation in Acts 28:25–27. By this, Luke shows us that the complete hardening and obscuring of the Jews, their final blinding, doesn't take place until they have heard the gospel not only from Jesus but from the disciples; it's only after the preaching of the disciples that we have the full hardening of the Jews. The combined book of Luke–Acts is clearly about Jesus and the church. But Luke wants to make a particular point about Jesus and the church. To see the point, we have to examine some of the structures of Luke's two-volume work.

Parallel Stories

The infancy narratives of Luke tell about the births of John and Jesus (Lk. 1–2). In both cases, the work of the Spirit is very much highlighted. John is filled with the Spirit from his mother's womb (1:15); the Spirit comes upon Mary (1:35); Elizabeth, Zecharias and Simeon all praise God in the Spirit (1:41, 67; 2:25–27); Jesus receives the Spirit at His baptism (3:22). Jesus says in His first sermon that the Spirit is on Him, and the Spirit drives Him into the wilderness, and drives Him back to Galilee (4:14). This of course fits with the opening of a two-volume work where the Spirit is going to be the power behind the early church. At the beginning of Acts, the Spirit is active, descending upon the disciples at Pentecost (Acts 2). In both Luke and Acts, the Spirit produces joy and praise. Luke begins with song, and the gospel also ends with praise, as the disciples devote themselves to worship (24:52–53). Luke's gospel also begins and ends in the temple. When the Spirit comes upon the apostles at Pentecost, they too are filled with joy, as they declare God's wonderful works (Acts 2:11; cf. 13:52).

The pattern in Luke–Acts is clear: first Jesus, then the church. Jesus receives the Spirit, then the church. Jesus comes with joy; then the church. Jesus preaches in the power of the Spirit; so does the Spirit-filled Peter. In the same way, the ministry of the disciples in Acts matches as it extends the ministry of Jesus. Luke moves through Jesus' Galilean ministry in chapters 4–9, which match up with the apostolic ministry in Jerusalem in Acts 1–6. In Luke Jesus heals a paralyzed man (Lk. 5), and in Acts Peter and John heal a man lame from his mother's womb (Acts 3). Jesus raises the dead (Lk. 7), and Peter raises a dead woman (Acts 9).

The clearest sign that the two books are structurally parallel is the long journey that closes both. Jesus' journey begins after his transfiguration, when Moses and Elijah discuss his "exodus" with him (9:31). Jesus sets His face determinedly toward Jerusalem for His "ascension," the rest of the book is a long march toward Jerusalem, trial, and death (9:51). Along the way, crowds begin to gather (11:29; 12:1; 14:25), and by chapter 14 he's leading a "multitude of crowds." Jesus is gathering the whole of Israel around him, and journeying toward the temple. This is paralleled by Paul's journey to Jerusalem. Paul is determined in the spirit (Spirit) to go to Jerusalem (Acts 19:21), and his travels through Macedonia and Greece here are part of a journey toward the temple. He endures a riot in Ephesus (19:23ff.), and then another riot in Jerusalem which begins at the temple (21:17ff.), where he is completing a vow and purifying himself. He is accused of preaching against the law and the temple (21:27ff.), and he's arrested. So far, the journey follows Jesus' journey toward Jerusalem. But of course, Paul's journeying is not finished in Jerusalem. He must move through Jerusalem, but his goal is Rome, and so from chapter 21 we have another journey narrative climaxing with Paul's preaching in Rome. The movement of Luke's gospel is toward Jerusalem and death and resurrection; the movement of Acts is from Jerusalem toward Rome. Jesus moves toward Jerusalem, while Paul moves toward Jerusalem, and then moves past Jerusalem toward Rome.

The heart of Luke's agenda is to explain and justify the turn from Jews to the Gentiles. Luke shows that the apostles turn from Jews to Gentiles only after the Jews have rejected the gospel and the Spirit twice—once in Jesus, and again in the disciples. Israel has two chances, and they reject Jesus both times. They reject Him when he begins to do and teach; they reject Him when, through the apostles, He continues to do and teach. Only then does Paul turn to the Gentiles. We can summarize the parallels of Luke and Acts this way:[1]

Luke	Content	Acts
1:1–4	Preface, with dedication to Theophilus	1:1–5
1:5–3:21	Time of preparation	1:6–26
3:22	Baptism with Spirit	2:1–4
4:16–30	Inaugural sermon	2:14–40

Local Ministry

Luke	Content	Acts
4:31–8:56	Galilee/Jerusalem	2:41–8:3
5:17–25	Lame man healed	3:1–10
5:29–6:11	Conflicts with leaders	4:1–8:3
9:9	Martyr: John and Stephen	7:54–8:1
7:1–10	Centurion sends for Jesus/apostle	10:1–48
7:11–17	Widow's son and resurrection	9:36–43

Journey

Luke	Content	Acts
9:51–53	Resolve to journey to Jerusalem	19:21
9:51–19:27	Missionary journey	13:1
9:31, 51; 12:50	Passion journey	20:3, 22–24
9:45; 18:34	Friends and disciples	21:4, 12–13
13:22	Ready to die in Jerusalem	21:13

1. The following outline is drawn from Victor Wilson, *Divine Symmetries: The Art of Biblical Rhetoric* (University Press of America, 1997).

Jerusalem, Arrest, Trial

19:37	Joyously received in Jerusalem	21:17–21
19:45–48	Visit to the temple	21:26
20:27–39	Dispute about resurrection	23:6–9
22:14–38	Farewell address	20:17–38
22:14–20	Last meal	27:33–38
22:47–54	Seizure by a mob	21:30
22:63–64	Slapped before high priest	23:2
22–23	Four trials before three courts	24–26
23:4, 14, 22	Declarations of innocence	23:9; 25:25; 26:31
23:6–12	Sent to Herod for questioning	25:13–26:32
23:16, 22	Opportunity for release	26:32
23:18	"Away with this man"	21:36
23:47	Centurion with a favorable opinion	27:3, 43
24	Fulfillment of Scripture	28
24:46–49	Sent to nations/Gentiles	28:28

Luke's journey narrative, stretching from Luke 9–19, is a chiasm:[2]

    A. 9:51–56: Departure/rejection
      B. 9:57–10:24: Following Jesus
        C. 10:25–42: Way to eternal life
          D. 11:1–13: Prayer
            E. 11:14–28: Signs of kingdom
              F. 11:29–36: Faith among foreigners
                G. 11:37–12:3: Stumbling blocks
                  H. 12:4–34: True riches, the Spirit
                    I. 12:35–39: Master returns
                      J. 13:1–9: Cost of discipleship
                        K. 13:10–30: Exiled home
                          L. 13:31–35: Jerusalem, Jerusalem

---

2. This is also drawn from Wilson, *Divine Symmetries*.

Good News to the Poor

Jesus begins His work in Luke, and His work is focused on ministry to the poor. Jesus' first sermon, in Luke 4, is preceded by the temptation scene and a genealogy, which ultimately identifies Jesus as "son of God." According to Luke 3:38, "son of God" means "Adam," and so Jesus' temptation is like Adam's in the garden. Like Adam, Jesus is tempted to eat forbidden food by turning stones into bread. Like Adam, Jesus is tempted to seize authority by bowing before Satan. The second temptation of Jesus is quite close to the temptation of Adam, since the tree of knowledge in the garden is associated with kingly wisdom, the ability to pass judgment. Adam seizes the fruit when he listens to the word of Satan, and Satan's word encouraged Adam to put God to the test: "Yea, has God said?" Like Adam, Jesus is tempted to test His Father's word, and to seize authority. Jesus is at a disadvantage. Adam had not been fasting. In fact, he had been encouraged to eat from the tree of life, and from all the other trees of the garden. Adam is tempted when he was fat and happy and well-filled, with no need to eat from another tree. Jesus has been fasting for forty days and nights. Adam is in a garden, but Jesus is tempted in the wilderness. The Son enters combat with Satan in the midst of a *fallen* world, a world under the curse of death; and yet still He triumphed.

Of course, Jesus is wholly unlike Adam where it counts: unlike Adam, He resists the temptation and keeps the fast that Adam broke. Instead of listening to the word of Satan, Jesus quotes the words of His Father back in Satan's face. Instead of obeying the serpent and worshiping and serving the creature, Jesus is faithful in serving and worshiping the Creator. Jesus' combat with Satan is a part of the accomplishment of redemption. As much as the cross and the resurrection, this is a once-for-all event. With this combat, Jesus, the true Seed and Son, begins to crush the serpent's head.

As we have seen in the chapter on Matthew, saying Jesus is the "Son of God" also connects him with Israel, Yahweh's firstborn (Exod. 4:23). Israel too was tempted and tested in the wilderness. Jesus is tempted for forty days, as Israel was in the wilderness being tested for forty years. The Scriptures He quotes in response to Satan all have to do with the exodus and Israel's wandering in the wilderness. "Thou shalt not live by bread alone" comes from Deuteronomy 8:3, and the full passage says "God humbled you and let you be hungry and fed you with manna which you did not know, nor did your fathers know, that He might make you understand that man does not live by bread alone but man lives by everything that proceeds out of the mouth of Yahweh." "You shall worship the Lord your God and serve Him only" is similar to the first commandment and also echoes Deuteronomy 6:12, where Moses warns, "watch yourself, lest you forget Yahweh who brought you from the land of Egypt, out of the house of slavery. You shall fear only Yahweh your God; and you shall serve Him and swear by His name." "You shall not put Yahweh your God to the test," is also from Deuteronomy 6, and the context refers to an incident in the wilderness: "You shall not put Yahweh your God to the test, as you tested him at Massah" (Deut. 6:16). Massah was the place where Israel tested the Lord by grumbling about a lack of water. Jesus enters the wilderness as the true Israel, and recapitulates the history of Israel. Like Matthew, Luke shows us that Jesus lives through Israel's history again, but reverses it. He does not grumble or break the fast, as Israel had done; he does not worship idols, as Israel did at Sinai; He does not put Yahweh to the test, as Israel had done at Massah and Meribah and countless other places. As the Last Adam and True Israel, He overcomes Satan and begins to reconquer the world.

Each of the temptations challenges Jesus' mission as Son ("if you are Son," 4:3, 9). Saying Jesus is "Son" means He is "last Adam" and "true Israel," but it also means that Jesus is the "Davidic king." In the Old Testament, the individual "son of God" was the son of David (2 Sam. 7:14), and this is what the Father refers to at Jesus' baptism. The Father's words are taken from Psalm 2, which prophesies about a Son who will be given the nations as His inheritance, a Son who will rule. Satan's temptations are all about how the Son is going to gain and exercise His rule. Satan offers Jesus things that He is going to inherit anyway—bread, authority, power. But Satan tempts Him to pursue those things in a wrong way. Satan tempts Jesus to attempt to become Lord in a way that is contrary to God's purposes.

Once He has triumphed over Satan, Jesus returns to Galilee in the power of the Spirit. He is impelled by the Spirit to come to His synagogue and preach. This sermon is in His hometown, Nazareth. Jesus comes to His own, not merely the Jews who are His own people, but to Nazareth specifically, but they turn against Him and are ready to throw Him off a cliff (4:24ff). This is the story of the Jews' reaction both to Jesus and to the church as Jesus' disciples (in Acts). This is a preview of the whole dynamic of Luke's two-volume work. The story is all about preaching of the good news, and Jews rejecting it.

Jesus begins His sermon by reading from the scroll of Isaiah:

> And the book of the prophet Isaiah was handed to Him. And He opened the book and found the place where it was written, "The Spirit of the Lord is upon Me, because He has anointed Me to preach the gospel to the poor. He has sent me to proclaim release to the captives, recovering of sight to the blind, to set free those who are oppressed, to proclaim the favorable year of the Lord." And He closed the book, gave it back to the attendant and sat down; and the eyes of all in the synagogue were fixed on Him. And He began to say to them, "Today this Scripture has been fulfilled in your hearing." (4:17–21)

The quotation comes mostly from Isaiah 61:1–2, and is concerned with the restoration of Israel from exile. Yahweh promises to send a servant anointed by the Spirit to lead Israel from captivity.

Jesus also quotes from Isaiah 58:6. The line about "release to the oppressed" is not from Isaiah 61, but Isaiah 58. That passage is about the true fast that Israel is supposed to keep, a fast that involves "dividing bread with the hungry" and "bringing the homeless poor into the house" and "covering the naked' and breaking the yoke of oppressors. The end of the passage refers to the Sabbath (58:13), and the whole description is a description of the true Sabbath and fast that Israel should enjoy. For Isaiah, as for Moses, Sabbath is about the giving of rest and relief to those who are needy, oppressed, naked, hungry. Jesus describes His entire ministry as the proclamation of Sabbath, this fast, this Jubilee. Disputes about the Sabbath are central to Luke's telling of the gospel story. The first time the Pharisees and scribes discuss how they can get rid of Jesus comes after He has healed a man on the Sabbath (6:6–11).

Anointed with the Spirit, Jesus claims to be Yahweh's agent for the renewal of Israel. But the combination of two passages shows that the restoration of Israel particularly means the restoration of those who are oppressed and afflicted. This is an especially prominent thrust in Isaiah 58. The fast that the Lord has chosen is a fasting from oppression, active breaking of yokes and burdens, releasing the captive.

From the very first, Luke tells stories about rich and poor. Jesus comes to deliver the helpless and the outcasts, to lift them up, and to topple the powerful and rich who oppress them. Both songs at the beginning of the book talk about overturning the order of Israel: the rich are sent away and the poor are exalted. Elizabeth has identified Jesus as "the Lord" and then Mary breaks into a song like the song of Hannah in 1 Samuel 1, a song that expresses the hopes of the faithful in Israel for an overturning of Israel's order. According to Mary's song, John is the new Samuel preparing the way for the coming of the new David, a new David that, Mary hopes, will overthrow the powers that exist in Israel. Zacchaeus appears only in Luke, as do Lazarus and the rich man. Luke records the Beatitudes differently from Matthew. Instead of pronouncing God's blessing on the "poor in spirit" He promises blessings to "the poor." Luke includes a great deal more about various outcast groups. Jesus spends time with sinners and preaches the gospel to the poor. There is more emphasis on women who are disciples. Luke alone tells us about the women who were helping Jesus in His ministry (Lk. 8:1–2), and he alone tells us the famous story of Mary and Martha (10:38–42).

Specifically, Jesus comes to challenge the power of Herod. Luke's story begins in the time of Herod, the days of Herod the Great (1:5). Though Luke makes this point only in passing, it is not just a chronological point. The "days of Herod" are days of considerable darkness for faithful Jews. Herod is a murderer, whose victims included members of his own family. He is a shifty politician who has an uncanny ability to anticipate where the political winds of Rome are heading, and change sides to take advantage of it. He is a builder of great monuments, many of them displaying his attachment to Hellenistic culture, and all of them requiring heavy taxation that crushes the peasants and poor of Judea and Galilee. He manipulates the priesthood and temple for his own political advantage. He is cruel, harsh, a brute, and, though he has been circumcised, he is ethnically an Idumean, a descendant of Edom, or Esau. Living under Herod, faithful Jews are eager for God to turn the world upside down. Rome is a problem for some Jews, but there is also a problem right in their own neighborhood, and they long for God to do something to renew His people.

If the Spirit equips Jesus to proclaim liberty to captives, the good news to the poor, and health to the sick, it is the same Spirit that enables the church to do so. After the Spirit comes at Pentecost, everyone sells property to provide for the needs of one another (2:43–47). The church becomes the place where the favorable year of the Lord has begun, the new community that is truly a community, a "commonality," sharing the Spirit and therefore sharing also material goods. Along with Paul, Luke is the great missionary theologian of the New Testament. Luke presents the history of the Christian *missio* and presents Jesus as the one through whom repentance and forgiveness of sins will be proclaimed to all nations, beginning at Jerusalem. Luke's gospel is also the one that pays most particular attention to Jesus' ministry to outcasts and the poor. Those two aspects of Jesus' work are closely connected in Luke. Rich and poor are economic categories in Scripture, but they are also covenant categories. Israel is the "rich" people, and Gentiles are "poor" and "outcast." The entire mission of the church is to the poor in this sense.

The phrase "acceptable year of the Lord" (Lk. 4:19) refers to the Jubilee year, the "year of release" (Lev. 25:10). According to Leviticus 25, Israel was supposed to have a Jubilee year every fifty years. During the Jubilee year, land that had been sold during the previous fifty years would return to its previous owner, and anyone who had become a slave or bond-servant would be freed. Isaiah uses this legal institution to describe what is going to happen when Israel is released from Babylonian exile. The land of Israel will be restored to its original owners (Israel), and the Jews who have been captive in Babylon will be liberated (see Is. 61:4–11). After the passage that Jesus quotes, Isaiah says:

> To grant those who mourn in Zion, giving them a garland instead of ashes, the oil of gladness instead of mourning, the mantle of praise instead of a spirit of fainting. So they will be called oaks of righteousness, the planting of Yahweh, that He may be glorified. Then they will rebuild the ancient ruins; they will raise up the former devastations, and they will repair their ruined cities, the desolations of many generations. (Is. 61:3–4)

Jesus has just defeated Satan in the wilderness, so the liberation that He announces is centrally about freedom from Satan's captivity. But the earlier chapters of Luke have set us up to expect Jesus to offer a political deliverance. He comes as Lord to overthrow the lords of the earth and to install the humble on thrones. Jesus comes to defeat the "enemy behind the enemy," but in defeating Satan, He also turns the social and political world of Israel upside down.

For Jesus, the favorable year of the Lord means that those who are "downtrodden" by the Herods and Pilates are going to be set free. And, more importantly, those who are in bondage to Satan and under the dominion of the curse are going to be released. The land, the whole earth, will be restored to those who become disciples of the Anointed One. This is the good news that Jesus brings to the poor.

Review Questions

1. How can we tell that Luke and Acts are two volumes of the same work?

2. Describe the parallels between the story of Luke and that of Acts.

3. What is the significance of Jesus' temptation in the wilderness?

4. What passage does Jesus read in the synagogue at Nazareth? What does the passage promise?

5. List some ways that Luke pays special attention to the poor and to outcasts.

6. What is the "favorable year of the Lord"?

Thought Questions

1. In Luke's account, Jesus leaves out part of the passage in Isaiah 61. What does He leave out? Why?

2. Using a concordance, find some passages in the Psalms that speak about the "poor." What does the word mean there?

3. Examine the chiastic outline of Jesus' journey narrative. What is in the center of the chiasm? Why?

A Sinner in a Pharisee's House[3]

Much of Luke's gospel is taken up with a journey narrative. But the journey is not just a journey. It is a movable feast. A number of chapters at the center of Luke's gospel show Jesus moving from one meal to another. One recent book

---

3. My interpretation of Luke 7 depends on Kenneth Bailey, *Poet and Peasant and Through Peasant Eyes: A Literary-Cultural Approach to the Parables in Luke* (Grand Rapids: Eerdmans, 1983) and Joel Green, *The Gospel of Luke* (Grand Rapids: Eerdmans, 1997).

on Luke's gospel is entitled "Lord of the Banquet," which captures both the emphasis on meals and also the emphasis on Jesus as "Lord," an emphasis distinctive to Luke's gospel. This fits with His sermon at Nazareth. One of the ways that Jesus shows His love and care for the poor and outcasts of Israel is through His meal practice. As we saw in chapter 2, the Pharisees are very concerned about whom they ate with, and Jesus is constantly violating their manmade taboos. Who Jesus eats with shows us who is part of His community, part of the Israel that is forming around Him. Jesus' table companions make up the Israel that will rise when the wicked rich of Israel are cast out.

But Jesus' behavior and talk at meals holds other lessons too. In the last scene in Luke 7, Jesus eats a meal in the house of a Pharisee, identified as "Simon" later in the story (v. 40). Just before the story starts, Jesus is talking about the way that the Pharisees and other Jews react to Him. They condemn Him because he is a "friend of tax-gatherers and sinners" (7:34). They complain that He eats and drinks with sinners, but in the very next scene Jesus is eating and drinking with a Pharisee at the house of a Pharisee. Luke's point is subtle. Does Jesus eat with sinners? You bet: He eats with Pharisees. This link between Pharisees and sinners has already been prepared by the previous chapter. In Jesus' sermon in Luke 6, He contrasts the behavior of His disciples with that of "sinners" on three points (6:32–34). Sinners love those who love themselves, but Jesus' disciples must love their enemies. Sinners do good only to those who do good to them, but Jesus' disciples must do good to their enemies without any hope for good in return. Sinners lend only to those who can repay, but Jesus' disciples must lend without expecting return.

Who are these "sinners"? Obviously, Jesus is talking about Jewish leaders (see Mt. 5:43–48). Think of the rhetorical effect here: Crowds are listening, and they hear Jesus say, "Sinners only love those who love them," and the people say, "Hey, that's what we do! He's saying we're sinners." Think also of how powerful the effect would be on Pharisees: He says that "sinners" give only to those who will repay, and do good only to those who do good to them: And the Pharisees who are listening to him are saying, "Hey, that's what *we* do!" The Pharisees like to classify unclean Jews, tax collectors, and others as "sinners." Jesus reshuffles and redefines their categories and includes them under the heading of "sinners." Jesus is eating with a Pharisee at the Pharisee's home: is Jesus a friend of sinners? Yes, indeed.

Why does Jesus eat and drink with Pharisees? Because He comes for sinners. It is equally interesting to ask why Simon the Pharisee invites him. Perhaps he is a "good Pharisee," a Pharisee who wants to follow Jesus. Luke 7:40 seems to indicate this, when Simon addresses Jesus as a "Teacher" or "Rabbi." But Luke has carefully written this story to give us that impression, and then later to undermine it. Overall, the scene leaves a different impression. Simon is definitely *not* a good Pharisee. On the contrary, he invites Jesus to his house, and then systematically insults him. He treats him as a low-life, barely worthy of Simon's notice, not as a respected and honored rabbi.

It is customary in first-century Israel for hosts to offer guests water for their feet, or for a servant to wash their feet. Jews of the first century wear sandals, and the dust of the feet is cursed and unclean. It is a ceremonial act too, since eating requires washing. Jesus says that Simon has not done this. Simon has not washed Jesus' feet, and that is a sign that he considers Jesus very inferior. It is customary too for a host to greet his guests with a kiss. If the host and guest are equals, the host would kiss the guest on the cheek; if the guest was a superior, an honored guest, the host might kiss his hands. A man greeting an honored Rabbi would definitely show honor by a kiss. But Simon has not kissed Jesus, and he shows him no homage as a teacher or rabbi. Though less common, anointing is sometimes done as an act of hospitality to guests. In the *Odyssey,* a bath and a rub-down with oil are standard rituals of welcome. When a guest is bathed and oiled, he is welcome to sit at table. Simon also fails to do this.

Simon's treatment of Jesus is nothing less than shocking. In Simon's case, it has to be a calculated insult. These customs are so important, and proper rituals of hospitality so central to ancient customs, that Simon would not do this without planning it. The contrast with the centurion could not be more stark. The centurion thinks he's unworthy to have Jesus enter his home (7:6). The centurion shows no hospitality because he is so humbled by Jesus' attention. Simon thinks that he's quite worthy for Jesus to enter his house, and that he's so superior to Jesus that he can insult and snub him with impunity.

Simon clearly is not honoring Jesus. So what is his agenda? Why invite him at all? Verse 39 gives a clue. Simon invites Jesus to share a meal with him so that he can test Jesus' prophetic gifts. He wants to see if Jesus can discern hearts and distinguish between the righteous and sinners. In response, Jesus shows that He is a true Son of the heavenly Father. He might as well have been struck on the cheek, but He does not retaliate in kind.

Simon's snub also explains the woman's actions. She was coming to show honor to Jesus anyway. When she sees Jesus come in, and observes Simon snub him, she rushes to Jesus, and makes up for the failures of Simon's hospitality. She does all the things that Simon fails to do, and goes a step further. Simon fails to provide water for Jesus to wash his feet, but the woman not only provides water, with her own tears, but washes Jesus' feet herself. She takes up the work of a menial slave, and she takes this role in relation to Jesus. Simon offers no kiss; the woman offers *many* kisses (v. 45), and she kisses his feet. This puts her in an even lower position. She is not merely treating him as a rabbi, but as Master and Lord. A conqueror puts his foot on the next of a conquered enemy, and when someone bows at the feet of another person in the Bible, they are saying "You have conquered me; I am your slave." That is the position the woman assumes. Simon refuses to anoint Jesus, but the woman anoints Jesus' feet with her perfume, with her aromatic ointment.

The woman not only identifies Jesus as her Lord, but there are hints of marital and sexual imagery here. The word "touch," used by Simon, can have a sexual connotation, and Simon perhaps thinks that the woman is making a sexual pass at Jesus. The woman also looses her hair, which was something a woman normally did only in the presence of her husband, unless she is a prostitute who treats every passing man as a "husband for an hour." She recognizes that Jesus is her bridegroom, her husbandly "Lord," and she offers herself as bride. She turns the meal into a marriage banquet.

Luke's story is clearly about the contrast of the Pharisee and the "sinner." The focus of this incident is on the contrast between the Pharisee's evaluation of the woman and Jesus' evaluation of her. The Pharisee condemns her as a "sinner" (v. 39), and he apparently thinks of her actions as actions of a sinner. He completely misunderstands what is going on in front of his eyes. He sees the lavish love of a forgiven and repentant sinner but he can only see the impurity that she might communicate, the scandal that might be involved.

Jesus does not deny that the woman has sinned. In fact, he affirms it when he says that she has "many" sins to be forgiven (v. 47). But her sins have been removed. The parable Jesus tells makes the point that she is a debtor whose debts have been forgiven. Though He says she is a sinner, Jesus treats her as a *forgiven* sinner. She shows unrestrained love for Jesus because she has been forgiven much. This incident also focuses on contrasting evaluations of Jesus. Simon the Pharisee doubts that Jesus can be a prophet, since He doesn't appear to know that the woman is a sinner (v. 39). Ironically, Jesus knows what Simon is thinking, which proves He *is* a prophet (vv. 39–40). Simon's reception of Jesus, furthermore, is minimal; he does not give Jesus the kind of hospitality that would be given to a truly honored guest. The woman, however, makes up for it, mimicking the customs of hospitality by washing Jesus' feet with her tears, kissing his feet, and anointing his feet with perfume. A woman, and a sinful one, responds to Jesus more discerningly than the well-educated Pharisee, just as a Gentile centurion knows the God of Israel better than the Jews (7:9).

Perhaps most importantly, the story is about contrasting evaluations of Simon, and by implication the Pharisees. By telling the parable and asking questions, Jesus forces Simon to admit that the woman's actions are a result of her having been forgiven much (vv. 40–43). The parable challenges Simon's own self-evaluation. As we have seen, Jesus often places his opponents in the parable, and forces them to see themselves as God sees them. Parables offer an opportunity for repentance. Jesus shows Simon that he has debts of hospitality as a host, debts that he has neglected. Simon has a lot to be forgiven for, since he has acted badly as a host. If he changes his evaluation of the woman, he'll have to recognize that he has acted abominably. The parable highlights the fact that Simon's main sins are *not* deliberate breaches of hospitality, as important as they are; the more serious problems are his self-righteousness, his hard-heartedness, his pride, the fact that he despises this woman who has been forgiven and received salvation, and his hostility to Jesus.

At the table in Simon's house, Jesus illustrates the sermon at Nazareth. She is among the "poor" that the Lord Jesus has come to rescue and liberate. Simon is among the rich and powerful who are going to be taken down.

Table Service and the Twelve

Jesus also uses meals to teach His disciples about their mission. At the beginning of chapter 9, Jesus sends the Twelve out to carry on His mission. The setting of this commissioning highlights the fact that Jesus sets the pattern for the mission of the Twelve. We have seen this pattern before. In Luke 4–5, Jesus performs a series of miracles (casting out a demon, healing Peter's mother-in-law, and causing a great catch of fish), and then calls Peter, James, and John as disciples. Jesus' initial call of the apostles is in the context of Jesus' ministry of release and rest, His ministry of Sabbath-giving. Again in chapters 8–9, Jesus performs a series of miracles (calming the sea, casting out demons, and healing a girl and a woman), and then commissions the Twelve on a mission.

This commissioning of the Twelve is integral to the gospel message and the gospel story. The gospels are not only about Jesus' ministry, but also about the Twelve. Luke is the story not only of Jesus but of the formation of the leaders of the early church. As we saw above, the need for new leadership for Israel has already been noted earlier in the gospel. Zacharias is the first character we meet in the story, and he is a priest who does not believe the good news from an angel of Yahweh. Throughout the following chapters, the leaders of Israel refuse to accept Jesus as the Christ. Instead, they begin to plot against Him. The formation of new leadership for the people of God is part of the good news. Soon, Israel will not be ruled by predatory priests and scribes, but by the Twelve, those whom Jesus called, trained, and commissioned to be His undershepherds.

Given this setting, it's not surprising that Jesus gives the Twelve authority and power to do what He has done. They proclaim the kingdom of God and perform healings, which is, of course, what Jesus has been doing throughout the gospel. They are "sent," just as Jesus is "sent" by the Father. Jesus is commissioned, and He commissions them. Jesus instructs them to treat unbelieving cities as He treated the city of the Gadarenes (9:5; cf. 8:38–40); if they reject the Twelve, the Twelve should depart. Jews in Jesus' time frequently shake the dust off their sandals when they reenter the promised land after being in Gentile territory. The dust of the Gentiles is cursed, and should not be brought into the holy land. Jesus is saying that the cities that reject the apostles are rejecting Jesus, and that therefore they are not really part of Israel. Leaving the city is like leaving Gentile territory; because they reject Jesus, they are going to be treated as Gentiles.

The most interesting part of the instructions to the apostles is the requirement that they take nothing on their journey. Traveling teachers and philosophers in the ancient world often take a staff and a wallet with them on their journeys, but Jesus says that the Twelve are not supposed to take even the bare minimum. This is sometimes seen as a kind of asceticism. Jesus wants His disciples to toughen up by denying themselves and refusing to take anything with them. During the Middle Ages, Franciscans used passages like this to prove that Jesus demanded absolute poverty from his followers. This doesn't fit the story of the gospel. Several of the Twelve were fishermen, who were not wealthy but also were not poverty-stricken. They could have used resources of their own when they followed Jesus. But when He sends them out, He tells them not to rely on their own resources. He does not tell them to use their money and wealth to fund their mission. If Jesus wanted them to take vows of poverty, it would have been more effective to instruct them to spend their money on the mission. Instead, He tells them *not* to spend their own resources on their mission.

Jesus' instructions force the Twelve to depend on the generosity of the people they minister to. The mission of the Twelve is funded much like the later mission of the church is funded. Paul makes tents for a living, working so that no one would have to support him. But Paul says that he has the right to be paid for his services as a minister (1 Cor. 9), just as a priest is paid for his ministry at the altar by receiving a portion of the sacrifice. Paul ministers in spiritual things for the people, and it is fitting that ministers should receive material support in turn. The only difference in the gospels is that the people of Galilee do not have advance notice that the Twelve are coming. But Jesus assures the disciples that God will provide for them through the people who receive them (9:4). Just as in the later church, the Twelve are "worthy of their hire," and are supported materially by those who receive spiritual benefit from them.

In depending on the people they serve, the Twelve are following the example of Jesus. At the beginning of Luke 8, we learn that several women support Jesus from their own funds. The Twelve are supposed to rely on the generosity of people too. Jesus is also giving them a lesson in trusting God to provide when they go out on a mission. This is the point that Jesus brings up later in the gospel, during the last supper (22:35): "And He said to them, 'When I sent you out without purse and bag and sandals, you did not lack anything, did you?' And they said, 'Nothing.'" They are sent without sufficient resources to support their work, just as they are later commanded to feed people with insufficient food. They must learn to say, with Paul, that the sufficiency is not of themselves but of God (2 Cor. 3:5). They must learn that they will lack nothing if they are on commission from Jesus.

Only then will they be qualified to lead the people of Jesus. Only then will they be ready to replace the unjust rulers that Jesus plans to overthrow.

Just as important, Jesus' instructions force the people who receive the disciples to respond. They need to express their acceptance of the gospel by offering hospitality. No one in Galilee can say, "I like what those Twelve apostles say, I believe it, but I'm not going to help them at all." If they don't receive the message by receiving the messengers, then the messengers will move on to other towns. Jesus forces reception of the gospel to take the specific form of hospitality. In short, receiving the apostles is receiving Jesus, and that means that receiving Jesus cannot be simply intellectual assent or agreement. It has to take the form of hospitality to His messengers.[4]

A final bit of training comes in the story of the feasting of the five thousand (9:10–17). Preaching and healing are important parts of their ministry, but ultimately the Twelve are called, like Jesus, to serve at table. The capstone of their ministry will be to perpetuate and extend Jesus' table fellowship.

This incident occurs shortly after the disciples return from their missionary journey. The apostles rely on the hospitality of others, and in the next scene Jesus demonstrates hospitality to the people gathered in Bethsaida to hear Him teach. The disciples receive hospitality, and that is part of their training. They learn to rely on God's provision. But receiving hospitality is not enough. They must give hospitality. They have been guests (as Jesus has been); now they must learn to be hosts. Here they fail. Jesus "welcomes" the

4. Later, Jesus instructs them to go out not only with wallet and staff, but even a sword (Lk. 22). The open and unarmed ministry is over: that gave people the opportunity to receive Jesus, but now the prophetic emissaries are going to be rejected and are going to reject.

people to Him (v. 11), and Luke uses a word associated with hospitality. But the disciples, when it is evening, want to send the people away to find lodging (v. 12), and Luke uses another Greek term associated with hospitality. They have been recipients of hospitality, but they have not learned to give it. They have received freely, but they have not learned to give freely.

The reason they are not good hosts is that they don't fully trust God. Jesus has all the people "recline" for the meal, taking a posture suitable for a banquet, and He serves as host. But the resources are meager, certainly not sufficient for a banquet. The Twelve are reluctant hosts because they don't believe there is enough to go around. They haven't learned the lessons of their missionary journey. When they go on their journey without wallet or food, they have all they need. They have sufficient resources as guests, and they need to apply the same lesson of trust to being a host. They need to rely on God as much for their giving as for their receiving. This is a lesson for every Christian: Jesus provides for our needs, but He also provides us with the resources to meet other people's needs. That is the whole point, since the mission of Jesus brings good news to the poor.

Review Questions

1. How does Jesus undermine the Pharisees classification of some people as sinners?

2. How does Simon treat Jesus? Why does Simon invite Jesus over to begin with?

3. What does the woman do to correct Simon's failures?

4. What is Simon supposed to learn about himself from Jesus' parable?

5. Why does Jesus instruct His disciples not to take any money with them on their mission? What are they supposed to learn from that?

6. Describe the connection between receiving and giving hospitality. How do the disciples fail here?

Thought Questions

1. How does Jesus' raising of the young man at Nain (7:11–17) fit into the gospel of Luke? Into chapter 7?

2. Luke 10 describes the mission of seventy disciples. How does it differ from the mission of the Twelve in chapter 9?

3. What does Luke mean by the "exodus" of Jesus in 9:31?

Table Talk, Luke 14

The table shows Jesus' ministry to the poor and sinners. The table is the center of training for mission—learning to receive and give hospitality. For Jesus, behavior at the table sets a pattern for the life of the disciples. In chapter 14, Jesus is again eating at the home of a Pharisee, and He uses this particular meal as an opportunity to describe the way of life that His disciples should adopt.

Jesus first observes the seating arrangements (v. 7), and the competition for good seats. Seating arrangements at ancient meals are very important, a matter of "honor" and "disgrace" (v. 8–9). Someone seated close to the host is exalted over more distant guests, and can boast in a closer relationship with the host. Seating has to do with honor and shame. A man invited to sit with the host at "high table" is honored, and those who were ignored feel the shame of humiliation. Honor and disgrace are *the* key motivations for ancient people (*men* especially). Winning the competition for honor is what made a man a hero, and this pagan competitiveness infects Israel, in a particularly Jewish way. Pharisees act like pagans when they compete for honor in holiness and piety.

They want to earn reputations for godliness that will bring them close to the divine "head of the table."

Jesus challenges that competitive honor-grabbing head-on. He's saying that there is a right way to be honored and to receive honor and a wrong way. The way he condemns is the way of Adam, who seizes an honor without permission and is exposed to shame. Jesus is saying, "Don't be an Adam, who grasped at a high place." Instead, Jesus says, the path to genuine and lasting honor is through humble service. Jesus uses this incident as an object lesson in humiliation and exaltation, and teaches the paradoxical truth that humiliation is the pathway to exaltation, service the way to authority.

This might appear to be just a question of strategy. It might seem that Jesus accepts the standards of the day and tells His disciples how to get ahead more efficiently. Jesus is showing His disciples a way to get *more* honor (14:7–11). But Jesus is taking a different tack. He's saying, "*If* you are seeking honor, *if* that's your goal, then the best thing to do is to take the lowest seat." Even on Pharisaical premises, they should humble themselves. But Jesus ultimately criticizes the whole system of honor and shame. The problem with the Pharisees is not that they are seeking honor, but that they are seeking honor from the wrong source. The exaltation Jesus mentions in verse 10 is not coming from other people, but from God. Jesus states a general principle that destroys the whole Jewish and pagan honor-shame system. The question is, Who exalts? Jesus' answer is, God the Father. Once you say that, then the honor system shatters. Competing for a good seat, strategizing for honors, wheeling and dealing— it's all folly. God lifts up and casts down, and true honor comes from seeking Him.

Jesus is doing more than giving good "social advice." Jesus criticizes the outlook of the Jewish leaders, who are vying and competing for favor with the Divine Host. They display their works and the strictness of their Sabbath observance and their utter ceremonial purity in an effort to win some praise from God. God is not impressed. Disciples must follow Jesus' lead. He humbled Himself, took the lowest seat, and therefore the Father exalted Him to His right hand.

Jesus criticizes the Jews for their behavior at the table, and then He turns to the guest list to see who has been invited (v. 12). His second observation about meals and discipleship is not directed to guests but to hosts. In the ancient world, banquets and meals are important ways of establishing social networks and, again, of gathering honor. Having an honorable person at your banquet enhances the honor of your banquet. When everyone sees that you have important people at your banquets, they'll want to be there too. As today, "partying" with the rich and famous is one way to become famous and perhaps rich. Plus, when you invite an important man to your banquet, you are buying yourself an invitation to his next banquet.

Jesus says that we should not think about hospitality in that kind of calculating way (cf. Lk. 6:30–35). Our hospitality should imitate the hospitality of God, who gives generously even though we can never repay Him and even though He needs nothing from us. Repayment is not evil or wrong. We should expect repayment and reward. But Jesus says that expecting a reward from another important person sets our expectations too low. When we invite a CEO or a movie star to dinner, we might be invited back. We will be rewarded by having a place at the table of a movie star. But that's not ambitious enough. Jesus says that inviting outcasts and the poor to our table wins a reward from someone far more luminous than a movie star. Hospitality to outcasts wins a reward from God.

The key issue is faith: Do we invite guests by sight, thinking about what rewards we get in *this age*? Or do we form our guest lists by *faith,* thinking about the rewards we will receive in the *resurrection?* Jesus is not merely speaking in parables. Jesus really wants us to construct guest lists for our meals and parties in this way: We should be looking out for the outcasts, the sick and lame and crippled, strangers and visitors and people who can never repay us. We should be having "sinners" to our tables, as Jesus does.

Finally, Jesus tells a parable that develops the analogy between the kingdom of heaven and a wedding feast (14:15–24). Jews recognize that the kingdom was a feast, but for many Jews, the guest list for the Messianic feast is very restricted. Some Jews interpret Isaiah 25, which speaks of a banquet for *all* peoples on God's mountain, in a way that excludes Gentiles. Others, like the Essenes at Qumran, explicitly exclude the lame, crippled, and poor, those who are physical and spiritual misfits, from the Messianic banquet. Jesus encourages us to invite *just those* people. The parable, which shows *God* bringing just these people to His table is even more astonishing to first-century Jews.

As with most of Jesus' parables, the parable of the wedding is mainly a commentary on His own ministry and Israel's response to it. He has sent the seventy ahead of him (Lk. 10) announcing that the feast is ready and issuing invitations, but many Jews make lame excuses and will not come. One man says he needs to look at a field that he has already bought, another that he needs to test oxen that he has already purchased. There is a grammatical shift between Luke 14:23 and 14:24:[5] Jesus moves from narrating a story in third person to a direct address. This is still part of the master's speech to his slave, but it is also the master speaking over the head of the slave to the assembled Pharisees. The master "steps as it were on to the apron of the stage

5. Green, *Luke,* 562, quoting Eta Linnemann.

and addresses the audience." This is an insult to the host of the banquet Jesus attends, and is meant to be. The host in the story is angry, but His anger leads him to expand His invitation even further (v. 21), to include the poor, lame, crippled, and blind. Guests will fill the banquet hall of the kingdom, but many in Israel will be outside.

Table and Mission

Jesus' tabletalk continues after His resurrection. Luke insists that the resurrection is a real event that took place in real history, and that Jesus' body was really raised. Luke certainly agrees that Jesus' resurrection was a pledge and promise that we will be raised on the last day. But the bulk of his resurrection story is taken up with something else, with the haunting story of the road to Emmaus. The main point of this story is about the mission of the church to the nations. This passage shows that the church is capable of mission *only* because the risen Jesus is among us. The church is equipped for mission *only* when the risen Jesus is *recognized* among us, and He is recognized at the table.

The story of the road to Emmaus is in part a journey story. It lines up with the flow of Luke's gospel as a whole. As we have seen, fully ten chapters of Luke's gospel are taken up with Jesus' journey to Jerusalem. Eventually, in Acts, Luke shows that the church journeys away from Jerusalem. The whole flow of the book of Acts moves from Jerusalem to Judea to Samaria to the uttermost parts of the earth. But the last episode of Luke is not the beginning of that mission. The two disciples who meet Jesus on the road have jumped the gun. They are already leaving Jerusalem, and it is clear that they are not leaving Jerusalem on mission. They are leaving Jerusalem dejected, disappointed, and perhaps even angry because all the hopes they put in Jesus have been dashed. They might be leaving Jerusalem in fear, fleeing because they worry that the Romans will begin the clean-up operation that often happened when a revolutionary leader was put to death. The two disciples of Jesus are fleeing from their mission. They leave not to be witnesses but to escape the danger of being witnesses.

As they travel, Jesus comes alongside and begins to talk with them, and they express their dejection and disappointment. They hope that Jesus was the fulfillment of Israel's dreams, and they express these hopes in terms drawn from the exodus. They describe Jesus as a prophet "mighty in deed and word in the sight of God," like the prophet predicted by Moses Himself in Deuteronomy 18. These disciples think that Jesus is this prophet, come to be the greater Moses. They also expect Jesus to "redeem" Israel (24:21). Redemption has to do with the liberation of slaves, buying them from slavery or delivering them from bondage. In the Bible, the word "redeem" always sends us back to the exodus when Yahweh intervenes on behalf of the enslaved firstborn son. The two disciples on the road know that Israel has again fallen into slavery, and they were looking forward to the new prophet, the prophet like Moses, who would free them from this new bondage and triumph over Israel's enemies. They are looking for the fulfillment of what Mary sings about.

All these hopes, and yet none of it has happened. The opposite happened. Instead of redeeming the people from bondage to the Gentiles, to the Roman overlords, Jesus has been subjected to a Roman execution. The crucifixion, they think, means that the Gentiles are still in charge, and that the Jews are still oppressed. A crucified prophet is not able to redeem Israel. A crucified Messiah is a failed Messiah, or so these two disciples think.

The disciples actually know even more than this. They know the entire story of Jesus, His miraculous life, His crucifixion, even His resurrection (24:18–24). They have heard reports of His resurrection, and they have heard the testimony of the women and also others (Peter) who had been to the tomb and found no sign of Jesus. In fact, they have the *entire gospel* in their fingers and on their tongues, but they are *still* dejected and defeated. More: The risen Jesus is walking beside them and they are still dejected. Neither the gospel story nor Jesus Himself among them is enough to turn them around so long as their eyes are closed.

How can Jesus break through this blindness? He does it as He has broken through during the entire gospel: By word and table. First He leads them through a Bible study to show that it is necessary for the Christ to suffer, die, and rise again. According to Jesus, this is precisely what the Old Testament predicts. Though the word is not used, the answer to their perplexity and confusion and dejection is a "typological" reading of the Old Testament.

We're not told in detail what Jesus taught these disciples on the road to Emmaus, but we can learn from the rest of the New Testament what kinds of things Jesus teaches. Jesus teaches the disciples that He is the Last Adam, the son of David, the greater Moses, a prophet like Jeremiah, the high priest after the order of Melchizedek, whose priesthood is better than the priesthood of Aaron. He shows them that the Christ is the sacrifice that fulfills and ends all sacrifice, a living temple and the tabernacle. The story of the Christ is the story of death and resurrection, of suffering and glory. Israel's history begins with the Lord raising up a living seed from the dead womb of Sarah. When Israel is "on the cross" in Egypt, when things are at their blackest, the Lord intervenes to save. When Israel is later attacked and oppressed by Midianites and Moabites and Edomites and Philistines,

God rescues them at the last moment. When Athaliah kills all the royal seed, the Lord preserves Joash in the temple so that the Davidic dynasty can continue. When Assyria overtakes the Northern kingdom and threatens Judah, the Lord raises up Hezekiah and sends out the angel of death against Sennacherib's hosts. Judah goes into exile, but the Lord raises Jehoiachin from the prison and gives him a seat at the table of the Babylonian king. When the bones of Israel lie decaying in the valley of exile, the prophet speaks to the bones and Israel is raised from the dead (Ezek. 37). Since the Messiah, the Christ, is the true Israel, Israel in person, His story is going to be the same. His story has to be a story of death and resurrection. It is *necessary* that the Christ should suffer and enter into His glory.

Strikingly, Jesus' presence and the teaching of the Word are not enough either. Jesus walks with the disciples, He teaches them everything concerning Himself from all the Scriptures, and *still* their eyes are closed. Still they are leaving Jerusalem. Still they are abandoning the mission that Jesus started, the mission to proclaim the gospel to the poor. Their eyes are opened only later, after Jesus sits to break bread with them (24:30–31). The Word without the bread is not enough to open our eyes to the living, risen Jesus. The Word without bread is detached from real life; the bread without the Word turns into a magic act. But when the Scriptures are taught and the bread is broken, then Jesus can be known.

Word and bread together open the eyes of these two disciples to be witnesses and equip them for mission. They have been leaving Jerusalem, but now they return (v. 33). They leave the other disciples, and are breaking away from the fellowship of the disciples, but now they return to join the Eleven. They are confused about the reports of the resurrection, and now they become witnesses to the resurrection, becoming the first humans who declare "The Lord is risen indeed" (v. 34). They have been traveling in the wrong direction; they are leaving Jerusalem but not on mission. Now they go back to wait for the Spirit. Their encounter with Jesus in Word and Bread equips them for mission, the mission that Luke will describe in Acts.

The final verses of Luke sketch out the dimension of that mission, which is also a fulfillment of Scripture (v. 47). Luke describes Jesus' journey toward Jerusalem as an "ascension" (9:51), since the ultimate goal of the journey is for Jesus to return to His Father (24:50–51). His ascension is the prerequisite for the coming of the Spirit, the "power from on high" (24:49). Through the Spirit, the disciples will carry on the mission that had been prophesied in the Scriptures, to proclaim "repentance for forgiveness of sins" to the nations (v. 47). "Repentance" is of course a personal obligation. Every sinner, confronted by the claims of Jesus, must turn from sin and unbelief toward God in faith and obedience. But we should not lose the political dimension of what Jesus says. Through Jesus, God is fulfilling the promise to Abraham that his seed would bring blessing to all nations. Part of that blessing is the proclamation of national and international repentance and reconciliation. In a world where nations are locked in seemingly interminable conflict, the only hope for the nations is through their union in Christ.

Easter is about hope for the nations. It is about the nations being gathered together into one family through Jesus, the family of Abraham. It is about restoring the nations to God, and calling the nations to repent and serve the living God. As the church knows Jesus, the Risen Lord, in the Word and Bread, she is prepared for the mission of preaching repentance and forgiveness of sins to the nations.

Luke's gospel is a large circle. It begins in the temple, with the angel's announcement to Zecharias that he would be the father of John the Baptist, and it ends in the temple, with the disciples of Jesus continually praising God. The gospel begins with the songs of Mary and Zecharias, and ends with the great joy of the disciples. Near the beginning of the gospel, Jesus is lost for three days and is found by his parents; he explains by saying "Did you not know that I had to be in My Father's house?" (2:49). Here at the end Jesus is found on the third day, and has to explain again that He had to be about His Father's business.

But the circle that Luke closes here is actually much bigger. At the beginning of human history, man fell into sin by eating fruit from a forbidden tree. Once Adam and Eve eat the fruit, "the eyes of both of them were opened, and they knew that they were naked" (Gen. 3:7). Luke gives us a similar scene: Jesus breaks bread with the two disciples "and their eyes were opened and they recognized Him" (Lk. 24:31). It is the first day of a new creation, a renewal accomplished in the resurrection of Jesus. On the first Easter, the Father not only says "This is My Son, the Righteous One." He also declares, "Behold I make all things new."

The Last Adam has undone the work of the first: The fall at the tree has been undone by the crucifixion on the tree; the sinful meal in the garden that brought death has been replaced by the meal in the village that brings life; the meal that opened eyes in sin has given way to the meal that opens eyes to see Jesus; and with the Word and the Bread, we are equipped to go to proclaim repentance and forgiveness of sins to the nations, equipped to extend the new creation to the ends of the old creation.

Review Questions

1. Why are the Jews so concerned with places at the table?
2. What is Jesus' alternative to the competition for honor?

3. Why do the Jews invite the people they do to meals?

4. Whom does Jesus tell us to invite to meals? Why?

5. What does Jesus teach the disciples on the road to Emmaus?

6. How do the disciples on the road to Emmaus finally recognize Jesus?

Thought Questions

1. What is the setting for the parable of the Prodigal Son (15:11–32)? How does that affect the way we read the parable?

2. Explain the parable of the unrighteous steward (16:1–13).

3. How does the story of the rich man and Lazarus fit into Luke's gospel as a whole?

Christian Diaspora

The church carries on the mission of Jesus. In Acts, the servant of the Lord continues working through the Spirit to deliver the poor. The Spirit comes on Jesus in order to announce good news to the poor, and that same Spirit comes on the apostles at Pentecost. The Spirit-filled church carries on the mission of Jesus to the poor.

Already at the beginning of Jesus' ministry, the "poor" includes the Gentiles, those who are outcasts from Israel, without God and without hope in the world. So long as Jesus is talking about the restoration of Israel, the Jews in Nazareth are excited about Him. But then he begins talking about Elijah and Elisha to Gentiles, to the widow of Zarephath and Naaman the Syrian. When Jesus starts saying that the "poor" Gentiles will receive the good news too, his home town folk take Him to the edge of a cliff and are ready to cast Him over. A prophet is not welcome in his hometown. This event at the beginning of the ministry is repeated in Acts 28. This is the climax of the book of Acts:

Paul is in Rome, but the Jews reject him, so he turns to the Gentiles. The last scenes of Acts thus show us the movement of Luke–Acts in miniature. The imperial breadth of the gospel is already noted at the beginning of Luke, since Jesus' birth is dated by reference to Roman rulers. Impelled by the Spirit, the church has gone to the uttermost parts of the earth to gather in the outcasts.

From the parallels of Luke and Acts, we can see that the lives of Jesus' disciples are shaped like Jesus' own life. Matthew has taught us that we must have righteousness, we must keep Torah in a way that surpasses the scribes and Pharisees, in the way that Jesus keeps Torah. Mark has taught us that this means taking up the cross and following the Son of God, the Strong Man, in His triumphant death. That's impossible for us, because our grip on life is too strong. But Jesus has secured the Spirit, and the Spirit is with Jesus, and the Spirit who is with Jesus is now with us. In Acts, the Spirit comes in the shape of Christ to shape us like Christ.

As a result, the history of the church in Acts follows very closely the history of Jesus. The disciples are living out the suffering/glory of Jesus in their own lives. Their lives are stamped with the imprint of Jesus' death and resurrection. Peter goes through a very similar experience to Jesus'. He receives the Spirit, preaches the kingdom, performs miracles, is arrested and opposed by the Jews. This is especially clear in chapter 12, when Herod (Agrippa) arrests Peter and puts him in prison. An angel releases him from prison, and he walks past Roman guards. When he gets to the house where the disciples are praying for him, a young woman comes to the door and recognizes him, but when she tells everyone else, they think it's a ghost. They don't believe that Peter has escaped. Finally, they are amazed to find him safe and sound. Peter tells them to report what's happened, and then he goes to another place, and in the next chapter, things move over to Paul's ministry. This is a repetition of the death (prison), resurrection, and ascension of Jesus.

Paul repeats Jesus' life too. Not only do we have Paul's journey toward Jerusalem and then to Rome, but there are more specific parallels: Paul is arrested in Jerusalem (as Jesus is); he is tried by the same courts that Jesus was (Roman, Sanhedrin, Herod); he is shipwrecked and survives (Jonah and Jesus); and then gets to Rome where he teaches unhindered.

At the hinge of Acts is the character of Stephen. He combines these themes. He is filled with the Spirit, his life is like the life of Jesus, and his life and death contribute to the expansion of the church to the poor throughout the Roman world. The description of Stephen marks him out as being Christlike. According to Acts 6:8 and following, he is full of grace and power, performs wonders, and shows wisdom and the Spirit. He refutes and silences the Jews who oppose Him, as Jesus does; he is accused of speaking blasphemously against the temple, as Jesus was; his death is like Jesus'. In rejecting Stephen's preaching, the Jews are rejecting the preaching of Jesus all over again.

The significance of this is reinforced when we look at the results of Stephen's martyrdom, which is a structural pillar of Luke's two-volume book. The book of Luke, as we've seen, has a trajectory toward Jerusalem: Jesus begins His ministry in Galilee and starts making his way to Jerusalem from chapter 9 on. The last of Jesus' temptations (in Luke's account) occurs in Jerusalem (ch. 4); the transfiguration is linked specifically to Jesus' going away toward Jerusalem; at the end of the gospel, Jesus tells the disciples to stay there until they receive the Holy Spirit. Once Jesus arrives in Jerusalem, the action stays there through the first six chapters of Acts. For over ten chapters, things are happening exclusively in Jerusalem.

All that changes with the death of the "second Christ," Stephen. In Matthew, Jesus' death and resurrection begins the dispersal of the Twelve. But in Luke, it's not the death of Jesus that leads to the dispersal of the gospel, but the death of Stephen. The mission of the church begins when Christlike disciples of Jesus share in His cross. From Acts 7, there is a shift in the directional flow of the story. Up to the death of Stephen, there is a centripetal movement toward the center, but now there's a centrifugal movement away from Jerusalem. Intriguingly, only Stephen's martyrdom is told in any detail. James the brother of John is killed by Herod (Acts 12:2); Peter's death is not told, nor Paul's. Stephen's death is the hinge of the mission of the church.

Stephen's sermon to the Sanhedrin reinforces the point. He retells Israel's story the way Jesus often does, subversively. He tells the whole story of Israel, but the focus is on Moses. All along the way, Stephen emphasizes that the Jews reject those sent to them. Joseph is hated by the patriarchs, though he is a true prophet, and though God is with Him. Even so, Joseph saves Israel by feeding them. The point is made even more precisely by the example of Moses, which comprises the long central section of Stephen's sermon. When Moses kills the Egyptian, he hopes that Israel will be delivered then through him. But the Jews don't want him to be ruler or judge, so Moses goes away. He comes a second time to deliver Israel, and this time, God has clearly designated the rejected savior as savior (Acts 7:35). Moses brings Israel out of Egypt. But the Hebrews still rebel against him, and in the calf incident, and God gives them up to idolatry. Here at the center of Israel's history is a story of the two comings of Moses. He is rejected in the first, and has to flee; he returns and delivers, yet is still rejected. In verses 51–52, Stephen brings the story up to his own time. He accuses his generation of Jews of resisting the Spirit as their fathers have done. They kill the prophets, and now have killed the Righteous One. Like Moses when he delivered the Israelite from the oppressive Egyptian, Jesus is rejected. Now Jesus has come again (by the Spirit, and through the Spirit-filled church, Stephen especially), and the Jews are rejecting Him all over again. They respond by killing him, proving his point!

This seems like a tragic conclusion to the story, but as Luke shows it is just the beginning. Jesus' death is just the beginning of the spread of the gospel to the poor. Filled with the Spirit and remade to be like Christ, the church shares that mission when her blood is mingled with that of Jesus.

Review Questions

1. What is Jesus' point in bringing up Elijah and Elisha in his sermon at Nazareth?

2. How is the mission to the Gentiles a continuation of Jesus' mission to the "poor"?

3. How is Peter's life like that of Jesus?

4. How is Stephen like Jesus?

5. Explain how the death of Stephen is a turning point in Luke's story.

Thought Questions

1. Looking at Acts 1–5, explain how the apostles are already being formed to be like Christ.

2. Do the early Christians believe in private property? Can you tell from Acts?

3. Compare the early chapters of Acts to the early chapters of Joshua. How are they similar? Why?

CHAPTER 7

JOHN [1]

seeing the
Father

John's gospel differs in many ways from synoptics. The synoptics emphasize the Galilean ministry of Jesus. All the gospels end in Jerusalem, but in the synoptics Jesus arrives in Jerusalem after a long trek from Galilee. In John, Jesus spends most of His time in and around Jerusalem. We get a whiff of a Galilean ministry in chapter 2, with the wedding at Cana; in chapter 4, with the healing of the son of a royal official in Capernaum; and in chapter 6, with the feeding of the five thousand and crossing of the sea taking place around the sea of Galilee. Otherwise, most of Jesus' activities are concentrated in and around Jerusalem.

Starting in 2:13, Jesus is in Jerusalem for a Passover at the beginning of the book. While there, He cleanses the temple. Even if this is the same incident as the one recorded in the gospels, it is out of chronological sequence. As we saw with Mark's placement of the exorcism in the synagogue, this sets

---

1. I have written on John more often in the past than the other gospels, and that presents a dilemma. I don't want to repeat what I've written elsewhere, but then again I think what I've written elsewhere was pretty good. I've compromised by using some material from *A House for My Name* (Moscow: Canon Press, 2000), small bits and pieces from *Deep Exegesis* (Waco: Baylor University Press, 2009), and articles on perichoresis, mainly published in *Credenda/Agenda*. For a complete portrait of what I think John's gospel is about, a reader should consult these other works.

the theme of the whole gospel. The story is about Jesus as the temple that gets destroyed and raised up in three days. Jesus' meeting with Nicodemus apparently takes place in Jerusalem as well (ch. 3). In John 3:22, Jesus and disciples are in Judea, where the disciples are baptizing. Chapter 5 brings Jesus back in Jerusalem for "the feast" of the Jews, and in chapter 7, He's back in Jerusalem for the Feast of Booths. The events of chapters 8–10 occur in the same setting, in the temple. Chapter 11 describes the raising of Lazarus at Bethany in Judea, while chapter 12 brings Him back to Jerusalem for good.

John's chronology also differs from the synoptics'. The synoptics show Jesus going to Passover at the end of His life to die and rise again, but in none of them do we see the adult Jesus attending the Passover more than that (though cf. Lk. 2:41–52). The events of the synoptics could fit into a single year of ministry. In John, however, there are several Passovers. In John 2, Jesus is in Jerusalem for Passover when he cleanses the temple. In chapter 6, there's another Passover, but Jesus is elsewhere, in Galilee, with his disciples. In 12:1, it is now six days before yet another Passover. It's possible that John is writing about only one Passover.[2] But there seem to be at least two Passovers, and at least two Feasts of Booths as well (chs. 5 and 7).

The ministry of Jesus is described in quite different terms in John's gospel. There are no exorcisms, few of the neat pithy sayings of Jesus that we know from the other gospels, and many of the most notable miracles are absent. There are marked differences in theological emphasis. John begins with

---

2. To fit all these into a single Passover, we would have to identify the Passover of John 2 with the Passover of John 12–21, and assume that Jesus did finally go to Jerusalem during the Passover of John 6. But that plays havoc with whatever chronological order there is in John's gospel.

the eternal Word of God, who becomes incarnate among men in Jesus, and Jesus is identified with the eternal God. At the end of the gospel, Thomas identifies Jesus as "Lord and God." John includes a series of "I am" statements that identify Jesus with Yahweh (6:35; 8:12; 9:5; 10:7, 14). John develops what scholars call a "Christology from above."

John emphasizes Jesus' sonship, and His relation to the Father, more than the other gospels. The other gospels do indicate that Jesus has a unique relationship with the Father (cf. Mt. 11:25–27). But this theme receives a particular accent in John, so that John becomes one of the leading sources in the New Testament for the doctrine of the Trinity. Jesus calls God "Father" four times in Mark, six in Luke, twenty-three in Matthew, and 107 in John; "the Son" is used as a designation for Jesus twice in Matthew, and once in both Mark and Luke, but eighteen times in John. Of course, it is not only the number of times that Jesus' unique sonship is mentioned, but what Jesus tells us about His relation to the Father. In John 5:19 and the passage that follows, Jesus defends Himself against charges of Sabbath breaking. He says the Son is dependent on the Father, and only does what He sees the Father doing. The Father is the model for the Son. The Son has complete access to the Father; the Father shows Him "all things" that He is doing. The Father gives the Son the powers that He uses in His ministry. Specifically, the Son has been given the power to raise the dead and to judge. Judgment and life have been given to the Son (5:30). In verse 36, He says that the Father works and the Son works too. When Jesus heals on the Sabbath, He's doing nothing but what He sees the Father doing.

There's also an emphasis on the gift of the Spirit, especially in the "upper room" discourse of chapters 13–17. This theme begins in chapter 3, where Jesus tells Nicodemus that he must be born of the Spirit, and the one born of the Spirit is like the wind. It is not the Spirit Himself who is like the wind, but the one *born* of the Spirit. When we encounter one born of the Spirit, we don't know where He comes from or where He's going. Jesus is *the* One born of the Spirit, and throughout the gospel people wonder where He comes from, who He is, where He is going. The first time Jesus appears in the gospel, two of John's disciples follow Him. Jesus turns and asks them, "What do you seek?" and they ask, "Where are you staying?" At the Feast of Booths in chapter 7, everyone is asking, "Where is Jesus?" and a dispute arises at the feast about where Jesus comes from. In chapter 9, after He heals a blind man, everyone searches for Him, asking "Where is He?" (cf. 9:28–9). Jesus says He will go away, and, as with Elijah, the Jews will search for Him, but not find Him. At His trial, Pilate asks, "Where are you from?"

In John, the Spirit is the "Paraclete," often translated "Comforter." This is a weak translation, since the word generally has a legal sense in Greek. A "paraclete" is an advocate for the defense, a defense attorney. For John, the Spirit comes to defend the disciples of Jesus by convicting the world—again, in a legal sense—of its own sin.

John also has a different eschatology, a different way of describing Christian hope, from the synoptics. In the synoptics, Jesus is the prophet pronouncing the doom of the temple. There is a hint of this in John 2, where Jesus says "destroy this temple." But John doesn't include the Olivet Discourse in John; there is no long sermon about the judgment to come. One reason for this is that for John, judgment is coming *now,* with the death of Jesus. The cross is the great *krisis* (the Greek word means "judgment") of the world (Jn. 12:30–31). Jesus tells us that judgment will be passed when Jesus is lifted up from the earth (vv. 31–32), and He is lifted up on the cross. Not only is the judgment occurring *now,* but those who believe in Jesus *already* have eternal life. It is not only a future gift, but a present one.

Finally, there's a distinctive view of the cross. The cross is often seen in the New Testament as the lowest point of Jesus' life. Jesus humbles Himself to the cross; He goes way, way down, and then the Father exalts Him (e.g., Phil. 2). But in John's gospel, the cross is not humiliation but beginning of exaltation. That's why Jesus emphasizes the type of death He'll die: He isn't buried under a pile of Jewish stones, but "lifted up" on the cross. His "lifting up" at His crucifixion begins His exaltation. We see this also in 13:3: His hour has come to depart "out of this world to the Father." The hour of Jesus is the hour of His departure, and when He departs He goes to the Father (14:12; 16:5, 10). But that "hour" is not the hour of Jesus' ascension. It is the house of Jesus' death.

This theme begins in John 3:13–15, at Jesus' nighttime dialogue with Nicodemus. Nicodemus misunderstands Jesus' words about being born from above, about being born of water and the Spirit. Jesus is a witness, like John, but Jesus is a witness of heavenly things. Jesus says He is able to bear witness of heavenly things because He has come from heaven. The One who descends from heaven is the One who will ascend into heaven, the Son of Man. The ascension of the Son of Man into heaven is an allusion to Daniel 7:13. Daniel sees a vision of the Ancient of Days, and one like the Son of Man goes up to the Ancient of Days to receive a kingdom and dominion over all nations. Jesus says that He is the Son of Man who has descended from heaven and will ascend into heaven. Verse 14 explains the character of that ascension to the Father: The Son of Man will be lifted up as Moses lifted up the serpent in the wilderness. In context, this is clearly a statement about the exaltation of the Son of Man. Like the Son of Man in Daniel, Jesus ascends and is exalted. But John also is talking about the cross. The Son of Man will hang from a pole, as the serpent did in the wilderness.

Elsewhere, "lifting up" refers to the cross: "And I, if I be lifted up from the earth, will draw all men to Myself. But He was saying this to indicate the kind of death by which he was to die" (12:32–33). In John's gospel, then, the cross is not a humiliation of the Son of Man, but the beginning of His ascent to the Father, His return to heaven. Elijah and Enoch may have gone into heaven, but none but the Son of Man who came from heaven will be lifted up in this way.

John has a roughly chiastic structure:

A. Prologue, 1:1–18
  B. Lamb of God, 1:19–34
    C. Discipleship, 1:35–51
      D. Marriage feast, 2:1–12
        E. Death and resurrection, 2:13–25
          F. Baptism, 3:1–21
            G. Meditation, 3:21–36
              H. Living water and worship, 4:1–45
                I. Healing, 4:46–54
                I'. Healing, 5:1–30
              H'. Living water and worship, 6–7
            G'. Meditation, 7:1–8:59
          F'. Baptism, 9:1–10:21
        E'. Death and resurrection, 11:1–57
      D'. Marriage feast, 12:1–26
    C'. Discipleship, 13:1–17:26
  B'. Lamb of God, 18:1–19:42
A'. Epilogue, 20:1–31[3]

The first twelve chapters of John concentrate on Jesus' "signs," John's word for "miracle." In these chapters, there are seven signs:

---

3. David Deeks, "The Structure of the Fourth Gospel" in Mark W. G. Stibbe, ed., *The Gospel of John as Literature: An Anthology of Twentieth-Century Perspectives* (Leiden: Brill, 1993), 94.

1. Water to wine, ch. 2
2. Child raised from deathbed, ch. 4
3. Paralytic healed, ch. 5
4. Feeding of five thousand, ch. 6
5. Crossing the sea, ch. 6
6. Blind man receives sight, ch. 9
7. Lazarus raised from the dead, ch. 11

There is a complex and overlapping background to this scheme. The number seven suggests a link with the seven days of creation, and the seven signs[4] match the seven days of creation fairly neatly:

Signs	Day of Creation
Water to wine, 2:1–11	Day 1: Light
Sick boy raised, 4:46–54	Day 2: Firmament
Heals lame man, 5:1–9	Day 3: Land emerges from water
Feeds five thousand, 6:1–14	Day 4: Rulers of heavens (king)
Walks on water, 6:16–21	Day 5: Birds/fish (exodus)
Man born blind, 9:1–12	Day 6: Man
Lazarus raised, 11:1–44	Day 7: Sabbath
Resurrection of Jesus	Day 8: Day after Sabbath

In turning water to wine, Jesus manifests His "glory" (2:11), which is associated with light. The man at the pool of Bethsaida had been hoping to be healed through the water, but Jesus proves that He is a greater healer than the pool. He is able to make the man emerge from the water as a new creation. Immediately after Jesus feeds the five thousand, the crowds want to make Him king (6:15), raising Him up as a ruler in the heavens. Jesus walks on water, the environment of some of the creatures of Day 5. Jesus heals the blind man

4. Calum Carmichael argues that John runs through the creation week in chapters 1–5, culminating in the healing of the paralytic on the Sabbath. See *The Story of Creation: Its Origin and Its Interpretation in Philo and the Fourth Gospel* (Ithaca: Cornell University Press, 1996).

by making clay and applying it to His eyes, reminding us of the creation of Adam in Genesis 2. Lazarus' resurrection brings relief and restoration from death, a great Sabbath, and Jesus' own resurrection at the end of the gospel takes place on the "day after the Sabbath," the eighth day, the first day of a new creation week (19:31; 20:19; 20:26).[5]

The entire book can be understood as a stroll through the tabernacle. The opening chapter, which introduces the "lamb of God" who comes to take away the sins of the world, brings us to the bronze altar for sacrifice. Chapters 2–4, with their focus on water, are at the laver. Chapters 4–7 center on the feeding of the five thousand, in which Jesus distributes the bread of the presence from the golden table. In chapters 8–13, John lingers at the lampstand, musing on Jesus as the light, and the Upper Room Discourse, especially chapter 17, displays Jesus as the intercessory priest, raising his hands before the golden altar. John is at pains to show us that the empty tomb is the new Holy of Holies. The slab on which Jesus body no longer lays is flanked by angels, like the ark, and Peter, like a high priest, is the first to enter.[6] On this scheme, the theme of light in John 9, already associated with creation and the Feast of Tabernacles, is given a fresh dimension, linked with the golden light, the lamp on the lampstand that is the disciple (cf. Mt. 5).

5. Robert Houston Smith likewise links the seven signs to seven of the plagues. In that sequence, the healing of the blind man corresponds with the darkness of the land. In Exodus, the death of the firstborn follows, while in John's reverse exodus, Lazarus is raised ("Exodus Typology in the Fourth Gospel," *Journal of Biblical Literature* 81 [1962]: 329-342). See also the proposal of M. E. Boismard summarized in Michael A. Daise, *Feasts in John: Jewish Festivals and Jesus' "Hour" in the Fourth Gospel* (Tubingen: Mohn Siebeck, 2007), 43.

6. W. Wiley Richards, *Riches from the Lost Ark: The Gospel of John and the Tabernacle* (Graceville: Hargrave Press, 1993).

Review Questions

1. How do John's geography and chronology differ from the other gospels'?

2. What does John say about Jesus as the Son of the Father?

3. How is John's Christology a "Christology from above"?

4. What does the word "Paraclete" mean?

5. What happens to one who is born of the Spirit?

6. How does John's treatment of the cross differ from the synoptics?

7. How do John's seven signs correspond to the seven days of creation?

Thought Questions

1. Compare John 2:13–21 with Matthew 21:12–17. Do you think they are describing the same event? Why or why not?

2. Why is the Passover setting important in John 6?

3. Why is it important that Jesus turns water to wine at a wedding? See 4:27–29.

The Word Was God

John's opening sentence is one of the best-known passages of Scripture: "In the beginning was the Word, and the Word was with God, and the Word was God." When John calls Jesus the "Word" of God, he is making several points. He clearly has the creation account of Genesis 1 in mind. John 1:1 quotes the phrase "in the beginning" from Genesis 1:1, and then adds that the Word created the world (1:3). The reference to light shining in darkness (1:4–5) also reminds us of the first day of the creation week. Throughout church history, some have interpreted the word "Logos" or "Word" as a philosophical principle. Some Greek philosophers speak about the "Logos" as the organizing principle of the universe, and some modern interpreters have gone so far as to translate the word as "logic": In the beginning was the "logic" or "reason."

Once we recognize that John is referring to Genesis 1, it is clear what he means. John may be aware of the Greek philosophical use of *logos,* but he's not primarily using Greek philosophical ideas. He's referring to the word that spoke the creation into existence. In calling Jesus the "Word," John is telling us that He is the Creator. By beginning his gospel with the words of Genesis, John is telling us that Jesus, the Word made flesh (1:14), is the agent of a new creation.

The Word of God is also the means by which the Father makes Himself known. This is implicit in calling Jesus the "Word." The Proverbs remind us constantly that our speech reveals our character, not just in what we say but in how we say it. Just as we reveal our character in the words we speak, so the Father has revealed His character in the "Word." God does use human language. He spoke on Sinai to Moses in language that Moses could understand, and He spoke to the prophets as well. But John is not writing about syllables of speech or sounds uttered. Rather, He is speaking about the Word of the Father who is a person, the second Person of the Godhead, who is God and who becomes flesh and dwells among us.

This personal Word of God has come, John tells us, to "explain" the Father: (1:18). The Word becomes flesh to interpret and explain, and exposit the Father's character to us, to reveal to us what the Father is like. John is fond of using words with double meanings: he uses words that can mean more than one thing, and he intends the reader to catch both of them. He's already used this technique in 1:5. He says that the light shines in the darkness and the darkness does not "comprehend" it. The Greek word for "comprehend" can mean either "understand" or "grasp" in an intellectual sense, but it can also mean "seize" or "grasp" in the physical sense of taking hold of someone. Which does John intend? As we read the gospel, we find that he intends both. Jesus speaks to the Jews, but they are in darkness and don't understand what He is saying. The Jews do not "comprehend" Jesus. Yet, the Jews also attempt to "seize" Him on a number of occasions (7:30–32, 44; 10:39; 11:53). But He slips through their fingers, until His hour comes. Since He is born of the Spirit, He is like the wind, blowing here and there, making sounds, but as impossible to hold in your hand as the wind is.

John intends the verb *exegesato* to carry various meanings as well. In the context, the Word "exegetes" the Father; but the verb is used in the first century to describe the rabbi's interpretations of the Law. John intends us to pick up that nuance. Jesus is not only sent to explain the Father, but in the process to explain the Scriptures. The two are connected. Jesus provides the correct exegesis of the Scriptures that reveal the Father. This is a continuous theme in John. Debates about the Scriptures are very common. In John 2:22, for instance, Jesus speaks about the destruction and rebuilding of the temple. He quotes from Psalm 69 (2:17). The Jews don't comprehend what He's saying, but the disciples tuck this away in the back of their minds. When Jesus rises from the dead, His disciples "believed the Scripture, and the word which Jesus had spoken." The resurrection gives a proper interpretation to Jesus' words, but also to the Scriptures of the Jews. Similarly, in 13:18, after Jesus washes the feet of His disciples, He announces that there is one among them that is a traitor. He quotes from Psalm 41: "He who eats my bread has lifted up his heel against me." The true meaning of this passage is again given by Jesus; the Psalm is about Judas and his betrayal. Similarly, throughout John's account

of the crucifixion, he refers to Scriptures being fulfilled. In
19:24, the division of Jesus' garments fulfills Psalm 22; Jesus
asks for a drink to fulfill the same Scripture (19:28); and
the fact that His bones are not broken is also a fulfillment
of Scripture (19:36–37). After the Roman soldier pierces
Jesus' side, John reminds us that this fulfills the prophecy of
Zechariah—the Jews will look on Him whom they pierced
(Zech. 12:10). Jesus does give verbal interpretations of Scripture in the gospel of John. He debates the meaning of certain
passages with the Jews. But His life itself is an "exegesis" of
the meaning of the Old Testament. He is showing the true
character of the Law in His life and death.

By calling Jesus "Word," John also is stressing Jesus' supe-
riority to Moses (1:17–18). John's statement that "no one
has seen the Father" refers back to the experience of Moses
on Mount Sinai. When Moses asks to see God, the Lord
responds, "You cannot see My face, for no man can see Me
and live" (Exod. 33:20). Moses is therefore shown the "back"
of God's passing glory, but not His face (Exod. 33:22–23).
Having become flesh, the Word expounds the Father to us
(Jn. 1:18; see 2 Cor. 3). It is no longer true that "no man
has seen God." On the contrary, Jesus says that those who
have seen Him have seen the Father (Jn. 12:45; 14:9), and
claims that His words and works display the Father's words
and works (Jn. 5:19; 12:49). In Jesus, the invisible God has
become visible, audible, tangible (cf. 1 Jn. 1:1).

John 1:14 implies another contrast. As everyone who has
heard a sermon on John 1 knows, the word normally translated as "dwell" can be translated as "tabernacled" or "pitched
a tent." The eternal Word moves into our neighborhood by
taking human flesh, and in so doing He shows the glory of
God. But notice: When the glory came into the tabernacle
in the Old Testament, everyone, including Moses and the
priests, evacuates the tent (Exod. 40:34–38; 1 Kgs. 8:10–11).

Now, the Word of glory descends in the tent of His flesh, and instead of fleeing "we beheld His glory" (Jn. 1:14).

Seeing the Father

John begins his gospel by stating that "no man has seen God at any time" (Jn. 1:18). This is a problem. For John, seeing is knowing (6:40; 11:45; 14:7), and knowing/seeing the Father and Son *is* eternal life (17:3). If the Father is hidden, then we can find no way that leads to life. We need some way to behold Him. For John, the good news is that there is such a way, and that the name of that Way is Jesus. When John speaks of the invisibility of God the Father, he is not primarily making a philosophical claim. God is invisible (see Col.1:15–16; 1 Tim. 1:17), but John's main point has to do with the progress of salvation in history. The Father has been invisible, until *now*. If you see Jesus, you see the Father too.

In chapter 14, Jesus explains that His "exegesis" of the Father is rooted in His eternal relation to the Father. The issue that dominates the discussion at the beginning of chapter 14 is the "way." Jesus has said He is returning to the Father (13:33; 14:2), and tells the disciples they know "the way where I am going" (14:4). Jesus Himself is "the way" to the Father (14:6) because the Father, the destination, is already and has always been "in" the way, that is, in the Son (14:7, 9–11). In Jesus, way and destination unite. Jesus can "show us the Father" because the Father is eternally in Him and He is eternally in the Father. The good news that the Father has shown Himself depends on the good news that the Father is in the Son.

What Jesus says about the "dwelling places" that He is preparing in His "Father's house" reinforces this point. Though often taken as a reference to heavenly dwelling places,

"Father's house" in John refers to the temple that is the body
of Jesus (2:16–22), which is the "Father's house" in the sense
that it is the place where the Father resides (14:10–11). The
Son is the permanent and eternal "home" of the Father, as
the Father is the eternal home of the Son. When the Son
comes into the world, we get a glimpse of the "home life"
of the Father with His Son. Through Jesus' descent from
heaven and His ascent back to the Father, the Father's house
becomes a home for believers. Jesus goes away to prepare a
place in His Father's house, in the temple of His body, for
believers (14:2–3). The word for "dwelling places" is used
elsewhere only in John 14:23, where it describes the *believer*
as the place where Father and Son take up residence. Jesus is
the dwelling of the Father, and becomes the dwelling place
for believers. Jesus becomes the meeting place of the Father
and His people. "In Him," in the house that is the Son, we
have family fellowship with the Father.

Jesus also talks about the mutual penetration of Father
and Son in John 17, and talks about the disciples in relation
to the Father and Son. Jesus offers a prayer for "those who
believe in Me through their word": "[I ask concerning] those
who believe in Me through their word that they may be one
even as Thou, Father, art in Me, and I in Thee, that they may
be in us, that the world may believe that Thou didst send me"
(vv. 20–23). The text moves from the scattered hearers of
the word, gathering them into a unity that reflects the unity
of the Father and Son. This unity is rooted in the disciples'
dwelling-in the Father and Son, a unity that manifests Jesus'
identity and mission to the world. Jesus prays that disciples
will indwell one another in a way that dimly mimics the
eternal indwelling of the Father and Son. More, the church
is unified in this way because she has become a participant
in the mutual indwelling of Father and Son. The church is
not merely image of the eternal dance of Triune life, but is
introduced to the dance as the bridal partner. This unity of

the church, further, is integral to the church's mission. If the church is not a place where the members "dwell within" one another's lives, the world will not believe that the Son "dwells within" and "came forth from" the Father.

For John, then, the good news is that the Father who has *not* been seen has *now* been seen in the Son, in whom the Father dwells. The Father who is not known has made Himself known in Jesus. Beyond this, the Father has not only shown Himself in the Son, in whom the Father lives, but has also brought us into the fellowship of Father and Son. The good news is that through the Son the Father has made room for us in Himself, through His Son.

Does the Father mourn and grieve at the grave of Lazarus? Jesus does. Does the Father fight self-righteous scribes and Pharisees, and call them liars and murderers? Jesus does. Does the Father give life and light and rest to the weary? Jesus does. Does the Father divide people? Jesus does. Does the Father lower Himself to redeem us? Jesus does. Does the Father strip off his garments and gird Himself to wipe our feet? Jesus does, and if you've seen Jesus, you've seen the Father.

N. T. Wright captured the point in one of his most beautiful passages:

> The Christian doctrine of the incarnation was never intended to be about the elevation of a human being to divine status. That's what, according to some Romans, happened to the emperors after they died, or even before. The Christian doctrine is all about a *different sort of God*—a God who was so different to normal expectations that he could, completely appropriately, become human in, and as, Jesus of Nazareth. To say that Jesus is in some sense God is of course to make a startling statement about Jesus. It is also to make a stupendous claim about God.[7]

7. *Jesus.*

Review Questions

1. What passage is John referring to in the first verses of his gospel? Why?

2. What does John mean when he says that the darkness does not "comprehend" the light?

3. How does the Son "exegete" the Father?

4. How is it possible for us to see the Father in the Son?

5. What does Jesus mean by the "dwelling places" that He prepares for us?

6. What is Jesus' prayer for the disciples?

Thought Questions

1. The first two chapters of John refer to a number of different "days" (cf. 1:29). How many days are there? Why?

2. What does John mean by the "darkness" in chapter 1?

3. Find two passages where Paul refers to the idea that disciples are "in" God.

Anointed for Burial

The raising of Lazarus is a turning point in the gospel of John. It is the culmination of Jesus' ministry prior to His death and resurrection, and it is the final sign that Jesus performs in the "Book of Signs." The raising of Lazarus is also the miracle that brings the Jewish conspiracy against Jesus to a head (Jn. 11:47–53). Because of the raising of Lazarus, many believe on Jesus, and this so alarms the Jewish leaders that they call a council meeting to plot his death. They fear that if they fail to suppress the Jesus movement, things will get so out of hand that the Romans will come against them to take away their temple and their nation. At the same time, they give orders that any Jew who sees Jesus should report Him so that He can be arrested. Everyone in Israel sees what is going on. They know that Jesus' life is in danger, and wonder if He will come to Passover at all. Everyone knows that Jesus will be risking His life if he comes to Jerusalem (11:54–57). Soon, the conspiracy extends to Lazarus (12:9–11), who must be eliminated because he is a walking, breathing witness to the life of Jesus, just like the blind man (ch. 9).

Though the Jews are making plans to kill Jesus, and enlisting the Jews to help them arrest Him, Jesus goes to Bethany, only two miles away from Jerusalem, six days before the Passover. He not only draws near to Jerusalem, but He later enters the city in a triumphal procession. Jesus takes the initiative in laying down His life. His life is not taken from Him. He enters Jerusalem as the good shepherd, who comes to lay down His life for the sheep, who lays down His life of His own will (10:18).

While Jesus is at Bethany, a supper is prepared for Him, and during the Supper, Mary, the sister of Martha and Lazarus, anoints Jesus' feet with perfumed oils and wipes His feet with her hair (12:1–8). As so often in John, this story resonates with other portions of the gospel. The event in 12:1–8 is already mentioned in 11:2, the beginning of the account of the raising of Lazarus. Before Mary ever anoints Jesus, she is identified as the woman who anoints Jesus. Again, in 12:1, we're reminded of Jesus' raising of Lazarus from the dead. These allusions back and forth between chapters 11 and 12 establish a thematic connection between them. Chapter 11 is about resurrection. Jesus is the resurrection and the life, and Jesus says that the Father glorifies the Son by giving Him the power to call the dead to life. This theme continues into chapter 12, where it is a reminder that the One who is anointed for burial is the One who raised Lazarus from the dead. And it shows that the one who can raise Lazarus from the dead after four days is capable also of taking up His own life again. He is the good shepherd in laying down His life; He is the good shepherd in taking it up again. The sequence in John 11–12 is from resurrection to burial. Even though Jesus is anointed for burial, resurrection in a sense comes first.

The fact that Mary "anoints" Jesus points to His resurrection. In John 9, Jesus mixed spittle with dirt and formed clay, with which He "anointed" the eyes of the man who had been born blind. The healing of the man is a rebirth. The man who had been born blind is now able to see; he has never seen before, but now he sees. It is like being born again. And, as mentioned above, Jesus heals Him by mixing spittle and clay, reminding us of Adam's creation. When the Word of God *anoints* the man's eyes, he sees and becomes a new man. Anointing is connected to resurrection again in chapter 11. When Jesus comes to Bethany after learning that Lazarus is dead, Martha rushes out to greet Him. Jesus assures her that Lazarus will rise again, and Martha answers, I know he will rise on the last day. Then Jesus tells her, "I am the resurrection and the life" and asks if Martha believes this. She does, and confesses the Jesus is the "Christ," the Son of God. "Christ" means "anointed one," and as the anointed one, Jesus brings resurrection, new life, power to overcome death. So, Mary anoints Jesus for His coming burial, but beyond that she looks with faith to the Christ, the anointed One, who raised Lazarus, and who is Himself the resurrection and the life.

Chapter 12 connects not only back to chapter 11, but forward to chapter 13. In chapter 12, Mary anoints the feet of Jesus with perfume; in chapter 13, Jesus washes the feet of the disciples. John 13:1–3 sets the scene for us. Jesus' love for His disciples, the good shepherd's care for His sheep, continues to the end. By washing the disciples' feet, Jesus shows that enduring love. Ultimately, the great expression of Jesus' love is His death for the sheep, and the washing of the feet depicts that. John emphasizes the fact that Jesus removes His clothing, and then puts it back on (13:4, 12). The only other reference to the removal of Jesus' garments is in John's account of the crucifixion (19:23). When Jesus removes His clothing in the Upper Room, He is foreshadowing the removal of His garments of glory on the cross. He lays aside His garments of glory and majesty to become flesh and to take on the form of a servant and to become obedient to death on the cross. He takes up His garments again, as a sign of the glory of the resurrection. By washing the disciples' feet, Jesus enacts the significance of His death and resurrection. And Mary prepares Him for this work by anointing and washing Him. In John, the humiliation is paradoxically also an exaltation. Jesus is never more Lord than when He is stripped as a servant.

Mary's action does not go unopposed. Judas objects to the waste of money, which might have been used for the poor. On the surface, Judas's objection has some plausibility. John tells us that the perfume was "very costly" and Judas estimates it could have been sold for three hundred denarii, about a year's worth of wages. This does seem an extravagant gift to offer to Jesus, where there is so much need in the world. Jesus' response, however, puts the question of the poor in it proper perspective. Care for the poor and needy is one of the chief duties laid upon the Christian church. It is part of the church's evangelistic mission, a central aspect of the church's worship. God calls us to His house and offers us His hospitality, and we are called to go and do likewise. But Jesus teaches that, however high and important this duty is, it is not the chief duty of the church. If the church considers this its chief calling, its true end, then the church's ministries will be distorted and unbalanced. The chief calling is to give ourselves in self-sacrifice to Christ, to offer everything we have and everything we are in service to Him. The chief end of man is to glorify God and to enjoy Him forever,[8] and only when the church expends herself for the glory of God will she truly be accomplishing the ministry that Christ intends for her.

John says that Judas is really motivated by greed. Though he covers his sin in pious words about the poor, Judas really wants the money for himself. In John's gospel, calling Judas a thief not only underscores the scope of his betrayal of Jesus, but also reminds us of the good shepherd discourse of chapter 10. Jesus is the good shepherd, contrasted with the thieves and robbers that have led the Jews in the past. Judas is such a false shepherd, a hireling, a thief and a robber. It is no accident that he objects to the preparation of the good shepherd for death, burial, and resurrection.

Mary anoints Jesus in preparation for His coming work as the Christ, the good shepherd, the resurrection and the life; she also anoints Him in preparation for His entry into Jerusalem. Jesus enters the city as the anointed One, the Christ, who has the power to triumph over death: He comes as the conqueror of death. The use of palm branches implies a few things about this event. Among the Jews of the first century, laying down palm branches is a way of greeting a hero. In the books of Maccabees, Judas is greeted by the crowds with palm branches as he enters Jerusalem. In the Old Testament itself, palm branches are associated not with the feast of Passover, but the Feast of Booths. Booths is the final feast of the Jewish religious calendar, taking place in the seventh month. During that feast, the Jews build booths or tents from the branches of trees, and palm trees are specified as one of the trees used (Lev. 23:40). Among other things, the Feast of Booths is a harvest feast, celebrating not only the bounty of the Lord's gifts from the field, but also

8. Westminster Divines, *Westminster Shorter Catechism* (London, 1648), Question 1.

looking forward to the final harvest of all the nations into the kingdom of God. In Zechariah 14 especially, the feast of booths represents the feast of the gathering of the Gentiles. When Jesus is greeted by palm branches, it is a sign that He comes as the one who brings peace to the nations, the One who subdues the Gentiles to the rule of God.

The Pharisees get it exactly right (12:19). The world is going after Jesus. The reference to Zechariah 9 reinforces this. The first part of chapter 9 describes a war of conquest. A conqueror moves from the far north of the land, southward along the coast, conquering Tyre and Sidon and the Philistine cities. There is devastation everywhere, but this conqueror enters Jerusalem in peace. Jerusalem is spared, and the king sets up Jerusalem as His capital. So Jesus comes as a conqueror of the nations. He comes as a king, but His kingdom is not like the kingdoms of this world. He enters the city not bringing a sword, but to offer Himself as a sacrifice for sin. He comes as the conqueror of the nations, but He does not come to conquer Jerusalem, except through His own self-offering. He comes as a conqueror, but one who is meek and lowly and seated upon a donkey.

These Things are Written

John begins his first epistle by saying that the life that was in the beginning drew near and became visible, tangible, and audible to the disciples (1 Jn. 1:1–4). In the incarnation, God shows Himself, makes Himself available for viewing, touching, kissing, conversing with. The people who know Jesus in that way died long ago, and we are left only with their written records. The evidence is compelling. We have records of eyewitnesses, evidence of the activities and responses to Jesus from the apostles, the evidence of the rise of the early church, the evidence of the inability of Romans and Jews to refute the apostles' claim that Jesus was risen. There is no better explanation for these facts than that the tomb of Jesus was empty on Easter morning, and there is no better explanation for the empty tomb than that Jesus rose from the dead. Unless we rule out the possibility of miracles and resurrections at the beginning of the discussion, there is no reason to reject the New Testament's account of the resurrection.

John himself writes his gospel, he said, so that those who read might believe, so that many centuries later we can still have the testimony of the eyewitnesses. But not everyone is convinced by the evidence, and even in the gospel story, not everyone is convinced by the testimony of the apostles.

Jesus' encounter with Mary Magdalene at the tomb is one example. Mary is an eyewitness to the resurrection. She sees Jesus standing in front of her, but doesn't recognize Him. She sees, but does not believe. This incident picks up on what is a recurring theme of the gospel: the theme of seeking Jesus. From the very first chapter, people are continually seeking Jesus. As we have seen, Jesus proves elusive. The Jews seek Jesus to seize and kill Him, but when the Jewish officers finally catch up with Jesus outside the garden of Gethsemane, they are so astonished that they have finally found Him that they fall to the ground. Others seek Jesus because He does miracles, providing bread to thousands; others because they want to have true and loving fellowship with Him. Jesus asks Mary the question that has been dominating the whole gospel: Whom are you seeking? Mary seeks Jesus not only to satisfy her own curiosity about where the body has gone, and in the context of the gospel she represents the believer's search for the Word made flesh.

Our appreciation of this scene is enriched by recognizing that part of the background to the scene here is found in Song of Songs 3:1–4. There, the beloved arises from her bed at night, and goes through the streets and squares of the city searching for her lover. When she finds him, she clings to him and will not let him go. The Song of Solomon is, of course, a love poem, but because the love of a man for a woman is an image of God's love for His bride, we can also say that the Song describes the love of the church or the Christian for her Lord. The beloved's search for her lover represents the diligent search of the believer for his God. So also in John 20. Mary represents the believer and/or the church searching for the elusive Spirit-filled Jesus. Finding Jesus requires a diligent search, a whole-hearted search.

However diligently Mary has searched, she does not even recognize Jesus when she finds Him. In part, this shows that Jesus has been transfigured by His resurrection. He is raised with a Spiritual body, ate and drank with His disciples, and could be touched and felt. He had bones and flesh even after the resurrection. Yet, His body is different. He has not merely been revived (as Lazarus was), but has entered into the new creation. He has received a Spiritual, glorified body, and therefore even those who were close to Him in His ministry have a difficult time recognizing Him.

More importantly, though, John records this incident to highlight the central importance of Jesus' words. Mary doesn't recognize Jesus, even though he's right in front of her. She doesn't understand what she experiences—*until* Jesus speaks her name. Jesus the Word comes to speak His Word, and the Risen Christ discloses Himself, and thus shows the Father, when He speaks the name of His children. Jesus is the good shepherd. He lays down His life for the sheep. He has authority to lay it down, and now He shows He has authority to take it up again. As the good shepherd, Jesus knows His sheep, is known by them, and He calls them by name. As the good shepherd, Jesus speaks so that the dead will hear His voice and come from their graves.

As we've seen, John regards the cross itself as a glorification. The cross is the "lifting up" or exaltation of the Son.
It makes sense for John to see the resurrection as part of
Christ's ascension. Jesus' words to Mary are puzzling, but
they imply that the ascension is very near at hand. Mary is to
tell the disciples that Jesus "is ascending" not that He "will
ascend" to the Father (cf. 20:17). Similarly, it makes sense for
Jesus to bestow the Spirit on the apostles on Easter. In Acts,
the Spirit is bestowed after the ascension and glorification of
Jesus, fifty days after Jesus disappears behind a cloud. John
also says that the Spirit is given after Jesus' glorification and
ascent, but for John the ascension/glorification has already
begun on Easter Sunday, the day of resurrection (20:22).
John does not deny that Jesus will ascend. As Jesus says in
the Upper Room, He is going away and will send the Spirit.
But John focuses on a different dimension of the Spirit. John
shows that Pentecost is all bound up with resurrection, that
Pentecost in fact begins with Easter. Specifically, Jesus gives
the Spirit on Easter to equip the apostles in their government of the church. The Spirit confers authority to forgive
or retain sins. Elsewhere in John's gospel, the Spirit is the
Spirit of truth. Jesus promises that the Spirit will lead the
disciples into all truth. He will speak only what He hears,
and disclose what is to come. This is the Spirit bestowed on
the apostles in the closed room on the evening of the day of
Jesus' resurrection.

This background makes Thomas's disbelief even more
damning. It is not merely that Thomas doubts the testimony
of men with whom he has spent a number of years in ministry with Jesus. In strictly human terms, we expect Thomas
to have some degree of trust in the other disciples. Disbe-
lieving good news from trustworthy friends is bad enough.
But Thomas' reaction is even worse. Thomas disbelieves
not merely the men who have been his close friends and

fellow-ministers, but he disbelieves those who have already been endowed with the Spirit of truth, who leads into all truth. Thomas doubts men whose truthfulness is supported not only by human testimony but by the testimony of the Spirit of God.

The point of this episode comes out clearly in 20:30–31. John describes the purpose of the written witness of the gospel. These things are written that you may believe. These things are written by the very apostles who first testify to Thomas about Jesus' resurrection, by one of that group on whom Jesus breathed out His Spirit. Believing their testimony is not just confidence in written records or reliable human testimony, but confidence that God the Holy Spirit guides the apostolic writers into all truth. John's message is: Don't be like Thomas, who refuses to believe the testimony of those who receive the Spirit and are witnesses to the resurrection. Don't be like Thomas, who refuses to believe until He has seen and touched Jesus. Rather, blessed are those who have not seen and yet have believed.

In writing his gospel, John is doing more than merely trying to convince his readers of the truth of certain events. He doesn't just want his readers to believe, but to believe in order to gain life. This is the good news of Easter: not just that a man was dead and came back to life, though this is true; not just that this event really happened, though it did. The good news of Easter is more: That the One who is Life submitted to death and conquered it. And therefore, those who believe in Him have life in His name. The Word of the Father has not been silenced by the grave, but speaks again, to Mary in the garden and, through John, across the ages to us.

Review Questions

1. Why is it dangerous for Jesus to go to Jerusalem for Passover?

2. Why does Mary anoint Jesus?

3. How is Mary's anointing of Jesus connected with the raising of Lazarus in the previous chapter?

4. When does Mary recognize Jesus? Why?

5. How does Jesus' description of the good shepherd inform the incident in the garden with Mary?

6. Why does John write a gospel?

Thought Questions

1. What are the soldiers doing to Jesus in John 19:1–6? Why?

2. Discuss the connections between Peter's betrayal of Jesus (18:15–32) and His restoration (21:15–23).

3. Can you harmonize John's account of the resurrection with the accounts in the synoptics?

4. Why are the angels arranged the way they are in the tomb (20:11–12)?

BIBLIOGRAPHY

Allison, Dale. *The New Moses: A Matthean Typology.* Minneapolis: Fortress, 1994.

Bailey, Kenneth. *Poet and Peasant and Through Peasant Eyes: A Literary-Cultural Approach to the Parables in Luke.* Grand Rapids: Eerdmans, 1983.

Bauckham, Richard. *Jesus and the Eyewitnesses.* Grand Rapids: Eerdmans, 2008.

Borg, Marcus. *Conflict, Holiness, and Politics in the Teaching of Jesus.* Harrisburg: Trinity Press International, 1998.

Carmichael, Calum. *The Story of Creation: Its Origin and Its Interpretation in Philo and the Fourth Gospel.* Ithaca: Cornell University Press, 1996.

Carson, D. A. and Douglas Moo. *Introduction to the New Testament.* Grand Rapids: Zondervan, 2005.

Daise, Michael A. *Feasts in John: Jewish Festivals and Jesus' "Hour" in the Fourth Gospel.* Tubingen: Mohn Siebeck, 2007.

Davies, W. D. and Dale C. Allison. *Matthew 1–7.* New York: T & T Clark, 2004.

Deeks, David. "The Structure of the Fourth Gospel." In *The Gospel of John as Literature: An Anthology of Twentieth-Century Perspectives,* edited by Mark W. G. Stibbe. Leiden: Brill, 1993.

Goulder, Michael. *Midrash and Lection in Matthew.* Eugene: Wipf & Stock, 2004.

Green, Joel. *The Gospel of Luke.* Grand Rapids: Eerdmans, 1997.

Hauck, Friedrich. "Parabole." In *Theological Dictionary of the New Testament,* vol. 5, edited by Gerhard Kittel and Gerhard Friedrich, translated by Geoffrey W. Bromiley, 744–760. Grand Rapids: Eerdmans, 1967.

Horne, Mark. *The Victory According to Mark.* Moscow: Canon Press, 2003.

Jordan, James B. *The Handwriting on the Wall: A Commentary on the Book of Daniel.* Powder Springs: American Vision, 2007.

Josephus, Flavius. *Antiquities of the Jews.*

Leithart, Peter J. *1 & 2 Kings.* Grand Rapids: Brazos, 2006.

———. *Deep Exegesis.* Waco: Baylor University Press, 2009.

———. *A House for My Name.* Moscow: Canon Press, 2000.

Marcus, Joel. "Crucifixion as Parodic Exaltation," *Journal of Biblical Literature* 125:1, 2006.

———. *The Way of the Lord.* Louisville: Westminster/John Knox, 1992.

Richards, W. Wiley. *Riches from the Lost Ark: The Gospel of John and the Tabernacle.* Graceville: Hargrave Press, 1993.

Robinson, J.A.T. *Redating the New Testament.* Eugene: Wipf & Stock, 2000.

Rosenstock-Huessy, Eugen. *Fruit of Lips: or Why Four Gospels.* Pittsburgh: Pickwick, 2004.

Sanders, E. P. *Judaism: Practice and Belief, 63 BCE–66 CE.* Harrisburg: Trinity Press International, 1992.

Smith, Robert Houston. "Exodus Typology in the Fourth Gospel," *Journal of Biblical Literature* 81, 1962.

Stassen, Glen. "The Fourteen Triads of the Sermon on the Mount," *Journal of Biblical Literature* 122, 2003.

Watts, Rikk E. *Isaiah's New Exodus in Mark.* Grand Rapids: Baker, 1997.

———. "Mark." In *Commentary on the New Testament Use of the Old Testament,* edited by Greg Beale and D. A. Carson, 111–250. Grand Rapids: Baker, 2007.

Wenham, John. *Redating Matthew, Mark and Luke: A Fresh Assault on the Synoptic Problem.* Downers Grove: IVP, 1992.

Westminster Divines. *Westminster Shorter Catechism.* London, 1648.

Wilson, Victor. *Divine Symmetries: The Art of Biblical Rhetoric.* University Press of America, 1997.

Wright, N. T. *Jesus and the Victory of God.* Minneapolis: Fortress, 1997.

———. *New Testament and the People of God.* Minneapolis: Fortress, 1992.

SCRIPTURE
INDEX

Made in United States
Troutdale, OR
05/16/2024